THE MONEY DIET

THE ULTIMATE GUIDE TO SHEDDING POUNDS OFF YOUR BILLS AND SAVING MONEY ON EVERYTHING!

MARTIN LEWIS

MONEY SAVING EXPERT

Vermilion
LONDON

1 3 5 7 9 10 8 6 4 2

Copyright © Martin Lewis 2004

First published in the United Kingdom in 2004 by Vermilion,
an imprint of Ebury Press
Random House UK Ltd
Random House
20 Vauxhall Bridge Road
London SW1V 2SA

Random House Australia (Pty) Limited
20 Alfred Street, Milsons Point, Sydney
New South Wales 2061, Australia

Random House New Zealand Limited
18 Poland Road, Glenfield
Auckland 10, New Zealand

Random House (Pty) Limited
Endulini, 5A Jubilee Road, Parktown 2193, South Africa

Random House UK Limited Reg. No. 954009
www.randomhouse.co.uk
Papers used by Vermilion are natural, recyclable products
made from wood grown in sustainable forests.

A CIP catalogue record is available for this book from the British Library.

ISBN: 0091894840

Designed by seagulls

Printed and bound in Great Britain by
Bookmarque Ltd, Croydon, Surrey

Martin Lewis, the UK's only Money Saving Expert, is a 31-year-old journalist who grew up in Cheshire and now lives in Shepherd's Bush, West London. He spends his life focusing on how to cut bills without cutting back. This is his first book.

Martin is in constant demand on TV and radio; including weekly slots on ITV1's *This Morning*, a Sunday Express column and regular phone-ins on Radio 2 and Radio 5. His highly energised delivery, unique primary source research and focused 'MoneySaving' philosophy means everyone wants to hear his strategies. In 2002 he set up a completely free website: www.moneysavingexpert.com. A year after its launch, without any advertising budget, nearly 150,000 people a month were visiting the site.

Before focusing on MoneySaving, Martin worked in the BBC's Business unit and has reported for BBC1, BBC Network Radio and even spent time as a Business Editor of Radio 4's *Today Programme*. Prior to that he worked 'for the other side' as a City Spin Doctor, advising major companies on how to communicate, and dabbled in stand-up comedy to 'relieve the tedium'.

Martin has a postgraduate degree in Broadcast Journalism from Cardiff University and is a graduate of the London School of Economics.

'The UK's Tightest Man' Philip Schofield, *This Morning*
'The UK's biggest Financial Anorak'
Paul Lewis, BBC Radio 4's *Moneybox*
'The Dumbledore of Debt' Paul Ross, *This Morning*
'If anyone can help, it's this man, Martin Lewis knows more about credit cards than possibly anyone else in the country'
Justin Rowlatt, BBC1 *Panorama*

Dedicated to the memory of my mother, Susan Lewis

Acknowledgements

Huge thanks to the whole MoneySaving community of www.moneysavingexpert.com. Their contributions, suggestions and thoughts are an inspiration. There are too many individuals to thank, so to represent them I've picked those contributors currently with the most Postings on the discussion boards. Thank you Galstonian, Andrea, Laminki, Pal, PurpleGreen, COS, Mini, Mark E, Mistralflow, MortgageMan, Payless, PakMan, Dannyboy and the Moderator.

Kind thanks for their astute comments on the relevant sections to Peter White & the Consumer Credit Counselling Service, Jill Stevens & Experian, Rudi Schlenker & London & Country Mortgages, Anna Bowes & Chase de Vere, Steve Playle & Trading Standards, Ray Boulger & Charcol. Special thanks to my uncle, Tony Tesciuba, for stepping out of the tax accountancy world and providing hardcore comment and number checking for the entire Diet.

And unexpected thanks to Starbucks. You may be shocked by this – after all, up to three quid for a cup of coffee ain't no MoneySaving. However, when I needed time and space to turn the mobile off, disconnect from the net and just think and write, Starbucks it was. It may be overpriced, but it provides plugs for my laptop, so on many occasions I wrote there for a whole day – buying just two cups of coffee. In other words, six quid for office rental. Bargain!

THE MONEY DIET
CALORIE COUNTER

**For a quick guide as to how much The Money Diet
can save you and how to prioritise your MoneySaving,
turn to page xiv for The Money Diet Calorie Counter**

CONTENTS

contents

contents

Part Two: The Crash Diet

contents

Part Three: Healthy Eating

contents

The Money Diet Calorie Counter

Use the following Calorie Counter to prioritise your MoneySaving. It brings together all the specific products detailed in the Crash Diet and Healthy Eating sections of the book. Find what you want, turn to the page, read the recipe, save the cash – it's as simple as that. Don't forget the Financial Fitness section though – read that, and you'll permanently hone your MoneySaving muscles.

TERMS EXPLAINED:

Time Taken: A rough guide, the purpose of which is to help you prioritise your time.

Typical Savings: The savings of course vary widely. The amount listed is a typical amount for someone to whom that specific recipe applies. For example, international phone calls: many people don't make any calls abroad, yet those who do tend to do so regularly, and could save £300 a year. Don't think of the amounts as an accurate guide, more as a rough scale of savings available for each recipe.

Difficulty Level: Incorporates both the practical difficulties and how complex it is to understand.

contents

INTRODUCTION

If you've just bought this book, why on earth didn't you borrow it from the library instead? If your answer is 'a book like this is so important I need it close by all the time', great. This is the key to the Money Diet – making smart consumer decisions while understanding others' agendas. If you bought it on impulse, then luckily it's a good buy anyway, as we've got work to do – and the money saved should easily outweigh the cover price. And, it shouldn't be forgotten – it enables me to continue to make a living!

Let me set out m'stall.

The Money Diet isn't Hard Work – the Work is All Done for You

The Money Diet is as little or as much work as you want: you decide how far you're willing to push it. The diet is designed so that those who want a quick cost-cutting hit will find the work's been done so it is immediately possible. And hardcore Money Dieters who want to become 'loophole spotters' and 'system screwers' will find techniques to tone their Money-Saving muscles, too.

The Money Diet is Not About Being Tight

It's about getting the best value. It isn't about 'stop spending', it's about 'spend better'. It's about preventing companies taking too many of our hard-earned shillings, about not spending more than you need.

The Money Diet is for Everyone, Not Just Those Who are Skint

It's *not* a 'what to do if you've got no cash' system. It's all about saving pounds without tightening your belt. If you've very little cash, it should stretch your money further. For those who are comfortable, it should enable you to buy or to save more. It's all about putting more money in your pocket.

The Money Diet is a Way to Get Your Own Back

Making rational decisions and understanding others' agendas are the engines powering the Money Diet. Without wanting to get too militant about it, most people have been taken for a ride for a very long time. My aim is simple: we spend our lives being screwed by companies for their profit. I want to show you how to screw them back.

I hope you enjoy the book, but most of all … I hope you save some money!

Martin Lewis, MONEY SAVING EXPERT

WHAT IS THE MONEY DIET?

Money affects every element of our lives. To get a cab or a bus? To get a pension or an ISA? To buy or rent a DVD? All are money decisions. Every time you spend, you can save, so the Money Diet's scope is huge.

For most people the Money Diet is just about how to get more for less. Yet, let's be honest, many people simply outspend their income. This is why it's a two-part plan. The first part comprises the pain-free steps to becoming a smart consumer – saving you thousands of pounds without any need to change your lifestyle. If after that there are more savings to be made, then I make no apologies for saying it may hurt and an effort is needed.

Now, I admit, grandiose money-making promises are common; usually in con-artists' adverts in shop windows, or spam e-mail. This book does not promise to make you millions – that's impossible. Its aim is to make the money you've got go further, just by showing you how to use it better.

A magazine once asked me to save its definition of an average family as much as possible, by tackling ten mainstream consumer finance products – the big, popular ones – in one go.

For a family of two adults, each earning £24,000, the spending on these ten products was estimated at a total

£17,000. By using what are the 'Money Diet' techniques it was possible to reduce this to £9,000. All in all, once you take into account the impact of tax on their salaries, this is actually the equivalent of a £6,000 salary rise each.

I will say now that it does require some action on your part – but it will be worth it. Your finances will be better. You will have the peace of mind of knowing that no one is taking you for a ride. But most important, think about the benefits. What would you give for a 10%, 20%, or even 30% pay rise? By spending your money more efficiently, you can make the equivalent of that gain. Think how many hours you'd have to work for 30% more pay ... A little bit of time spent taking on the banks, building societies, retailers, service companies (and virtually anyone else who is trying to make a profit from you) is therefore time well spent.

HOW TO DO THE MONEY DIET

Like any diet, the recipes depend on what you like – and how quickly you need it to work.

There are three main options:

1. The Financial Blitz

If you're roaring keen to save a huge pan of cash or in dire need of sorting out your spending and debts, do it all in one go.

2. The Slow Burn

If you'd rather spend the day listening to fingernails being scraped down a blackboard than deal with your money, this is for you. Do it right, and you'll hardly notice, but after a year, you'll end up having massively cut your expenditure.

3. Blitz and Pieces

Politicians would call this 'the third way'. Start with the big and easy savings, but then just take it one step at a time over the year.

HAVING A MONEY BUDDY

Whichever regime you choose, it doesn't have to be a solitary affair. The Money Diet is a perfect example of a problem

---

The Money Diet on www.moneysavingexpert.com

For those who are looking for the best products at any time, my website www.moneysavingexpert.com is completely free and designed to aid the Money Diet. The web is easily updatable in a way a book isn't. So read the guides here, then if you've got access to the net, check out the site for the very latest independently selected Best Buys for a range of product categories.

---

shared is a problem halved. Start the Money Diet with a friend – it makes the research easier and perhaps adds a level of competition about who can save the most. Money can on occasion be tricky; it has to be understood. I hope that by reading this book everything will quickly become clear. But if you do get stuck, you should be able to get through any tricky bits together.

BEFORE YOU START

It's important to know what the Diet's different parts do and how and when to use them.

Part I: Financial Fitness for Life

This is about how to mould your money-saving muscles to save cash on anything and everything. A journey through your money, how to deal with it, and how to stop companies getting one up on you.

This was the most difficult section to write. My father tells the story that as a little boy I knew all my times tables only weeks after starting infant school. Yet for years after, while I got the sums right, I struggled to explain how. Until now saving money's always been 'telling the answer'. Yet 'Financial Fitness' aims to show you how to think like a MoneySaver with the Money Diet's Ten Golden Ingredients.

Part II: The Crash Diet

Here it's all done for you. A practical product-by-product guide to getting the best deal, how much you can save, and how long each will take. The Calorie Counter on page xiv details all this in a simple table. With it you can start the big savings straight away.

Part III: Healthy Eating

Mortgages, credit cards and personal loans – 'Healthy Eating' covers debt from all angles, from debt crisis to how to make a profit out of credit cards.

The reason I wanted to dedicate an entire section to this is simply that debt is paying money for money itself, rather than any greater purpose, so cutting its cost is the purest form of money saving.

Now let's take a closer look at your three Dieting options.

1. THE FINANCIAL BLITZ

The idea of sitting down and spending a day rummaging through paperwork and finances to find the best deals makes *me* salivate with glee. For some bizarre reason this isn't a commonly shared feeling. For those of you for whom tackling finances is the emotional equivalent of fingernails screeching down a blackboard, don't worry. A few simple steps will make it as painless as possible.

PLANNING

Read 'Financial Fitness for Life'. The 'Money Diet Budgeting Technique' (page 29) is a very good way to start. After that move on to 'The Crash Diet' to ensure you take product-providers to the very extreme and get the best deals, and to 'Healthy Eating' if you are in debt or, if you're debt-free, how to profit from lenders.

Gather the papers. Collect all the paperwork and documents relating to all your different money matters, so everything is in one place.

Establish current rates and prices. Make some phone calls and establish what the rates and credit limits you are paying are, so you have as much information as possible to hand when you start.

Choose the day. Every day isn't equal. The most important thing is that businesses should be open, ready and able to talk to you. Thus the very best day is a weekday, and the best time to make your calls is mid-morning or mid-afternoon when the phone lines are least busy.

If you can't do the Financial Blitz on a weekday – after all, time is money – the next best day is a Saturday. Then again (he writes smiling) there's still a lot you can do on a Sunday … any day is better than none.

Time and travel. For some things you might need to head out to the shops, so make sure you've got time to be able to get there. If it's all too much, split this task over a couple of days.

PREPARATION

Paperwork. Lay *out* the paperwork, and compile and collate everything, so that it's all to hand and nice and easy to see.

Use a 'to do' list. Prioritise the areas you want to tackle. The 'Calorie Counter' on page xiv shows you the potential savings on different types of products.

Facilities. A phone is incredibly important, but if possible also use an internet connection to speed up the research (see 'Talk to People', page 94).

EXECUTION

Big 'n' easy. Why not alternate big savings with easy savings? This way, once you've got a big saving under your belt, you can take a breather with an easy one next. This should keep you going – though regular breaks and a little food are helpful, too.

Running total. As the money saved starts to flood in, keep a running list of the savings so far. It may sound like an extra effort, but when you can see the amount of extra cash you'll have, it will enthuse you and motivate you to keep going. Think about what you could spend the money on, or simply how much money you will have in your bank account. It's empowering and stimulating and helps keep your resolve firm.

2. THE SLOW BURN

Whereas the Financial Blitz is like circuit training in a gym, the Slow Burn is more like a couple of lengths in a pool every fortnight.

PREPARATION

Understand. The most important thing about starting the Slow Burn is understanding the philosophy of the Money Diet. When you have the time (on the train, bus, plane, beach, waiting to pick the kids up, when there's nothing on the telly) read through 'Financial Fitness for Life'.

While the Slow Burn doesn't advocate looking backwards to repair all the problems in your money matters, it does encourage you to say, 'From now on, I am always going to get the best possible deals.'

EXECUTION

Stop and think. Every time a bill pops through the letter box, every time you sign up for something new, every time you buy something – rather than just automatically renew, pause. Say, 'Today I am going to improve my finances.' Do this with every product and gradually the overall picture changes.

As a rule of thumb, always tell yourself, 'I will check out three providers, not just one option.' This alone can revolutionise your finances.

Keep a money diary. Make a list of when and how much you save every time you've done a transaction. Use this to keep a running total and you will be amazed at the end of the year.

Things change. Do remember that sometimes situations change. Even if you've already switched a product, when each bill comes through from one quarter to the next, it's worth looking at it and asking, 'Am I still doing the right thing?'

3. BLITZ AND PIECES

When you've just bought this book and still have the Money Diet ethos running through your veins, do a Mini Blitz.

PREPARATION

Follow the 'Financial Blitz' guide for preparing to save. As for what to tackle, I would choose a mix of big and easy savings. Take on the big ones and save immediately, take on the easy and quick for a few extra pounds. Always choose based on your own priorities, but just to help if you're not sure here's a selection.

- Gas and electricity ('Crash Diet', page 149)
- Balance transfer credit card ('Healthy Eating', page 296)
- Mortgage/remortgage ('Healthy Eating', page 252)
- Savings accounts (cash ISAs) ('Crash Diet', pages 156 & 160)
- Water bills ('Crash Diet', page 154)

EXECUTION

That's the 'Blitz' bit, and after seeing the scale of savings, you'll have bags of enthusiasm for the 'Pieces' part. Now follow the Slow Burn and change everything in simple and easy stages.

PART 1

FINANCIAL FITNESS FOR LIFE

HOW TO SAVE MONEY ON ANYTHING

THE TEN GOLDEN INGREDIENTS

Ensuring financial fitness for life involves more than just getting the best of every product. That works for the short to medium term, but what really drives continued savings is changing your mentality so that every time your fingers fondle loose change, you're going to be as smart a consumer as possible. Becoming a successful Money Dieter has two sides: taking yourself on and building up your financial muscles.

The first involves throwing aside financial fears and phobias and learning that money isn't a scary monster lurking in the cupboard, but simply a tool – and one you can easily master. That's why the first five ingredients focus on taking control of yourself and your spending urges.

Building up money-saving muscles does sometimes involve a fight. The opposition are product providers and service companies whose goal is to make as much money from us as possible. Our task is to stop them; that's why the second five form my 'self-defence class'.

1. You're In Charge

Don't be scared. It's what they want! The easiest way to lose a game is by not knowing the rules. But they really aren't that difficult. Be confident, be informed and take a tiny bit of thought each time you spend or make any financial decision *(page 18)*.

2. Prepare Your Pocket

Money is a two-sided coin. Know how much you can afford to spend and you win the toss. On one side is debt, which is simply paying money out of your salary after you've bought something, but you have to pay interest on top. On the other is saving – which is simply paying money out of your salary before you've bought something, but this time they pay you interest *(page 27)*.

3. Know Thyself

We're all different. And this is a secret weapon. Providers tend to look and make their decisions based on the conglomerated masses, but by knowing yourself and finding your niche you can play against these averages, and win *(page 54)*.

4. Be a Better Shopper

Retail therapy, at a price you can afford, is possible. The first thing to do is target your own 'gotta have' impulses. Control them and you can have more for less. Every time you shop, follow the right money mantras to discipline yourself *(page 69)*.

5. Forget Loyalty

Fact: No one financial services product-provider is top of the table for more than one product. Therefore, by definition, two products from one company means at least one of them isn't the best. Forget loyalty; it only pays them, not you *(page 82)*.

6. Talk to People

We live in a time of unrivalled access to information, yet as consumers most of us simply avoid taking advantage of this. STOP! Know what you are doing and you'll be the winner. It's a question of research, evidence and simply talking about money *(page 94)*.

7. Haggle

There's no such thing as a fixed price. The ticket price is purely an indicator of what you need to pay. Legally they don't have to accept it, so you don't need to pay it *(page 107)*!

8. Holler

You have rights, use them! Just because you buy cheap doesn't mean you've no right to good service. And just because you've been with a company for a long time doesn't mean you should let them take you for granted. If they do, move on *(page 117)*!

9. Think Through their Logic

Shopping around isn't enough – you may just get the best of a bad bunch. To really see through their charades ask, 'How do they make money from me?' and 'How much do they make?' *(page 130)*.

10. Find the Loopholes

They make money out of you. So always ask, 'Can I make money out of them?' Companies assume everyone is lazy and apathetic; if you're not, you can surf a wave of offers to make money. Go on, twist their terms and conditions. You've everything to gain *(page 136)*.

The next 10 chapters will describe each one of these golden ingredients in simple terms, teaching you how to think about and act with your money.

£ one
YOU'RE IN CHARGE

Don't be scared. It's what they want! The easiest way to lose a game is by not knowing the rules. But the rules really aren't that difficult. Be confident, be informed and use a tiny bit of thought each time you spend or make any financial decision.

DON'T LET THEM TAKE CONTROL

I called up to book a hotel the other day. I knew where I was going and I knew roughly what standard I wanted. There were two that fitted the bill. When I asked the cost, the first one said, 'That will be £60 for the night please, sir.' The next: 'That will be £60 for the night, please, sir, including, of course, our full breakfast, porterage service and unlimited use of our swimming pool and gym.' It was a no-brainer.

But then I had a thought. So I re-dialled the original hotel, and asked, 'What's included in the price? Do you have a porterage service? Do you offer a full breakfast? And do you have a gym and a swimming pool?' And slap me down with a wad of fivers, as I suspected, it offered all those services, and all were included in the price. The only difference between the two hotels – *the second one had sold it better*.

We must take charge and set our own agenda if we don't want companies to lead us by the nose. The sales patter the hotel used is known as 'sandwiching': as when telling a customer about a sandwich, don't just mention the filling, tell them about the bread too. So it's a beef and horseradish sandwich on freshly baked wholemeal bread straight from the oven and covered with sesame seeds.

Yet for every sales manoeuvre there's a counter-manoeuvre. When you look at a sandwich, always compare the bread anyway. If the packet doesn't describe it fully, find all the information, to make the best choice. By taking a considered decision rather than being sold to, you take control.

All Money is DIY Money

Financial blinkers are a curse. Many people abrogate the responsibility for their own money and finances, whether formally or informally. Some hire an independent financial adviser; some simply leave it to their husband, wife, partner, child, parents, grandparents, uncle, aunt or anyone else, if they can get away with it.

Realise, though, that even if you hand over the reins to someone else, it's still *your* money and ultimately *you* must take charge. Even if that person knows more about money than you do, just let him or her guide you. Don't ever let somebody tell you what to do – not even me. This book is here to coach, guide, encourage, train, motivate and edify you; it suggests answers, solutions, methodologies and tactics – but ultimately the decision is always yours.

There's nothing wrong with taking advice, but always question it, and trust your instincts. In many walks of life, advisers make mistakes. Investment advisers or stockbrokers may know more about investments than you, but they don't know your future. Think about the factors that affect you, and remember that even close family members, friends and partners have agendas, thought-processes and terms of reference that differ from yours. You must make the decisions about your life, and you must make the decisions about your money. You are in charge.

Things Change

Now let me add something unpleasant. If you are married, it may not last for ever. You may get divorced, or your partner may die before you do. In either event, if you've never taken control of your money before, you will find yourself dealing with it, alone, and probably with less income, during a stressful time. This is a tragedy you mustn't allow to happen. Take an interest in your joint financial affairs right now, build up your understanding. You will, in any case, have lost nothing but a little time and you will have learnt a great deal. Knowledge is the best insurance.

FROM ICE CREAM TO PENSIONS: DON'T BE SCARED

Go on holiday, buy the kids a prezzie, visit a friend, have a drink on the way home from work – each affects your pocket. While many people say they hate making money decisions and consciously try to avoid them, unless you're spending the day sleeping in the park, it's impossible to avoid money. Yet most money decisions don't scare us, because we don't think of them as being 'financial', and as we're not scared when we think the decision through, we do it correctly.

However, when we hit the big stuff – the products that affect all our lives and delineate how wealthy we are – the financial fear factor is high. You hear it all the time: 'I don't understand,' 'I never know what to do with my cash,' 'I'm the worst person in the world with money.' Often it is said as a boast. Of course, in my life I hear it more than most; people say, 'You can't help me, I'm terrible with money.' This seems slightly strange logic to me – more sensible would be, 'You can't help me, I'm superb with money.' If you are trash with your cash, fantastic – the savings available from the Money Diet are huge.

While being bad with money is one thing, not dealing with it is criminal; it's the financial equivalent of self-harm. If you always ignore the price and never think about the cost, then you're probably always struggling with money. If you throw bills away without looking at them, your finances are probably critical. That one act alone slides a knife across the neck of your credit score. If that's you – STOP. You've done well getting this book, now it's time to take a deep breath and start repairing the damage. It can, and will, get better and easier.

As you'll discover, the differences between buying a stakeholder pension and an ice cream aren't that big.

THE FIVE-SECOND MONEY MAKEOVER

Having all the necessary information simplifies and improves decision-making. Throughout 'Financial Fitness for Life' I'll be introducing techniques to aid the process, but ultimately it all boils down to a single core concept – the 'five-second money makeover'. Which is: before you carry out any transaction, think 'What are the questions I should ask?' and once you've thought of them, ask them.

Asking should be pretty easy. Simply open your mouth and start speaking. Yet many of us feel stupid asking questions. This affects everyone. As a professional know-it-all, I panic when I need to ask a question. It's the fear that everyone else will know the answer and think your question bloody stupid. The other day, a pizza menu included 'Fontina' cheese – something I'd never heard of – was it a (yuck) blue cheese? After two deep breaths I asked and it was answered without a fuss. If it's a choice between your pride and your wallet (or palate), bite the bullet. When I was first taught to be a journalist, they always said, 'Remember to check who, what, where, when, how and why.' So ask questions – and this book is full of the kind of questions you should ask.

This is so important I really want to stress it. Ask questions! Ask questions! Ask questions! A lack of information is the prime weapon product providers wield to put one over on us. Questions disarm them, and empower us.

THE LIST OF THERE'S NOTHING WRONG WITH ...

1... bringing sandwiches to work if you're on a budget. Don't be embarrassed; do it with pride. Maybe if you start the trend your work colleagues will find financial freedom too and do the same. And if anyone asks why, don't say, 'I can't afford to go out and buy lunch every day,' say, 'I'm budgeting because I want to spend more on things that are more important.'

2... asking your partner how good your, and their, finances are. Knowledge of your own financial situation is crucial. You need to be assured that, independently as well as together, you would be fine. This isn't selfish. If you care about your partner, assure yourself their financial fitness is good too. Remember, they might not be as good with money as they think they are, and two heads are always better than one. So take charge of your future, and while you're doing so, look out for them, too.

3... asking for a discount. There's nothing to lose. No one ever gets thrown out of a shop for politely asking for a reduction. No one ever gets hung up on for asking to pay just a little bit less. So why not have a go, and see how much you can save? (See 'Haggle', page 107.)

4... asking for money you've lent to be paid back to you. It was generous of you to help your friend out, so why be embarrassed to ask for your money back if you need it? One easy way, when you lend the money, is to set a time and a date for when you will ask for it back. Be upfront – it's much less embarrassing than beating round the bush. A quick 'Hey, remember that £20 you borrowed from me – any chance you've got it? I could do with it now' is more polite and easier to deal with than obfuscated hints. If they were bold enough to ask you for a loan, you can be bold enough to ask them for it back.

5... not splitting the bill evenly. Why do we have meals with friends in restaurants and agree to split the bill evenly, even when some drink or eat much more than others? If someone generously wants to pay for all, great, but by splitting evenly perhaps you're unwittingly making a debt-ridden, financially strapped friend pay for your wine. While technically the best solution is for everyone to calculate what they owe, that's a complete nightmare. My technique is what I call 'the Easy

Honour System'. At the end of the meal, everybody should contribute what they think they owe, including the tip. Most people get it roughly right, but of course when you total up you'll almost always be short – it's human nature. So divide the shortfall by the number of people – let's say there's £50 difference and ten friends, everybody then puts in an extra £5. It may not be completely accurate, but it's a quick and easy way for people to pay near enough what they should. It helps you budget, without losing friends or looking too mean.

6... asking family for an interest-free loan, if they can help. Too often people hide their debts. One guy I worked with was paying hideous rates of interest on his loans. He was only young. He spoke to me, looking for help. When we talked through the options it turned out his parents could quite readily pay the cash, but he simply hadn't told them he was in trouble. As he had no other access to cheap credit I asked him to speak to his family. While there was a little bit of embarrassment, his parents lent him the money, and interest-free. If necessary, it's fair for family members to charge a low but reasonable interest rate. After encouragement the young man signed a formal document to establish that it was a loan, not a gift. This transported him out of financial trouble immediately, without losing too much family face.

7... asking friends how much they've paid for something and where they got it from. There's nothing wrong with freely trading information. The fact that we all like to keep quiet about our finances helps us all get ripped off. Friends often have similar interests, so when they do something or own something that you might want to do or own too, ask

---

Martin's Money Memories: She Already Had the Lipstick On

Caroline is a WPC with London's Metropolitan Police. She's in her mid-thirties, with two kids. She was one of my first 'Money Makeovers' on *This Morning*.

She described herself as being absolutely abysmal with money. But when we sat down, she started talking about her mortgage. Having watched the programme, and listened to me spouting on, she had already changed her provider. And that change alone had meant a saving of over £1,000 a year. Then we came to credit cards and loans. Again the same, another annual £1,000 already saved.

Now, of course, there was more that I could save her. I'm not suggesting that everybody will make these kinds of savings right off the bat. The very best deals take time and some expertise. Yet even without any help from me, Caroline had saved herself a good wodge. And most people, just by taking a little time, can generate an equivalent scale of saving. It's all about deciding, perhaps for the first time in your life, to take charge of your finances and do it yourself. If it's a kick up the backside you need, then hopefully, as you read *The Money Diet*, you'll feel the thwack!

---

them, 'How much did you pay, and where did you get it from?' It sets up an easy point of reference for the future. And make sure they feel free to ask you the same. (See 'Talk to People', page 94.)

8... *saying 'I don't understand'*. Being confused is an easy way to get ripped off. If the person explaining something to you understands it, so can you. Make them explain it step by step until you get it. There's nothing wrong with going back to basics. Everyone should be concerned that you are making the right decisions based on the right facts, and therefore should always make time to ensure you understand them.

9... *saying no.* Don't be sold to out of politeness, and don't accede to pressure. You're in charge, only you know your financial situation, only you live your life, only you can decide what's right for you – don't let others browbeat you into a decision. Sense isn't common.

two
PREPARE YOUR POCKET

Money is a two-sided coin. Know how much you can afford to spend and you win the toss. On one side is debt – simply paying money out of your salary after you've bought something, yet shelling out interest charges on top. On the other is saving – simply paying money out of your salary before you've bought something, but this time being paid the interest.

'I'M ALWAYS SKINT AFTER CHRISTMAS'

Sitting in a bar with a well-paid friend who works in the City one cold January evening, I suggested we order some food. She turned to me and said, 'Would you mind if we just got drinks? I'm skint.' Now, she earns good money so I was quite surprised by this. Why was she skint? Her answer, 'Christmas, of course.' 'And?' I asked again. 'What do you mean, and?' she said. 'It's just been Christmas. I've spent loads of money, I'm skint.'

Now, you're probably thinking, what's he going on about? Christmas is a good reason for spending. The festivities, the presents, going out, office parties, meeting people, and the excuse to spend and shop. So I'd like to point out a little fact – Christmas happens on 25 December every year; it's not unexpected. Yet many people try to pay for it out of December's money, and this is often doomed to failure – leaving a post-Christmas credit hangover to accompany alcohol's mists.

AVOID A SPIRALLING FINANCIAL DESCENT

Let's look at the potential consequences of what my friend did. All her spending on food, drink, gifts and décor was in the pre-Christmas run-up – the time when shops traditionally charge the most. When January rolls round, the sales are on and it's the cheapest time to buy. In her job she needs to look good and feels the need to buy designer clothing. But she has no money left to take advantage of the bargains, so she has to wait, and instead buy her clothes later in the year – meaning it costs her a lot more, dropping her finances down yet another step. So by the time next Christmas arrives, she's still paying for the last one. And thus starts the spiral.

Budget, Plan, Prepare

The weapons to fight spiralling finances are budget, plan and prepare. These aren't necessarily easy, but are easily necessary. Even those lucky enough to have a bigger income than expenditure will benefit.

The Piggybank Technique

Piggybanks are an extremely clever idea. They sit in the corner of the room and you put money in them. You don't really notice the absence of the money as it disappears from

---

Forgotten Gold – Don't Lose Your Payrise

When we get a pay rise, we feel richer and we liberalise our spending habits. This means we rarely actually feel the gain. It's forgotten gold. After all, most people tend to think they should be paid roughly three times what they currently earn. Unfortunately, if we got that rise, soon afterwards we'd still believe a three times pay rise was due again. It's our own personal inflation.

The way to deal with this is 'shrink to fit'. As soon as you get a pay rise, rework your money so you actually gain. Allocate increased savings and provisions immediately, before you adjust your expectations. Follow through the Money Diet budget plan, put your newfound wealth towards a good financial future. Otherwise it's just fool's gold.

---

your pocket. Yet gradually the coins add up, waiting for the proverbial rainy day.

My Money Diet budgeting technique is inspired by piggy-banks, as will become apparent.

The Mr Micawber Corner

'My other piece of advice, Copperfield,' said Mr Micawber, 'you know. Annual income twenty pounds, annual expenditure nineteen nineteen six, result happiness. Annual income twenty pounds, annual expenditure twenty pounds ought and six, result misery. The blossom is blighted, the leaf is withered, the god of day goes down upon the dreary scene, and — and, in short, you are for ever floored. As I am!' (From David Copperfield by Charles Dickens)

The debtors' prisons of Dickens's day may have left us, but attempting to spend within your means is as tough as ever. Remember that money is a two-sided coin – that debt and savings are opposite sides of the same coin. Know how much you can afford to spend and you win the toss. On one side is debt, which is simply paying money out of your salary after you've bought something, with the added burden of interest. On the other is saving – which is simply paying money out of your salary before you've bought something, but this time they pay you the interest.

Proper planning will help turn debts into savings, shifting the odds in your favour.

A FOUR-STEP 'HAPPINESS' PLAN

There are four simple steps to keep your expenditure below your income. You can follow these alone, or as part of a couple or family. Just be consistent – if you start them for a couple, make sure you fill in the total spending for both, down to the smallest article of clothing. Do it alone, then only put in your proportion of any rent or mortgage.

Step 1: Don't Trust Your Bank Account

Bank accounts are devious and cunning beasts. When you get paid, they seduce you into believing the cash in there is the cash you have available to spend. Yet this wanton temptation is a terrible vice. Bank accounts lie!

We spend money in many ways and over many time periods. Purchases are daily, weekly, monthly or one-offs. However, your bank account presents only a snapshot of how much money is in your account at that moment. It ignores where you are in your money cycle – receiving your salary and paying your bills don't necessarily coincide. It also forgets that though Christmas comes but once a year, its cost should be spread all year round; so should holidays. Yet knowing the logic is no protection – so let's move to step two.

Step 2: Discover What Your Real Monthly Spend Is

It isn't as obvious as it seems, and it's important to incorporate all the real demands on your income. To help this, I've developed the Money Diet Monthly Calorie Counter.

You'll see a detailed chart on page 33. All you have to do is fill it in. (Those already using computer packages can simply adapt these.) After each category you can choose whether to enter the spending as per week, per month or per year – just fill in whichever is appropriate. Don't panic if you don't know exactly how much you spend on something. A good guess is better than giving up.

Some pointers:

Only count things once. Some spending may overlap – if you've already counted it, don't count it again.

Overestimation is better than underestimation. Honesty pays dividends. Fight that very human temptation to lie to yourself about your spending, and if you're not sure pick more not less. If you overestimate you'll have money left over, rather than still being short.

Don't forget anything. There's always bound to be something you spend on that's not on the list – have a think and make sure you fit it in, either in an 'others' section or the 'odds and sods' at the end. If you're struggling, do it over a week's daily activities. This will help remind you where your cash goes.

Money-save while you write. As well as counting the calories, as you write the numbers down, always ask yourself, 'Is this really the best deal I can get?'

Okay – now fill in just Part A of the chart. Once this is completed, work out what your real monthly spending is by filling in Part B of the chart, the 'monthly total' column. To do this you will (probably) need a calculator.

For things in the Per Week column: Multiply the amount by 4.33 (the average number of weeks in a month) and put the answer in the 'monthly total' column.

For things in the Per Month column: Move the answer straight over to the 'monthly total' column.

For things in the Per Year column: Divide the amount by 12 and put the answer in the 'monthly total' column.

Now total up each section and write the answer below.

Home total per month _____

Insurance total per month _____

Eats, Drinks & Smokes total per month _____

Transport and Travel total per month _____

Debt Repayments total per month _____

Savings & Investments total per month _____

Family total per month _____

Fun and Frolics total per month _____

Big One-Offs total per month _____

Clothes total per month _____

Education, Courses and Classes total per month _____

Odds and Sods total per month _____

Total Monthly Expenditure _____

Money Diet Monthly Calorie Counter					
	FILL IN FOR PART A			**PART B**	**PART C**
	Per week	Per month	Per year	Monthly total	Monthly desired
HOME					
Mortgage/Rent					
Household maintenance					
Home & contents insurance					
Council tax					
Water rates/Meter					
Gas bill					
Electricity bill					
Oil bill					
Home phone bill					
Internet bill					
Mobile phone bill(s)					
Cleaning products/cleaner					
Garden maintenance					
Other home					
TOTAL HOME					
INSURANCE					
Level-term assurance					
Private medical insurance					
Healthcare cashback scheme					
Pet insurance					
Travel insurance					
Gas & plumbing cover					
Other insurance					
TOTAL INSURANCE					

Money Diet Monthly Calorie Counter					
	FILL IN FOR PART A			**PART B**	**PART C**
	Per week	Per month	Per year	Monthly total	Monthly desired
EATS, DRINKS & SMOKES					
Food shopping					
Eating out					
Coffee/sandwiches out					
Pet food					
Drink for home					
Drinking out					
Smoking					
Other eats, drinks & smokes					
TOTAL EATS					
TRANSPORT AND TRAVEL					
Rail/bus/coach/taxi					
Car maintenance					
Car insurance					
Car tax					
Petrol					
Other car					
TOTAL TRANSPORT					
DEBT REPAYMENTS (just the average amount repaid, not the total debt)					
Car loan repayments					
Personal loan repayment					
HP repayments					
Credit card repayment					
Other loan repayment					
TOTAL DEBT REPAYMENTS					

(REMEMBER DO NOT DOUBLE COUNT:
If you've noted your spending elsewhere, then don't add it in the debt repayment column)

Money Diet Monthly Calorie Counter					
	FILL IN FOR PART A			PART B	PART C
	Per week	Per month	Per year	Monthly total	Monthly desired
SAVINGS & INVESTMENTS (how much you pay in, not how much is in there)					
Saving schemes					
Mini cash ISAS					
Investments					
Buying shares					
Pension payments					
Other savings/investments					
TOTAL SAVINGS					
FAMILY					
Childcare/playschemes					
Babysitting					
Children's travel					
School trips					
Other family					
TOTAL FAMILY					
FUN AND FROLICS					
Hobbies					
Pet costs					
Fitness/sports/gym					
Shopping for fun					
Big days out					
Books/music/DVDs/ computer games					
Cinema/theatre trips					
Family days out					
Other fun and frolics					
TOTAL FUN AND FROLICS					

Money Diet Monthly Calorie Counter					
	FILL IN FOR PART A			PART B	PART C
	Per week	Per month	Per year	Monthly total	Monthly desired
BIG ONE-OFFS (for things spent less than once a year, divide the total by the number of years and put it in the per year column)					
Cost of Christmas					
Cost of summer holiday					
Cost of winter holiday					
Cost of birthdays					
Cost of new sofa/kitchen/ TV/other electrical					
Other big one-offs					
TOTAL BIG ONE-OFFS					
CLOTHES					
New clothes					
New children's clothes					
Work clothes					
Other clothes					
TOTAL CLOTHES					
EDUCATION, COURSES AND CLASSES					
Your courses/classes					
School fees					
University tuition fees					
Other education costs					
TOTAL EDUCATION					
ODDS AND SODS (anything that doesn't fit anywhere else)					
Regular charity donations					
Tax and NI provisions (self-employed only)					
Newspapers & magazines					
Dentistry					
Optical bills					
Complementary therapies					
Other odds and sods					
TOTAL ODDS AND SODS					

Step 3: Work Out What You Can Spend Each Month

You've got your answer ... are you shocked? Don't worry –
almost everyone is. It's almost always more than you thought.
This is because lots of money floats away through direct
debits, standing orders and cheques without really entering
our consciousness. Plus those big one-offs aren't usually
counted this way, so when you add them in, it can hurt.

Don't panic, though. Let's see if your spending is affordable,
by discovering what your income is. It shouldn't be as tough,
but here's a table to help. All figures should be after tax.

How much do you earn each month?	
Income	After tax monthly earnings*
Average earnings from employment/ self-employment	
Incomes taken each month from savings/investments	
Pensions and annuity payouts (state and private)	

Benefits, including child benefit,
   child tax credit, income support,
   council tax benefit	

Gifts or help from family or friends	
Other	
TOTAL	

*If the income isn't monthly, then use the same system as in the Calorie Counter (left) to work
out the monthly equivalent you receive.
*If you're self-employed, then use untaxed earnings and fill in the tax and NI provisions in the
Calorie Counter.

At this point it's back to Mr Micawber.

Your income is bigger than your expenditure – 'happiness'.
If your income is bigger than your expenditure, HOORAH.
Apart from jumping up and down for joy, you're also relatively
safe in the knowledge you can afford to save a little more or
treat yourself a little better. However, that isn't a reason not to
do the Money Diet or not to plan. Just because you have spare
cash doesn't mean you should throw it away.

Your expenditure is bigger than your income – 'misery'.
This tends to be a more common outcome. You're probably
saying '*wooaaah*' – or maybe something more colourful – do I
really overspend by that much? And you're right to be
shocked, because it is a problem. Continued overspending
isn't sustainable: you will get into debt, with more and more of
your salary going to pay interest, leaving less and less to
spend, making it even worse. It's time to cut your expenditure.

There are two ways:

Pain-free. This is the prime Money Diet aim. Use the cheapest and best-value products and services to mash down your
spending. Do the Crash Diet and follow the Healthy Eating
Guide. If you're doing this exercise as part of the financial
blitz, great. Before you do anything else, make the product
changes and then re-do the table with the new figures.
Hopefully, it'll reduce your personal deficit.

No pain, no gain. If switching products isn't enough, then it's
ouch time – you need to cut your spending. This has to be
done honestly, though; don't arbitrarily cut down your paper

spending unless you mean it. If you then think 'Damn it' and end up spending more than you've put aside, this whole exercise is lost.

Painless pain. There are many spending cuts that shouldn't hurt much – saving a little less, eating out a little less, taking control of your phone habit, turning the lights off as soon as you leave the room. Taking videos/DVDs back to the rental shop on time. Filling the petrol tank when it's still half-full, to give you time to shop around for the cheapest (use www.aapetrolbusters.com to locate it). These are the types of things people typically laugh at when they explain to me how bad they are with money. Stop laughing. Pay attention to them. Then start smiling.

All spending reductions hurt. However, I make no apology for saying that they are necessary and you must spend within your means. This is about continually running through your expenditure until you have cut out everything you can.

The cappuccino contract

To cut back, use Part C – the MONTHLY DESIRED spend column in the table – to set yourself a limit for each category. Once done, that's your new limit. You need to be conscious of it. Stick it on a pinboard, and always be aware of what you're doing.

Alternatively, use the old 'spending diary' and note down every time you spend, no matter how small. When you look back, you'll be surprised at how much you spend on the tiniest of things. I call this the 'Cappuccino Contract' because you may need to agree with yourself from now on no more cappuccinos – that £2 every day at work is £500 a year.

Unfortunately, it may be necessary to cut back on a lot more than coffee – going out, new clothes or a take-away may be too expensive. Be creative and thoughtful, but ruthless. This is one of the most important decisions you'll make. And always remember, £10 a month mightn't sound much, but saving £120 a year is worthwhile.

Sometimes we need shouting at or scaring. So let me do it here. If you're not convinced of the need to manage your money, turn to 'Debt Crisis', page 335. Read some of the stories. It may be that getting the bus instead of a taxi could just tip the balance in your favour.

Step Four: Trust Your Piggybank

Your budget is set – now to make it easy as possible to stick to it. To do that we must turn 'It's the beginning of the month. I can go shopping, hoorah!' into 'It's the end of the month. I've got money left, I'll go shopping.'

You may laugh at the thought of ever having money left at the end of the month, yet stop spending at the beginning of it, and there may be more than you think. The trick is to take temptation out of your path with a wee bit of organisation.

This is where my piggybanking comes into action. It's about putting your money into different piggybanks, or in practical terms, different bank accounts, each designated for certain types of spending. Every month, as soon as you are paid, siphon off the right proportion of money (according to your planned budget) into each of these accounts.

The accounts you choose depend on your particular spending patterns, but let me use an example to explain. Let's assume you set up the following five accounts in addition to your normal day-to-day account.

- Bills (including mortgage)
- Family food
- Holidays
- Christmas
- Savings

When I say different accounts, I literally mean using separate current accounts at your bank. Even better – put the cash in a savings account (preferably high-interest) with easy withdrawal facilities so it will earn decent interest too. There's usually no problem having more than one account at one bank, and there's definitely no problem having a few accounts at different banks. You could even just do it by allocating amounts on a computer or paper, as long as you keep it up to date and stick to your plan. Do whatever you feel most comfortable with.

Once you have the new account, automate moving the budgeted amount of money there on the day (or day after to be safe) you are paid. This can be done by direct debit, standing order or manually.

The goal here is to leave in your main account only the money available to spend, and no more. The other accounts will have the money in to meet specific demands on your cash. Of course this may mean that now you can see you can't afford the first-class holiday you wanted, but the truth is you couldn't before either. At least now you'll vacation with the peace of mind that you won't suffer the rest of the year because of it. Do this and at last your bank account is finally trustworthy.

1. Different piggybank banking accounts
The piggybank technique is all about honing it to your own

needs. Each account is a box separating its spending from all others. This controls the impulse to overspend. Use accounts that fit in best with what you want to buy – for example, you might use a 'Major Purchases' account when you want to buy a new washing machine to see directly what you can afford to spend. To help, I thought I would explain a few options – but there are as many different accounts possible as there are ways to spend.

2. Holiday spending

There's absolutely nothing wrong with going on holiday, but there is something wrong with trying to pay for it all in the month before you actually go. A holiday is an annual expenditure that needs planning by putting aside a little bit of money each month.

Let's say you take two holidays a year costing £1,000 each, for both the travel and spending money (easily done with a family). That's £2,000 a year, the equivalent of £166 a month. If, each month, you put this aside in a special account, when it comes to buying your holiday, the money is waiting for you. You will know exactly what the limit on your holiday spend is, and be able to enjoy it without the worry of knowing you're going to be skint.

3. 'Rainy day' fund

Everyone needs a rainy day fund (known in financial circles as an 'emergency cash fund'). You never know what's going to happen in your life. In truth, we should all have three to six months' income saved away, so that we're ready for any emergency. This does sound a huge amount, and it's not the type of thing you can save up in a year. But there's nothing wrong with starting to siphon money away for a rainy day. (For a more sophisticated method, see 'Healthy Eating'.)

4. Shopping and big purchases account

If you are a shopper, put some money in a special account for big purchases or clothes shopping. Start to build it up and you will know what you've got available to spend. It may even allow you to make the one-off big purchase that you've always dreamed of. It could be a car, a TV, a DVD player, a designer suit, a dress for a wedding. It could be anything, but now it won't have to come out of your day-to-day funds.

You can even have two 'buying' accounts, as long as they're correctly budgeted. For example, a big purchase fund and a shopping fund for monthly spending – an especially useful system for those people who habitually get out the plastic and spend without thinking.

5. Savings account

A savings fund is slightly different from a rainy day account, because that's for *emergencies*. A savings account is putting money away for your future. As you never know what's going to happen, it's a good idea to have money put aside for your children, or simply for a treat for yourself.

6. Christmas account

This is the one that's crucial for my friend: the Christmas fund. Make a habit of putting cash aside for Christmas each month, and you can have a good time without having to worry about debts in January or missing the sales.

THE TRANSITIONAL STAGE

This budgeting technique works a treat when it's up and running. However, it's important to acknowledge that moving from unplanned to planned finances can be difficult. Changing over from your old habits to new ones does take a little bit more discipline. If you've old debts to pay off from past poor planning, this can leave your finances tightly squeezed during this stage. It's worth the investment though – take a couple of months of slightly less jangly pockets and in the long run your money life will be a whole lot easier. You'll know what you've got to spend, and you will have more money when you need it. If you do it right there will be no more 'I'm always skint after Christmas' and you will be able to shop in the sales. There will also be less 'We really can't afford that holiday.' Dare I say it – I know it's a boring word – 'sensible' planning actually will mean you have more.

TAKING THE DISCIPLINE UP A LEVEL
Piggycash Technique

For those who need it there's an even more stringent way to enforce this discipline, taking the main Piggybank Technique, and turning it into the Piggycash technique. Rather than having the money sitting in your current account, to really enforce some self-discipline, withdraw a set amount of cash each week, and no more. If you are going to do this, the best time is a Monday morning – that way you know 'spend now and there's nothing for the weekend'. This also means that if you've done well during the week, you can reward yourself by spending the cash that you've got left once you come to the weekend.

Cash-Machine Inflation

It's a phenomenon of our age. When most of us want cash, we put our plastic in the hole in the wall, and it magically appears. Yet ... let me ask you a question: do you now withdraw more money each trip than you used to? Personally I don't like carrying too much in my wallet, so I usually take out quite small amounts. Even so, it used to be £20, but now it's £30 a time.

The interesting thing, though, is I tend to spend the £30 in the same amount of time as I did the £20. This is cash-machine inflation.

The truth is, we often consider one trip to the cash machine counts as an actual amount of money – let's call it a HIT (Hole In The wall). The number of HITs in a week tends to be reasonably static, so reducing the value of a HIT can help govern your expenditure. In other words, get less cash when you go to a cash machine. If you usually take £50, start taking £40 out.

This might all sound slightly simplistic, but it does work. We tend to use the amount of money we've got in our pocket to judge the actual amount of money readily available to spend. If there's less there, you can't spend as much, or at least you need to make the extra effort of going to the cash machine to get more out – and this hassle in itself is good as each trip is a vivid reminder you've been spending money.

Use a Debt Buddy

My piggybank technique is a good way to manage your money. Unfortunately, you may find controlling your spending beyond self-regulation. Either the debts are racking up, or you find it really difficult to keep control of your cash. If this is the case it's time to pour a bucket of cold water over your spending.

A classic technique is the 'spending diary'. Simply write down *every single thing* you spend in a notebook, so you know exactly where your money is going and how much – if anything – you've got left. Unfortunately, this simply isn't a powerful enough tool for some people.

I've a solution, and it's inspired by the guilt-ridden faces of my friends whenever they come to ask for money help and admit dire spending habits. It's called 'debt buddying'.

Hopefully, you have at least one friend who is good with money, or at least quite conscientious. What you need to do is ask them if they will sit down with you, once a month, and go through the amount of money you've spent. If you're young, really want to turn the heat up and are really, really brave, you could always make your debt buddy a parent!

I can almost hear the cries of 'way too embarrassing'. Of course you don't want anyone to see what you've spent – that's the point. The mere fact your buddy will see where your money has gone acts as an extra conscience to prevent you from spending on frivolous or unnecessary things when you are stuck for cash. Of course you could lie and not write things down, but that defeats the purpose – the debt buddy is there to help you help yourself.

The Double Dip

The final trick in the Money Diet cash-machine-cracking arsenal is 'the double dip'. To do this don't ever put the cash in your purse or wallet. Instead move it around so you don't always instantly know which pocket/bag it's in. This means it'll take at least a double dip to retrieve the cash, adding valuable extra thinking time to delay the impulse to spend.

Martin's Money Memories: There's Nothing Wrong With Flying Concorde

One of my scariest professional memories was an appearance on ITV1's *Loose Women* – a show with four female presenter panellists, and an audience full of women. Being the sole man in a room full of women usually has an appeal. Yet when I was introduced with the words 'Guess what? We've got a bloke joining us. He's going to be talking about shopping. And he says you're all useless at it', it felt similar to climbing K2 with non-stick shoe soles.

The truth is I'd never actually said women were bad shoppers, my actual point was everyone – men and women – can be much better shoppers. But TV doesn't like bland phrasing, and so the challenge was set.

It went well at first. My initial tactic was to explain that cutting the cost of the boring stuff like gas, electricity and telephone bills means more shopping cash in your pocket. The discussion whizzed along until Claire Sweeney, one of the presenter panellists, was asked, 'What's the most you've ever spent on a dress?' To the aghast faces of the audience she replied, 'I think £3,000.'

They turned to me and said, 'I bet you've got something to say to her about that!' The subtext being, 'Come on Mr Money Saving Expert, we've heard you introduced as the tightest man on television, have a go at Claire.' However, MoneySaving is more subtle than that, so I asked her, 'Why did you spend that much?'

It turned out the dress was for a specific concert appearance, part of her job, and an exclusive one-off from a designer that she really liked.

In other words, she'd bought an item which was necessary and wasn't available anywhere else, so there was no way to get it more cheaply. It was a planned and considered expenditure from someone who could afford it. So my reply was quite simple: 'There's nowt wrong with what Claire's done. MoneySaving isn't about being tight – there's nothing wrong with flying to New York on Concorde and returning on the *QE2* providing you can afford it; there's only something wrong if you pay £7,000 for it when you could have got it for £3,000.'

This is the basic Money Diet philosophy. If you budget, prepare and plan, know what you need and can afford it, there's nothing wrong with treating yourself. If it makes your life more pleasurable, go on, enjoy it.

THE LIST OF MERRICK'S EIGHT MONEY-SAVING WEEKS

You're about to get access to a unique MoneySaving diary. 'Merrick' is a 31-year-old man who lives in the South of England and earns around £22,000 a year. As a regular contributor to the Chat Board of www.moneysavingexpert.com, when he heard he might be due to be made redundant, he decided to concentrate on his spending and radically reduce it.

Using the information available from the site, and the help of other Chatters for hints and tips, he started to diarise his weekly savings.

With his very kind permission here follows an edited version …

Week 1: Clearing up the mess

I am deep into a relationship. My girlfriend wants to move back to England from Canada and we want to set up home next year. So today I have looked at my finances (and they are a mess) and changed a few things that I pay out monthly.

£10 union membership cancelled. I have never used it.

£2.50 clothes insurance. Never claimed and don't need it.

I have changed the following as well:

Taken a three-month payment holiday from a loan I have (11% APR) and will put the money I'm not using on that into paying a sizeable chunk of my store card (28%) off.

Moved a credit card balance to a six-month 0% interest rate. Cut up all but one card and my current account card.

Used the 'aapetrolbusters' website to find a garage I travel past regularly and estimate savings of £200 a year.

(Martin's note: www.aapetrolbusters.co.uk is a website I recommend, run by the AA, in which you plug in your details and it tells you the cheapest petrol stations in your area.)

Looked at my daily expenses (food, mainly) and decided to take sandwiches to work as well as drinks. I estimate savings of £3 a day (food is expensive in London).

I am going to stop driving the car to the station. Will only save me 50p a day by switching to public transport, but is probably just as quick.

Noticed that pizzas are about a third the price I pay in Asda if I cook them myself. Estimate savings of £120 a month.

Total savings per year (excluding credit cards which I cannot work out): £1,920 (estimated), and I will probably save a bit more because my priorities have changed and now must save for a house.

Week 2: A glossy cut

This week, I have looked at magazines. I buy a computer magazine monthly for its advertising. This works out at £39 a year. By subscribing, I pay just £23.97. A saving of about £15 a year. Not a fortune, I know, but every little bit helps.

Week 3: Water palaver

In my personal pursuit to find a way to keep the same lifestyle but cheaper, I have this week looked at several things and the biggest shock to me is water. I drink a lot of bottled water during the day at work (can't trust the tap stuff) and buy one 500ml bottle going to work and one coming back at 89p a bottle (London is expensive). This equates to £8.90 a week.

But by buying a 6-litre pack of water at Tesco for £3.49, I would save on the year around £280.

(Martin's note: This comment provoked a great deal of debate on the Chat Board. One major argument stemmed from the cost of using water filters rather than buying the

water at all – and overall that was calculated to be cheaper. Others simply said buy one plastic bottle of water, and once it's finished just fill it up from the tap or (if available) purified water from work.)

Week 4: Ringing up the savings

Hoorah, I have changed my overseas telecom provider. I phone my girlfriend twice a week in Canada for two hours each time. I spend £100 a month phoning Canada, but by switching to Telediscount, that will come down by 75%.

Brilliant or what?

(Martin's note: Telediscount is a cut-price telecom provider that can be accessed from any phone. At the time of Merrick's writing it was my recommendation as the cheapest way to call Canada. See 'Crash Diet', page 222.)

Week 5: Electric savings

Well, Sunday was strange. I had to defrost the freezer. Being a single male, I am not too well versed in the ways of kitchen appliances. So, after defrosting, these blue marks numbered 1 to 10 appear on the side wall of the freezer (chest freezer). 'Wonder what they are?' Look in the manual and slap me if it's not a marker for setting the freezer – i.e., if the package for the food says it has to be stored at number 3, you switch the dial to number 3.

Now, I haven't a clue how much I am going to save, as it has been on setting 10 for the last three years, and I never have more than half of it full with food. So off I go to look at other things in the house. And here is what I discover:

- Video – used once a week at most, so now it's unplugged when not needed.

- Three courtesy lights outside – changed the time they stay on from seven minutes to two minutes each.
- TV – never to be left on standby.
- I have started turning lights off when I am leaving a room. Can't quantify savings, but one evening the girlfriend phoned and we spoke for two hours and I actually turned off the light in the study when I went to phone her (three spotlights).
- Washing machine – had an economy setting. Now using that for all my knocking-about clothes.
- Switched on 'powersaving' on my PC. Monitor now switches off if I am away for more than five minutes.

I haven't a clue what I will save, but my goal is to save and at the same time not change my lifestyle too much.

(Martin's note: There are loads of ways to save energy use, helping you and the environment – energy-saving light bulbs and better draught insulation are two to think about. As for the money, the biggest and easiest saving all of us can make is to move to the cheapest energy supplier – check out 'Crash Diet', page 149.)

Week 6: A view to save

I audited my Sky TV package and found the following: Film Four and TVX (for the lads) I don't watch. Which equates to about £13 a month I am paying for unwatched channels. I'm thinking of keeping a diary of what I watch for a week to see whether I have all the right packages.

Looked at my DVD collection and find I pay about £50 a month on DVDs I watch once, maybe twice. The upshot of it all is that I actually joined Blockbuster. Saving around £35 a month by renting rather than buying.

So this week's cost-saving is around £570 per year.

Okay, I haven't got as many nice DVDs on my shelf, but I am a hoarder so they would be dead money anyhow.

Week 7: 'Get rid of your junk'

Last Sunday I had to go up to the loft for some suitcases. Now, while there, a load of boxes fell over. This prompted me to start sorting out my junk. And believe me, it is junk.

I have always done a little selling on eBay, and decided to be totally ruthless and get rid of anything that I didn't need.

(Martin's note: www.ebay.co.uk is an auction site which, among other things, enables you to sell anything you like on the internet and people can bid on them.)

The sum sales total so far is £395 (after taking out all the various costs) and I still have another similar amount of items to list.

So this week I say, hopefully, I can dispose of £1,000 of rubbish and pay off my store card (28.8%). This will save me the £40 a month I currently pay on it.

I am going to tackle the shed and garage after the loft, and hopefully expand on this.

(Martin's note: Store card debt is almost invariably the most expensive form of debt on plastic, with rates up in the 30%s. My only problem with Merrick is that in week 1, he should have moved this debt onto the 0% credit card via the balance transfer ahead of any other debt, as it is the most expensive.)

The final amount I made on eBay from junk in and around my house was (drum roll, please) £874.80 after all expenses.

My mum has now asked me to get rid of all my junk at her house. So a lot more selling coming up.

The money is to be paid off my store card and this means I

am now debt-free on store cards. I've cut them up as well. There's a store with a beautiful plasma TV round the corner and I don't want to be tempted.

Week 8: Keep the savings in the family

Had the distinct pleasure of taking my nephew to town last Saturday. While walking through the shopping centre, he says, 'Uncle Merrick, can I have a Playstation magazine, please?'

Now he had been good and was no trouble, so I agreed. He then says, 'Let's go to the market then.' It turns out that our town market has a guy who does last month's magazines for around half the shop price.

Savings could be quite substantial for those with kids, as he also does comics and other kid-related stuff (stickers, etc). I guess the lesson is 'Spend a morning learning your town and save money.'

After clearing all the rubbish from the spare room (see eBay, last week) I was left with a nice room with a bed, double wardrobe, TV and large desk in it.

Now what to do with it?

I was in the pub Wednesday, and a friend who is constructing a rail link mentioned the lack of affordable rentable accommodation.

He has now moved into my spare room at £50 a week, and left his place that was costing him £80 a week.

He saves and I gain.

Thanks to my zeal in saving, I am now making money.

three
KNOW THYSELF

We're all different. And this is a secret weapon. Providers tend to make their decisions based on the conglomerated masses, but by knowing yourself and finding your niche you can play against these averages, and win.

No two people are the same, whether it's fingerprints, DNA or spending habits. Fortunately, those people trying to flog us things or push financial services forget that, and the Money Dieter can use this to gain an advantage.

Finance has become 'massified' – big institutions are dealing with huge numbers of people at the same time. They usually treat people identically, making easy assumptions. One of the most common, and often correct, is the assumption that most customers are apathetic and ill-informed – and by targeting this side of people's personality they can supercharge their profits. At certain times companies even use actuarial risk tables which divide us up into easy-fit demographics, and attempt to predict our behaviour.

Yet, they're wrong: there's no such thing as one-size-fits-all, we're all different, with different life stages, family situations, incomes, likes, habits, risk profiles, spending habits and decision-making criteria. And just as in buying clothes, knowing the size, style and colour that fit and suit you means you look better, knowing who you are and how you behave gives you the edge – simply by choosing what's right for you, not them.

SELF-KNOWLEDGE

There are three steps to climb to really push home your self-knowledge advantage over providers:

Step One: Getting to Know You

The most important question is, are you an active or passive Money Dieter? To stretch this book's analogy slightly, it's a bit like saying, do you want to exercise by walking more briskly to or from work, or are you itching to pump iron and sweat to maximise your savings?

Just like with real exercise, most of us tend towards good intentions and poor delivery. How many people do you know who have a gym membership and yet never go? In itself this is a fitness and financial problem – after all, gym membership is expensive – but when it's not just the gym, but your entire money matters you're deluding yourself over it's a much more severe problem.

Coolly and clinically assessing your own behaviour is crucial. Good powerful resolutions are great but – look back – are you the type of person who follows your resolutions? Do you set goals and achieve them? If not, you are better off being less ambitious and choosing long-term easy solutions rather than following the cutting-edge power-playing techniques.

To help you, in this book I separate the easy and the best solutions. Easy isn't wrong. It mightn't deliver the same savings as the best solutions, but it takes less work. And it's much better to go for the easy solution if you honestly don't think you will be able to put in the effort for the best.

Be a tart or have a stable relationship?

Enough psychobabble gobbledegook, let me put this in practical terms. Take the tricky world of credit cards – as you'll see in 'Healthy Eating', page 283, there are more MoneySaving recipes here than anywhere else, but let's focus on interest rates for those with decent credit scores who need to borrow. There are two different interest-cutting offers for everyday spending. The best way is to be the consistent 0% player, applying for a new 0% intro offer each time the old one runs out, moving from one card company to another. This is the classic strategy of the credit-card tart. And I'm happy to proclaim loud and proud that 'I am a tart.' Frankly, if I weren't, I shouldn't be writing this book. Card companies hope that once the 0% interest ends you'll continue to keep your money with them, so they can smile all the way back to the (their own?) bank.

Credit-card tarts thwart this easily and simply by moving money from 0% card to 0% card (see 'Healthy Eating', page 296).

The second route is for those who prefer a stable relationship to tarting. Here you just stick with a card that has a low standard rate, around 8%, over the long term.

So what happens if you don't know yourself well enough and get it wrong? Wannabe tarts who go for 0% offers but don't remember to switch will be seriously out of pocket. Take a look at the table opposite.

Who are you?	What do you do?	Interest charged on £1,000 debt*				
		After 6 months	After 1 year	After 18 months	After 2 years	After 5 years
The Tart	Continually rotates 0% cards	£0	£0	£0	£0	£0
Failed Tart	Starts on 0%, forgets to change, and ends up on 18%	£0	£86	£180	£282	£1,105
Stable Relationship	8% the whole time	£39	£80	£122	£166	£470

*For ease of illustration, I've assumed the debt starts at £1,000 and is never paid off. In truth that would never happen as there are minimum payments.

The real Tart wins by a mile, but the Failed Tart is the big loser. Even after just one year, someone in a Stable Relationship does better than the Failed Tart, and after five years the difference is enormous. Picking the wrong card for you can be an absolute financial disaster – and is exactly what card companies want.

Always remember – MoneySaving fervour can feel like a forgotten fad in six months' time. So be very careful to analyse yourself before choosing.

This pattern stretches way beyond credit cards – it hits virtually every product out there. Take savings accounts (see page 156) – here the choice is between riding the wave of top rates by switching from account to account, or settling for a good, steady, high rate which tracks the Bank of England base rate.

It even impacts Personal Finance's blue whale, mortgages. Either remortgage to a better rate time and time again or just stick with a low standard rate, keeping the payments consistently low.

All this boils down to asking yourself: 'Am I willing to do the work required for the very best results or am I happy to stick with good, solid, safe and easy?'

There's no right or wrong here, there's just you!

Step Two: You Know You Better than They Do

Product providers can do all the statistical number crunching in the world, but they'll never know as much about us as we do. This knowledge deficit can be manipulated to pay cold hard cash. Think through the things that specifically affect you in a different way from other people.

This is most effective in the world of insurance. Here prices often depend on actuarial risk tables, which predict how individuals behave so insurance can be priced accordingly. It's done by statistically looking at the standard behaviour of the masses. Yet you can predict your behaviour better than they can.

Let me introduce a moment of culture here. Purely to show off, you understand. The phrase 'Know thyself' was born as an inscription on the Oracle of Apollo at Delphi (well, the ancient Greek equivalent was, anyway). The most tangible MoneySaving benefit of 'Know thyself' is with mobile phone insurance. This provides no symmetry at all as Apollo was the god of music, and surely his wrath would have been awakened by the tin-toned faux 'tunes' mobiles play.

Yet there is an Olympian-sized gain from self-awareness. If a phone's lost, stolen, cracked or crushed, insurance will cover you – but more important is the question whether it's worth insuring in the first place. There are some whose mobile phone has been safely clipped to their waist belt for five years; it's never been damaged or stolen and no one ever gets near it.

Then there's me. On average I lose a mobile phone three times a year. Don't ask me why – I'm good with money but bad with phones. If you're a waist-belt clipper, you may be smiling smugly, but hold on a second, because if you've got mobile phone insurance, did you know you're subsidising me? In fact you're paying for my lost phones. And I'd really like to say thank you.

Let me explain. Mobile phone insurance prices are not based on any of the standard risk factors – age, sex, gender, occupation, where you live, health or, most important, whether or not you've lost your mobile phone before. This means my insurance payments haven't risen beyond the average, even though my phone is more difficult to locate than Shergar. Waist-belt clippers pay the same as me, as the overall cost is

---

Martin's Money Memories:
'You Were Very Handsome' – Good, Fair, Unbiased Opinion

My first trial appearance on *This Morning* was a truly nerve-racking affair, not the being on telly, but the fact that if I did well, I might get a regular slot – a long-held ambition. After the show, I decided I needed an honest, unbiased critique of my performance. So I called my grandmother.

'What do you think?'

'Oh, Martin, you were very handsome,' Grandma said.

'But what about what I said, did it make sense?'

'Well, I didn't understand it, but you were very handsome. And my friend Dorothy Leverhume called and she said you were very handsome, too.'

'But, Grandma, isn't she going blind?'

'Yes, Martin, but she said you sounded very handsome.'

worked out by the market's, not the individual's, average loss. This is where the cross-subsidy comes in – those who never lose partially pay for those of us who are losers.

That's why it's important to ask, do you really want or need mobile phone insurance? Of course the past never predicts the future, as all financial communications must rightly tell us. But, if you've not lost your phone in the last five years, the chances are pretty unlikely you're going to lose it in the future. It's always possible, but I still suspect you're less likely to lose it than I am, so should you really pay for the insurance? This means you could choose to 'self-insure'. Here, instead of paying premiums, you put money in a savings account, so in the eventuality that you lose your phone, there's ready money to pay for it and it's earning interest. After a number of years, if you've never lost the phone, you can take some cash out and enjoy it. People like me, of course, should get mobile phone insurance – as I pay substantially less in insurance than for repeated replacements. As I know my own behaviour and demands, I have a policy that gets me a new replacement phone straight away.

There is a middle ground. Cheaper mobile insurance is available free with some bank accounts or by simply adding 'all-risks' cover onto your household insurance (this covers objects taken outside the home). Neither of these systems provide as quick a replacement mobile, but they do offer cheap peace of mind.

This 'playing against the average' works across a range of risk-based policies. For example, adopt this tactic for private medical insurance: if you're fitter than a fiddle and healthier than humanity, why not just put money away in a bank account for potential treatments and self-insure again? For peace of mind, you could also hedge against any serious problems by getting a private medical insurance policy with an incredibly high excess, such as you pay the first £5,000 of any treatment. This means it's very, very cheap, but if you have serious problems, you're covered.

Step Three: Forewarned is Forearmed, So Stay One Step Ahead

Who is the first person you tell when you discover you or your partner is pregnant? Parent, friend, grandparent, cousin, aunt, uncle, work colleague, secret friend you meet every day on the bus and chat to, lover?

It may be any of these, but it certainly isn't your bank, credit-card provider or insurance company. This means you've a good few months of advance knowledge. The same's equally true of other life changes – moving house, changing or quitting work, leaving for a sabbatical all affect your finances. And at any of these crucial transitional life points you have the upper hand over the banks and building societies. You know what's likely to happen, they don't.

Sticking with the original example, pregnancy. If you or your partner is pregnant, the likelihood is that you or she will quit work for a minimum of six months. During this time you will credit score substantially lower, because of decreased income. (See 'Credit Scoring', page 242.) So if you need to borrow money, apply while you are still in work. This should mean you score more highly and have better access to cheaper credit, something probably useful during maternity leave.

This means we must become educated fortune-tellers. 'Know yourself' becomes 'know your future'. And whenever you know more than the bank does, take full advantage.

The No-Butts Guide to Smoking

Know the Cost of Your Habit

Do you smoke? Are you aware of its impact on your finances? Before you think I'm about to rant, actually smoking isn't always as bad for your wealth as it is for your health. Don't get me wrong, usually being a smoker means you pay more and your finances burn, but occasionally, lighting up is a bonus.

This isn't even about the more-than-four-quid-a-day (£1,500 a year) a 20-a-day smoker pays for cigarettes. Ignoring that, quit smoking and you could pay over £26,000 less for your financial products over 20 years.

Smoking impacts any product where the price depends on the likelihood of illness or death. Common medical opinion is that the benefits of exercising, eating well and losing weight combined pale into insignificance compared to the benefits of quitting smoking, as the risk from most smoking-related illnesses decreases rapidly after you give up.

What is a 'Non-Smoker'?

To qualify as a non-smoker you normally have to declare you have been smoke-free for at least a year. Cigarettes, cigars, roll-your-owns and pipes all count as smoking for most policies. Always notify providers when you quit smoking, and again after you've been smoke-free for at least a year.

Most policies rely on your honesty when it comes to declaring whether you smoke. Lying is easy and results in cheaper premiums, but can be disastrous when it comes to making a claim. It's at this point that medical or other evidence of your habit is likely to be discovered. Your provider can and probably will legitimately refuse to pay out and not even refund your premiums. Even people who have almost, but not completely, stopped smoking may be detected and lose out this way.

Quit smoking and as a non-smoker you'll save money on the following:

Term Assurance: This is the cheapest type of life assurance. It only pays out if you die within a set period. (See 'Crash Diet', page 198.)

(Other life assurance policies are much less affected by smoking as, unlike term assurance, they're investment-based – it's their underlying performance, not whether you light up, that counts.)

Approximate non-smoker cost-saving: 40%

Private Medical Insurance (PMI): PMI provides medical treatment and hospital accommodation. You'd think its costs would be massively upped for smokers. They're not. Providers usually make a detailed analysis of your health, even if only via a phone questionnaire. Smoking-related health issues or signs are therefore taken into account in their own right, leaving the actual fact that you smoke as a side issue, hiding the real cost.

Approximate non-smoker cost-saving: 5%

Permanent Health Insurance (PHI): Often called 'income-replacement plans', these pay a proportion of your normal salary if you're incapable of working after a set amount of time. The payments stop once you return to work.

Approximate non-smoker cost-saving: 25%

Critical Illness Insurance: Pays a one-off lump sum if you're diagnosed with a critical illness. These policies have the biggest smoking price-differential – this indicates how much bigger the risk of serious illness is for smokers. The increased cost also reflects the fact that, unlike PHI, the payment is all in one big lump sum.

Approximate non-smoker cost-saving: 50%

Annuities: Up to now it has been all bad news for smokers. However, at retirement the situation can change. I'm in no way advocating people should start smoking, but if you are a smoker and about to retire, it's worth considering the timing of when you give up. The main bright spark for nicotine lovers is that smokers get better annuity rates, and these better rates can add nearly 10% a year to your retirement income.

At retirement, you're legally obliged to spend at least 75% of a money purchase pension fund buying an annuity, which pays you each year until you die. The rate depends on your fund size and on how soon you're predicted to die; therefore smokers, with their reduced life expectancy, can receive substantially higher rates. For a 60-year-old woman in 2003 with a £100,000 fund, the best-paying smoker's annuity pays £800 more a year than the best non-smoker's annuity – that's 10% extra, and over 20 years means a gain of £16,000.

Bizarrely enough, some smokers lie and claim they're smoke-free when they get their annuity, both out of guilt and mistakenly believing it's the 'correct' answer. This may cost them a fortune. However, there's no point in non-smokers grabbing a fag just before retirement, as you normally need to have smoked continually for ten years to get special rates.

Annuity providers rely on your honesty, as it's difficult to detect how long someone's been smoking for – but remember, lying is fraud. On the other hand, if you are a smoker, there's nothing preventing you quitting the day after you've set up your annuity contract, as payments are fixed at this point. Therefore, if you are about to quit just before retiring, consider holding off.

THE TEST OF ARE YOU A MONEY DIETER ALREADY?

As we're moving through the Diet now, I thought a little test of your instincts would be in order. Answer the following questions by selecting the best fit. Keep a note of your answers and find out your score using the table at the end. Then you'll know whether you're a true Lean, Mean Money Diet Machine.

1. It's Sunday afternoon, a friend's mentioned a way to cut your gas and electricity bills by 20%. It should take about 20 minutes. Would you:

a. Put it on your list of things to do and have a quick peek?

b. Know you've already finessed the best supplier by using internet comparison tables?

c. Take a trip out for a bite to eat – a Sunday's simply too good to waste on utility bills?

2. You're buying a new wide-screen TV because the old one is on its last legs. Do you:

a. Buy *Whose TV?* magazine, research the technology needed to optimise it, then go to the nearest shop that sells it and grab it?

b. Walk into Dixons or Comet and buy the cheapest one that seems to fit the bill?

c. Scan the internet using shopping robots for the cheapest price, having already done the technical research to ensure you're getting the model you want at the lowest price?

d. As c, but then take the quote to the high street and barter with every shop, playing them off against each other in order to get it cheap and instantly?

3. You're in the pub and that rather intense money-focused friend of yours intriguingly asks you what rate you're paying on your mortgage. Do you:

a. Reel it off instantly?

b. Not have a clue?

c. Not know the rate, but know where your mortgage form is and how to find out?

4. A market research company stops you in the street and asks you what an ISA is. Do you answer:

a. It's a way to invest money in the stock market?

b. It's Italian frozen water?

c. It's an Individual Savings Account that allows you to save or invest tax-free in cash, shares or life assurance?

d. It's an Individual Savings Accounts, and while many people tout it's tax-free, they ignore the fact there is moderate tax to pay on share dividends, plus of course there's share stamp duty within a self-select ISA?

5. You are about to pay for some cinema tickets. You open up your wallet and there are your credit cards. How many?

a. Two. A Visa and a Mastercard.

b. Four. All high-street cards, on which you only make the monthly minimum repayments, and the debts now stack up to £14,000.

c. Nine. All have had debts on them, but you only ever pay 0% interest, continually rotating the debt via balance transfers and saving the money you're not spending in a high-interest savings account to make a profit.

d. One card. Your bank's, and you pay it off in full every month.

6. The telephone bill arrives. It's £95 for the month, a lot more than you want to spend. How would you cut it?

a. Look into switching provider, do some research and find the best plan.

b. Move house nearer your friends so more of your calls are local.

c. Forget changing products, deciding instead you'll just cut down slightly.

d. Do the research, first switching the main phone-line tariff, then making a note of the 14 different call providers to find which is cheapest for each type of call.

YOUR SCORE

1. a. 3 b. 5 c. 1
2. a.1 b. 2 c. 5 d.10
3. a. 5 b. 1 c. 3
4. a. 3 b. 1 c. 5 d. 10
5. a. 2 b. 1. c. 10 d.3
6. a. 5 b. 0 c. 2 d. 10

MONEY DIET POINTS

5-12: *Obese* You're obviously quite happy to throw your money away, and it seems you don't know your ISA from your elbow. If you're very rich, fine – though it won't last. If not, you need to start taking more of an interest in your finances. Then again, you've made a great start by getting hold of *The Money Diet*. Well done on making the first move.

13-25: *Need exercise* You try not to overspend, but you don't want budgeting to rule your life. There are lots of easy ways for you to save without too much effort, though. The one-off methods in the 'Crash Diet' will pay dividends.

26-48: *Trim, lean and fit* A great score. You care about how much you're spending and make sure you always get value for money. There are always ways to ensure companies make less profit out of you though, and some of the more cutting-edge techniques in later chapters should be able to teach you a few more tricks.

48-50: *International money athlete* You're willing to go to extremes to cut your bills, and you've knowledge levels to match. In fact, you should probably be writing this book rather than reading it! For you, money is more important than time. You're the type of person who turns their windscreen wipers off when you go under a bridge to save energy. Your bills and costs will enable you to have a better lifestyle, but will you ever manage to get off the internet in time to enjoy it?

51+: *Unbelievable* Your scores are not as good as they may seem at first. The maximum possible on this questionnaire is 50. Be very careful. You're the type of person who'd go out and buy 10 colour TV sets, because you only need one licence. Pay a bit more attention to your cash, seek advice, don't just jump straight in there and assume you're doing it right.

four

BE A BETTER SHOPPER

Retail therapy at a price you can afford is possible. The first thing to do is target your 'gotta have' impulses. Control them and you can have more for less. Every time you shop, follow the right Money Mantras to discipline yourself (see page 71).

Do the Money Diet and you will have more in your pocket, possibly to lessen debts, but maybe also to spend and enjoy. The next step is about being a better shopper, so that when you spend, your cash stretches further and you can have even more.

Now I must admit, I'm quaking as I write this. You see, for many people, shopping is not money, but sport – it is a prime recreational activity. This is only wrong if it goes out of control – then it can ruin lives, and stop you shopping ever again. I promise not to ruin your enjoyment, if *you* don't either!

Becoming a better shopper is a mix of knowledge and self-discipline.

Martin's Money Memories: Cheap and Cheerful, Darling

Backstage at *This Morning*, I was chatting to two top TV stylists (who will remain nameless) also on the programme that day. Before long my appearance was being deconstructed. Overall the verdict was 'Casual's good, but you're overly so.'

Then, item by item:

Jumper: 'It's a good shape, but the wrong colour.' It cost me £55.

Trousers: 'Totally the wrong choice, wrong shape, wrong cut, wrong colour.' They cost me £99 (though admittedly I bought them in a sale for £49).

Shoes: 'They're cool, and seriously funky, where d'ya get them?' They cost me £10, bought the evening before in an emergency, from a nearly empty high-street store's rack.

RETAIL SNOBBERY: MORE EXPENSIVE ISN'T BETTER!

You see two stereos, one is priced at £50, one at £150 … which is better? Admit it, your instincts say the more expensive one must be – after all, there has to be a reason it costs more. This is a retail snobbery we've been hypnotised into by marketeers, false pride we have to let go of. Judge a product on whether it suits you and your needs, not purely on how much it costs; pricey may be better, but it isn't automatically so.

FIGHT THE IMPULSE!

Let's be honest, when you shop, it's not what you need that's the problem, but the things you don't need; it's when the 'gotta have' impulse rises from your belly and a desire to spend springs from your loins. The child inside says, 'I want, I want,

I want,' and once that little voice is heard, it's virtually impossible to stop.

Impulse-cracker 1: Martin's Money Mantras

I've a couple of easy-to-remember mantras for you to chant to yourself when you are about to spend. One for those who are short of cash, and therefore need to be long on self-discipline, and one for those who can, within reason, pretty much buy whatever they want.

Martin's Money Mantra I – for the skint

Do I need it?

Can I afford it?

If an answer is 'No' or 'Don't know' – STOP!

Quite simply, if the answer to either of these questions is no, don't buy it. If you don't need it, don't buy it. If you can't afford it, don't buy it. If you haven't checked it's cheaper anywhere else, don't buy it. You need every penny. If it's 'yes', 'yes', 'don't know', then go now and check (see 'Talk to People', page 94). Now if you make the purchase, you will know you're doing the right thing.

Martin's Money Mantra II – even if you can afford it

Will I use it?

Is it worth it?

If an answer is 'No' or 'Don't know' – STOP!

This may sound just a little bit harsh – after all, you can afford it. But the funny thing is, sometimes we make purchases purely out of desire, yet get no real benefit apart from the pure shopping buzz. Are you really willing to shell out for that buzz? So ask: 'Will I use it?' If not, don't buy it.

'Is it worth it?' Even if you will use it, will you use it enough to justify the cash? If not, don't buy it. In economic terms, this is known as 'opportunity cost'. What else could you do with the money, and would you enjoy that more? Take a look at your wardrobe, book shelves, shoe rack and CD collection – are there clothes or shoes hardly ever or never worn, unread books and unlistened-to CDs? With this Money Mantra you may have spent the cash on something else instead, and gained more fun or benefit.

Finally, have you checked if it's available anywhere else? If you haven't, if you can spare a little time do so, especially with a big purchase. The savings could be huge, leaving more money in your pocket for other things.

Remember the mantra that is appropriate to you, and as you are about to take 'it' to the till, repeat it to yourself.

Sometimes time is money

Now don't think I'm being a complete party-pooper here. I realise that at certain times money mantras are unrealistic. To quote the old cliché, time is money – and when you're in a rush, buying quickly can be cheaper than buying cheaply.

For example, if you're holding a party and need new music, I would of course suggest using a shopping robot on the internet to find the cheapest prices (see 'Crash Diet', page 153), then trying three or four high-street stores to ensure you're getting the best deal. Yet if the party is tonight, and you're rushing to get home to prepare food, getting the CDs in the first shop may be the MoneySaving move – if it means you can use public transport not a taxi; you have more time to cook so food isn't wasted; or you've more time to shop for a good deal on booze and snacks. All of these are valid reasons.

However, this realism isn't an excuse for *never* getting the best deal. Realism works both ways. Don't just say, 'I don't have time to save money today,' unless you also follow the more difficult 'I don't have the money to save time today.'

Impulse-cracker 2: Powerful Shopping Technology

Impulse-cracker 2 is a high-tech piece of communication equipment. A flat two-dimensional optical tablet, with a specialised marking instrument to direct your shopping.

It's called a shopping list. Before you leave home to be subjected to marketing ploys, clever shop layouts and tempting special offers, sit down and work out what you're going out shopping for and how much you can afford to spend on it. It doesn't matter whether it's clothes shopping on the high street, buying a new computer, or a supermarket session. There's an old adage – never go food shopping when you're hungry. Well, don't shop for *anything* unless you've defined your appetite. Make a list and stick to it. By deciding what you want *before* you go, and before you're enticed by all the various goodies on offer, your purchasing decisions will be more effective.

There are of course always exceptions to a rule. Spotting a substantial bargain while shopping, something that you were planning to buy another day, may rightfully loosen the purse strings somewhat, but not of course without following the Money Mantras first.

Impulse-cracker 3: Price Tag Scanning

What I'm about to say causes a physiological reaction in a few women that makes them arch one eyebrow and give me a look so sceptical it makes Jeremy Paxman look like a wilting violet. However, if you're willing to try, it can work.

Price tag scanning is a simple idea, and is especially good for clothes shopping, though it can be used on anything. Rather than looking at the clothes first and then the price tag (or worse, not looking at the price tag until you get to the till), check the price tag before looking at the clothes.

This may sound silly. Of course you'll see the clothes when getting to the tag, but in most clothes shops, garments are massed and squashed together. If you're buying a pair of trousers – having, of course, decided beforehand how much you can spend – run your eyes across the tags. When you spot something within your price range, pull it out and have a gander to see if you like it. Where the price is too high, don't even look at the item. Don't tease yourself. Don't let that inner voice seduce you into spending more than you can afford – as soon as you say to yourself, 'I have to have it', you've lost. Either you're going to spend more and self-delude with the old 'I'll buy this now and spend nowt next week' or you'll leave the shop disappointed and with regrets. The price tag scanning technique will stop you putting yourself into this position in the first place.

Impulse-cracker 4: Blind Branding

This is one especially for designer doyens. It's just a simple one-off game to play with a friend. Go to a shop and get the friend to pick out a number of branded and similar but unbranded clothes. Ask your friend to show them to you in such a way you can't see what brand it is. Now pick the one you prefer. Do this five or six times. How many of your preferred choices are branded? If, as is likely, it's only about half, ask yourself, 'Is branded always better?' I will admit, fashion is the one area where brand has a value, because the

Martin's Money Memories: Sometimes My Advice is a Load of Cobblers!

I was out shopping with one of my best friends. Something she doesn't particularly enjoy, as shopping with a Money Saving Expert takes some of the fun away. Her big love is shoes, she adores them and has a large number sitting at home waiting for her. This particular day was a 'boots' day. There were two pairs in the shop she was yearning for.

The decision for her wasn't whether to spend, but which of these knee-length, high-heeled black leather boots to go for. At this point I intervened and looked at the prices. The pair on the left cost £60, the pair on the right cost £130. Instantly she decided, of course, that the £130 pair were the best and the 'gotta haves'.

Putting my spend-buster hat on, I decided it was time for drastic action. I nipped to the cash machine, shoved my card in and took out £70 in crisp notes. Running back to the shop, for fear she was already at the till, I grabbed both pairs of boots. Look, I told her, this is the real decision you're actually making: either this pair of £130 boots here on its own, or this £60 pair but with this £70 in cash. Her eyes widened and she said, 'I'd never thought of it that way before,' leaving me sitting there smugly, thinking 'Money Saving Expert on the case! Job's a good 'un.' Ten seconds later she was off to the till with the £130 pair. Ah, well, you win some, you lose some!

brand itself can be fashionable even if the clothes aren't. However, often well-made unbranded fashion clothing can mean you look just as good. If money's tight, de-labelling pays.

Fashion is fleeting

It always amazes me that people on a budget save up to fork out for really expensive fashionable clothes, knowing they'll soon have passed their peak and will never be worn again. Fashion is transitory, so fashionable garments tend to have a limited life, therefore buying cheap and often can be a better strategy. This is magnified when it comes to the bizarre trend of high fashion for very young children. First, kids grow, and second, they don't recognise the brands, so why not wait and save your cash for when they're old enough to demand designer – which they surely will.

Impulse-cracker 5: Retail Therapy at a Price You Can Afford – the Game

Shopping is sexy, it's fun and it's enjoyable. It's also extremely dangerous when you don't have any money. So if you're on a cost-conscious budget but love to spend, and retail therapy is a hobby, here's a little challenge just for you.

Shopping is about both the activity and the acquisition of new things. Now, I can't recreate that perfectly, but there is a way to at least *try* to satisfy yourself at lower cost. If you feel the shopping urge, go to the shops, but only take a pound or two, or maybe if we're being generous, three or even four – and challenge yourself to use that very small amount of money to buy something frivolous, useful, or both.

The Game. To find the most enjoyable thing possible from all the shops.

The Aim. To provide your spending buzz fix at the cheapest possible cost.

This Money Diet game tries to do for spenders what a nicotine patch does for smokers. It won't always work, but anything's worth a try.

DANGER! SALES!

Sales are wonderful for money-savers, but they also hold a measure of danger. Bagging a discount doesn't automatically mean you're saving money. In the panicked, fevered rush to grab sales bargains, it's easy to buy lots of things you don't really need. A suit that's 50% off is a great deal, but a bad buy if you never wear it.

As I'm neither stupid nor brave enough to bring up shopping gender differences, I thought I would re-print a joke floating round the internet:

'A man will pay £2 for a £1 item he needs.

A woman will pay £1 for a £2 item that she doesn't need.'

Things often look different outside the sales than in. And while you still retain all your statutory rights, you have no right to return goods simply because you don't like them. Shops normally grant us this privilege, but they often withhold it in the sales. That's why when sales shopping it's even more important to shop smart, because you can't change your mind.

Money Diet Quick Fact Snack: When to BOGOF!

Bogof! No, not you! BOGOF stands for 'buy one, get one free'. And in some circumstances these are a 'must buy'. This applies when the BOGOF or 3-for-2 or half-price deal is on consumable goods you use regularly that don't go off, like toothpaste, razors, toilet paper and batteries. If you see these offers, grab as many as you can store. To put it in stock-market terms, a 3-for-2 offer (on something you'd spend on anyway) is a 50% return risk-free. An amazing investment.

TOP FIVE TIPS FOR THE SALES

- Decide what you want before you go.
- Set a budget of exactly how much you can spend.
- Don't buy on impulse, stick to a list. Use the Money Mantras.
- Cheap isn't automatically a bargain. Good deals are great, but just because it's cheap doesn't mean you should buy it.
- Remember, overextending yourself in the sales and getting yourself into costly debt can be more expensive even than the full price.

THE LIST OF WHAT SHOPS REALLY MEAN

Two for the price of one/buy one get one free
Meaning: The goods are half price.
Why it's cunning: You're obliged to buy two, not one, so you spend more money than with a simple 'half price' offer, doubling the retailer's sales, and you shift their stock.

Three for the price of two
Meaning: A third off.
Why it's cunning: You need to spend double what you would have spent. Though they're discounting, they're moving more volume. Also they've sewn up all your purchasing requirements for that product for the foreseeable future. In other words, if you drink one orange juice carton a week, it's guaranteed your next three weeks' worth is bought with it. Similar offers on this theme include 'buy one get second half price' and 'buy two for £5'.

50% extra free
Meaning: A third off.

Why it's cunning: This one's my favourite, it's just so damn clever. It's a numbers game. Add 50% to a product and in fact it means you're only selling the produce a third cheaper. Add 30% to a product and you're selling it 25% cheaper. This is simply the way the numbers work – so the store advertises an offer where the customer bonus looks much more generous than it is.

We'll match any other store's price

Meaning: Very little – it tells you nothing about whether its price is good or not.

Why it's cunning: While it says, 'We'll ensure you've got the cheapest price,' actually *you* have to ensure you've got the cheapest price. The shops know you won't do the work. So you've a false sense of security that you've got the cheapest goods you possibly can (see 'Price Promises', page 135).

Up to XX% off

Meaning: Very little – very few goods are at the maximum discount.

Why it's cunning: 'Up to' is a retailer's favourite. The headline discount looks much bigger than it is. In the summer sales I went to four fashion clothes shops all offering 'Up to half price/50% off' deals. I surveyed the average discount on ten items in each, and almost uniformly they only discounted an average of 15%. As a rough rule of thumb, therefore, divide the 'Up to' price by three to see the real average discount.

Shop with us and earn loyalty points

Meaning: Tiny discount on everything you spend.

Why it's cunning: Loyalty is a very clever phrase – obviously and simply it keeps you shopping at the store. Remember, though, that just because you get a couple of pence in the pound's worth of loyalty points, it doesn't automatically make it a good deal. Always think of loyalty points as just a very small discount off the purchase price – and compare this to what's charged elsewhere. (See page 84.)

An extra 100 loyalty points if you buy this

Meaning: £1 off (assuming a point is worth 1p).

Why it's cunning: The shop is giving you a discount, but ensures you must return to the store to spend it. Usually when you do that, you buy other things too. Plus, as you're spending the discount in its store, though it feels to you like it's worth a pound, the shop is only giving away its cost price on the goods, so this 'discount' hits its profits much less than the headline figure. Even better for the shop, it's likely that when you're there again you'll earn bonus points again and need to return to spend them too – perpetuating this purchasing circle.

Lingerie shop sale! Knickers coming down

Meaning: It's a good pun.

Why it's cunning: Because it enabled me to smuggle a dodgy double entendre into the book.

More people choose us than anybody else

Meaning: We're the biggest brand.

Why it's cunning: Just because a company has persuaded more people than anyone else to buy its product doesn't mean it is cheaper, better or more reliable. It probably means they've got the biggest advertising and marketing spend. Most of us make the wrong spending decisions a lot of the time, so following the masses is no guarantee of success. These signs run a spending shiver down my spine, and maybe a little unfairly my instinct says 'avoid', but if the brand or company's only real selling point is that it's popular, it can't be that good.

Consistently low prices
Meaning: Absolutely nothing.

Why it's cunning: It's a nice, easy, unsubstantiated claim. It has resonance, but there is no reference point as to what consistently low prices are. On whose terms are they cheap? Compared to whom? For what products? This is a big retailer's ploy to make us feel confident. Often it's backed up with specific examples of cheap prices, yet these are of course specially selected. When you see this sign, blink, ignore it and carry on.

Here's our ranking over the last five years
Meaning: You'll never know what it means until you read the small print.

Why it's cunning: It's not just shops that use slogans. This technique is used by unit trusts and investment funds. Be very, very careful with these, and not just because past performance of shares isn't a good indicator of future performance. I spotted a billboard advert which in big bold capital letters listed one fund's position in its category over the past five years as something like 1st, 2nd, 1st, 4th and 1st*. This looked like razor-sharp performance, yet the asterisk (*) at the bottom noted this was its 'quartile performance'. In other words 1st just meant it'd been in the top 25% of similar funds; 2nd meant it came somewhere between the 25 and 50% of funds, and 4th meant it was actually boasting about being in the bottom 25% of performers!

five

FORGET LOYALTY

Fact: No one financial services product-provider is top of the table for more than one product. Therefore, by definition, two products from one company means at least one of them isn't the best. Forget loyalty; it only pays them, not you.

BE LOYAL TO YOURSELF

Let me reiterate the fact at the top of this page. There is not one product provider who is top of the table for more than one product. Thus, if you have two or more products from any one provider, only one of them can be the top, and the rest, at best, are second-best. And when it comes to saving money, even second-best is worst.

Loyalty is important for companies: it's an easy way to help boost their profits. Dealing with loyal customers is easy; it takes less time, less management and provides consistent income. This can be a bank's current account customers, specific trainer brand buyers, a credit card's users, or Marks & Spencer's knickers wearers – anything.

Loyalty is so important to banks that they even use it as a critical measure of profitability. They compare how many different products each customer has; the more products, the more profitable they are.

Loyal customers aren't as sensitive to price changes – firms know it takes a quantum leap to displace their custom. This means they make more money out of them, with less marketing spend, and use their continued custom to subsidise attracting newcomers.

Firms' attention, gimmicks and, most important, best offers are focused on *new* customers. The phrase 'introductory offer' is common parlance, but 'existing customer offer' is heard about as commonly as 'FA Cup Winners Northwich Victoria'. New customers get access and eligibility to services existing customers don't. So why be loyal?

Credit Card Companies Will Pay £40 to £80 for Your Custom

Credit card companies are willing to pay roughly between £40 and £80 to gain a new customer. This is paid in the form of introductory 0% offers, freebies and cash, etc to encourage you to join them, or in marketing and advertising in order to introduce the new customer to their products. Ask yourself a question:

'Do I want to be the person whose custom is paid for, or the person who gives it away?'

Remember, once they've got your loyalty, they've got you. So to be a smart and savvy consumer and save money. Forget loyalty.

Who Are You Being Loyal to, Anyway?

Before becoming a journalist, I worked in the murky world of financial public relations – almost exactly the opposite of what I do these days. One day I heard the Scottish entrepreneur Sir Tom

Farmer, then owner and Chief Executive of Kwik-Fit, being questioned by City analysts about his company's latest acquisition.

He had bought a chain of outlets very similar to Kwik-Fit, yet, rather than rebranding them all as Kwik-Fits, he planned to operate them separately and keep their existing name. When asked why, to paraphrase his answer, he said, 'I believe in this world you're always going to have competition, and if there's going to be competition I may as well own it.' Everyone laughed, but underneath the humour is the truth.

Money Diet Quick Fact Snack: Dis-Loyalty Cards

Any shop worth its salt (and many that aren't) has loyalty cards. Yet never, ever, ever choose where you will shop simply because it has a loyalty scheme.

'But,' some may say, 'loyalty schemes are good, they give us discounts, we enjoy them.' Hmmm. At their hub, loyalty schemes are discount schemes. If they pay 1p in the pound, that's a 1% discount. If, as with the Boots Advantage card at the time of writing, it's 4p in the pound, it's an effective 4% off all your Boots shopping. Great! Yet it can mean diddlysquat.

Imagine you walk into Boots and there's a shampoo priced £2. Use your loyalty card with its in-effect 4% discount, and it actually costs £1.92. Yet, in a neighbouring shop, the shampoo could be priced at £1.80.

If this is the case Boots, even with its 'Advantage', isn't cheaper. Yet loyalty cards somehow mist our clinical decision-making. It's worth pointing out, even if after the loyalty discount it was the same price, you'd still be better off shopping elsewhere – as that means you'd have 8p extra cash rather than points, and cash is much more flexible and usable. This of course is a piddly sum, but over time piddly pays.

Therefore the rule is simple. When shopping in a place with a loyalty scheme, always use the card, just never base your choice of where you're going to shop on loyalty, only on value.

Money Diet Quick Fact Snack: Same Company, Twice the Price

Multiple brands are big bucks. They enable one company to target you in many different ways and push their profits to the extreme. One of the doyens of this is the Halifax Bank of Scotland Group. As well as the two big bank brands in the title, it also owns Esure, Intelligent Finance and Birmingham Midshires. Yet though it's all one big company, try getting house insurance quotes and see if one big company gives you one low price. Of course it doesn't: for one sample the range went from £125 to £242. Go to one brand and then another with the same company and the price can nearly double.

Multi-ownership is everywhere. Do you know who owns the company that you're dealing with? Travel agent Going Places is owned by My Travel. Direct Line is owned by the Royal Bank of Scotland, as is NatWest. The Abbey's credit cards are really run by MBNA.

If you want a mobile phone, why not try Dixons or Curry's or PC World or The Link? But they're all the same company. Does trying these four really count as shopping around? Actually it means the marketplace isn't as competitive as we think. And, worse, it allows different companies to use different brands to target different customers. So even if you want to be loyal – who to?

NOT JUST WHO, BUT HOW?

To bang another nail in loyalty's coffin, remember providers charge different people different prices. Stretching my memory back to Mr Hallis's A-level Economics class, I remember being taught the term 'price differentiation' – a holy grail for companies. In a perfectly profitable world a company would charge each and every customer the maximum they'd willingly pay.

Way back then, this was unthinkable, but with hi-tech number-crunching and internet technology it's starting to happen. The most obvious area is 'rate for risk' – where the lower credit risk at which you're assessed, the less you're charged. At least this has a certain logic to it. Yet price differentiation can be much more divisive, with pricing based on our access to information. The most stark example I remember was with Lloyds TSB's loans a couple of years ago.

Borrow £10,000 from it via the internet and it charges 8.7% or £2,750 in interest over five years. Borrow £10,000 by walking into a branch and you'll pay 15.9% or £5,140 in interest over five years. Yet worse is to come. Anyone responding to a mailshot from Lloyds' subsidiary Black Horse would've been charged 19.9% or £6,540. All for the same size loan, from the same company at the same time.

This means don't just think 'who' but also 'how'. Again, forget loyalty; in this case long-standing existing branch customers fare much less well than newcomers who happen to have a computer. The argument that 'they've given me a good deal in the past, they will do so in the future' should be consigned to history.

Loyalty's Greatest Weapon – Beware Brands

Brands are created by huge marketing spend. We pay for this spend in the form of higher prices. Yet a successful brand means the company can charge even more on top. So we pay double.

Brands are simply a way for companies to increase our spending and their profits without adding any real extra value. League tables show different brands perform differently for different products, whether it's cars, electronic goods or clothes. One brand doesn't uniformly come top of the product league. Yet people continue to think that if a brand's product is good in one area, then a different product from the same brand will be good too. Even though this product may have been made in a different country, with different techniques and standards. After all, why should a company with a good airline be any good at making vodka, mobile phones, or mortgages?

Brands subtly tap at our natural psyche. Purchasing decisions are neither art, nor science, but instinct. When we make quick decisions, usually we don't have all the facts, we short-cut the process based on past experience, trust and guesswork.

Let's use the murky world of politics to demonstrate. You turn on the television and there's a debate amongst a group of politicians, on a subject you know nothing about. If asked their opinion, even after listening for a short time, most people would echo the thoughts of the person from the party they tended to support – even if they didn't yet understand the argument.

There is nothing wrong with this – it's a perfectly rational way to behave. Essentially it is 'I usually think the way they do, so on this subject I probably will too' – after all, until we know better, what else do we have to go on?

It's this implicit instinctive loyalty that the people who manage brands try and tap into. So that when we don't have the time, or more usually inclination, to think about our purchases, we will simply follow brand loyalty and stick with what we know.

Stop. Don't do it. This is what they rely on, and they use huge, weighty marketing and advertising teams to back it up.

Supermarket Brands – Sheer Genius

In a modern supermarket there are usually four brand levels: 'the no-frills or basics brand', the 'supermarket own brand', 'the mainstream brand' (e.g. McVitie's Jaffa Cakes') and 'the premium brand' – like Tesco Finest.

A round of applause for the sheer marketing genius. This stratified system automatically allows supermarkets to justify huge variances in price. When we judge, often it's not based on experience, but on the brand. So when Tesco says 'This is Tesco Finest' we believe that because we had a good Salmon en Croûte, the Peppered Steak will be fantastic too, even though they may have been made in factories thousands of miles apart, and that if we choose to pay the higher price, we'll get a finer feast. This means we let them tell us what 'good' is. It's any salesman's dream. Packaging and placement provide the pricing.

This isn't to say there aren't differences in produce and production quality. Yet there is no uniform guide to quality. This is something we need to judge ourselves.

The Downshift Challenge: Don't worry, I'm not about to tell you to always buy 'no-frills'. Yet I want to challenge you to try to downshift. Quality is worthwhile, and can justify expense, but are you really getting it? To check – slip out of your shopping habits and occasionally try something one level cheaper. Sometimes you'll like it, sometimes you won't. For me, I don't notice the difference between no-frills and supermarket own-brand baked beans – yet I'd never dream of drinking no-frills diet cola, nor would I wipe my bottom with ultra-cheap toilet roll.

This is about finding what fits and costs less. Next time you want tinned spaghetti, get four of your normal, one supermarket own-brand and one no-frills and try them out. Downshift savings can be huge – take a look at this sample from different shops on the same day.

Bread 800g Loaf

Kingsmill 83p each

Supermarket own-brand 69p

Supermarket no-frills brand 28p

Tea 0.25Kg

PG Tips £1.88

Supermarket own-brand £1.25p

Supermarket no-frills brand £0.49p

Long Grain Rice 1Kg

Uncle Ben's £2.15

Supermarket own-brand 82p

Supermarket no-frills brand 55p

Skin Lotion

Vaseline £2.90 (200ml)

Nivea £2.99 (250ml)

Pharmacy own-brand £1.59 (250ml)

London Hair Cut

Vidal Sassoon £42

Toni and Guy Essensuals £39

Fish £27

Mr Toppers £6

Sunglasses

FCUK £56

Boots Dial 45s £20

Boots Fixed Tint £10

Superdrug Fashion Tint £3.99

Take just one of the above examples. If you used one packet of rice a week, over a year Uncle Ben's would cost £112, the supermarket own brand £42, and the no-frills brand £28. Are you really sure the extra £44 or even £58 is worth it? Try the downshifting challenge to see.

They work constantly to shift our focus away from product and onto brand. Exactly the opposite of what the real Money Dieter should do. To defeat brand power, we must move outside our comfort zone, and be more rational in our purchasing.

THE TEST OF HOW LOYAL YOU ARE

This is all about testing whether you gorge on loyalty. Before each product or service you will see a little box. If you have that product, then write in that box how many months you estimate it was since you last compared it to alternatives to see if you're getting good value. It's not about always changing, it is about often checking. If you don't have the product or service, don't fill the box in.

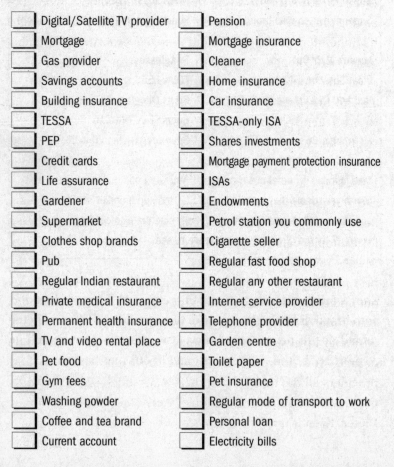

☐	Digital/Satellite TV provider	
☐	Mortgage	
☐	Gas provider	
☐	Savings accounts	
☐	Building insurance	
☐	TESSA	
☐	PEP	
☐	Credit cards	
☐	Life assurance	
☐	Gardener	
☐	Supermarket	
☐	Clothes shop brands	
☐	Pub	
☐	Regular Indian restaurant	
☐	Private medical insurance	
☐	Permanent health insurance	
☐	TV and video rental place	
☐	Pet food	
☐	Gym fees	
☐	Washing powder	
☐	Coffee and tea brand	
☐	Current account	

☐ Pension
☐ Mortgage insurance
☐ Cleaner
☐ Home insurance
☐ Car insurance
☐ TESSA-only ISA
☐ Shares investments
☐ Mortgage payment protection insurance
☐ ISAs
☐ Endowments
☐ Petrol station you commonly use
☐ Cigarette seller
☐ Regular fast food shop
☐ Regular any other restaurant
☐ Internet service provider
☐ Telephone provider
☐ Garden centre
☐ Toilet paper
☐ Pet insurance
☐ Regular mode of transport to work
☐ Personal loan
☐ Electricity bills

YOUR SCORE

Add the total number of months in all the columns together, then divide it by the number of boxes you've filled in. For example, if the total number of months is 721, and that is in 32 categories, then your score is 721 divided by 32, which equals 23. Then look at the list below to see how well you've done.

MONEY DIET POINTS

Over 25: Flushing it down the loo You are almost invariably paying too much across the entire range. Either that or you've had one product for such a long time it's prehistoric. Your big advantage, though, is that there's room for huge savings – doing the Money Diet should reap massive rewards for you.

15–25: Stuck in the mud Not brilliant: you've checked some things recently, but more are needed. Why not focus on the really big numbers in the list, the things that you never change, and see if you can reduce the average? There's money to be saved here.

8–15: An open mind Pretty good. There are always things you need to look at more often. Credit cards and savings accounts, for example, can be changed every six months or more often. Always remember, focus on the methodology and having the best products. You can probably squeeze a few more pennies out and get a few more pounds in.

Less than 8: More churn than butter You spit in the face of customer loyalty. Congratulations! I'm assuming when you do change, you do your research and move to the very best providers all the time. If not, there's not much point in changing frequently. Congratulations, you're a successful Money Dieter. Keep it up.

LOYALLY PERSUADING US TO BUY MORE, MORE, MORE

'Annyulneed'

In my chequered youth, I had a good few jobs. Petrol pump attendant, waiter, barman, yet the most useful for my Money-Saving education was three months spent as a salesman. I glamorously sold caravan awnings (the tent bits to stick on the outside of a caravan). The lead salesman, James, a slick-tongued Scotsman, taught me a clever trick: suggestive selling. When someone had just made an expensive awning purchase, and while they were focused on it, he said I should say, 'And you'll need ...', picking another product to add on. This worked over half of the time, bagging me lots of commission. I flogged caravan kettles, floor mats, and even portable TVs with 'And you'll need ...' The quicker I blurted it out, the less time customers had to question it, so my patter soon morphed into *annyulneed*.

Insurance providers turn this consumer disaster into an art form. Get a credit card *annyulneed* card protection insurance; take a mortgage *annyulneed* life insurance, *annyulneed* buildings and contents insurance.

Sidecar Profiteering

Yet *annyulneed* is just the beginning. In the grown-up big-bucks world of flogging us money products it's developed into an even more powerful trick I call 'sidecar profiteering'. It works like this. Advertise good-value competitive products to suck customers in. Then use a quick *annyulneed* to persuade them to accept an add-on good.

However, while the main product is good value, the 'sidecar' product is nearly all profit. But as the add-on's face value is lower it attracts less scrutiny. It's brilliant, and most of the time it works.

A classic example is the travel insurance on a package holiday. The market is competitive, so travel agents have to keep holiday prices quite low. But buy a holiday, *annyulneed* travel insurance. Say yes and it may cost another £100 for a family on top, even though similar cover is available elsewhere for around £25. This means that although the travel insurance is much cheaper than the holiday, it's also much more profitable. Yet the customer is still considering the big purchase price, not the add-on. (See 'Crash Diet', page 204.)

'Sidecar profiteering' is a game of wits. The patter's drafted by experts, so it's unsurprising we often fall for it. It's very common with payment protection insurance on personal loans, as the cost needn't be included in the interest rate. Providers flog dirt-cheap loans, then add dirtily expensive insurance on top, costing possibly thousands over the full life of the loan, often much of it pure profit. (See 'Healthy Eating', page 324.)

This leads to one basic rule: *Make a unique decision each time you decide to spend.* Don't follow brand loyalty, don't follow any loyalty. Don't start buying one product and then immediately buy another.

Mix 'n' Match is the Solution

Why not get a personal loan from one company and stand-alone payment protection insurance from another? Get your mortgage from one provider and your mortgage life assurance from another? It can apply to anything – get your DVD player from one retailer, but the scart lead from another. Just because you've made a big purchase, don't forget to use the same money-saving logic on the small ones, too.

six
TALK TO PEOPLE

We live in a time of unrivalled access to information, yet in our lives as consumers most of us simply avoid taking advantage of this. STOP! Know what you are doing and you'll be the winner. It's a question of research, evidence and communication.

I'm constantly surprised that most normal human beings don't seem to relish digging through reams of numerical data, putting it in a spreadsheet and crunching the minutiae. Yet I've decided to abstain from any talk of statistical analysis, and instead focus this chapter on quick, easy and effective ways of finding out if you're getting the best deal.

You may be wondering about the title 'Talk to People'. Originally it was 'Research, Research, Research' but I changed my mind. The most important form of all research is communication, talking to people. Whether it's face-to-face, by phone, e-mail, sign language, letter, fax, text message, internet chat room, memo, semaphore, instant messenger, morse code or post-it note, we must make sure we converse.

REACHING OUT

To find the best information we need to reach out.

Method 1: Breaking the Last Taboo

Talk isn't cheap. If you gathered ten of your friends together in a room, and asked them about any form of financial decision, usually at least one of them would have a clue about the subject, probably would have done it themselves, and possibly would have some pointers. Yet time and time again we all try to reinvent the wheel.

Talking about money is one of the few taboos left in modern society. I don't understand it – why is it rude or vulgar to ask: How much did you pay for it? Did you manage to get a bargain? How did you barter? How much is it worth? What bank do you use? What kind of accounts have you got with them?

Many people have made decisions I've never faced, just as I've made decisions they never have. By failing to ask 'How much did you pay?' we deny ourselves incisive terms of reference for future decision-making. Knowledge is built through conversation and discussion. The reality of a friend's financial history is more lively and easy to understand than anything else.

Let me make a clarion call to change this. Don't be embarrassed. Talk, ask and be open about your money and your finances to friends and family. It's a great way to gather information and help build your knowledge, and you may also find they're able and willing to help in ways you hadn't imagined.

So, apart from reading *The Money Diet*, the first thing to do when starting any new project is talk to your friends and family about it – shared experiences are invaluable. Of course, they're not always right, but then who is?

Martin's Money Memories: How Much Do You Earn?

'Don't ask, don't tell': that was the rule about discussing your salary in my first job after university. Of course, new and inexperienced, I obeyed, at first.

After a year or so, I did start talking, though. And one day I was surprised to learn that a colleague, who was asked to work under me, turned out to be earning nearly twice my salary.

The bosses were right – talking about it sowed dissent and displeasure, yet the fact I knew the difference wasn't the cause, it was the catalyst. The real problem was the fact I was paid less. After all, if we worked for the fun of it, they wouldn't pay us anyway. So, armed with the knowledge, I had a valuable bartering tool to try and bump up my salary.

If a colleague asks you what you earn and you're working in the same company, don't be so shy. As with all money issues, knowledge is power.

Method 2: the Internet

The net tends to either scare people or make them salivate thinking about tapping their fingers on the magical keyboard. It offers an unparalleled wealth of immediate knowledge – the problem is knowing how to find it, filter it and trust it.

For the web savvy, the internet is an amazing tool. However, even for complete beginners there are some easy ways to gain. (See page 104.) It is often said you can't trust information on the internet. Not true. Don't confuse the delivery mechanism with the source. If the info is from a reputable source, the fact that it is on the web makes no difference.

There is a range of ways to find information on the web.

1. www.moneysavingexpert.com

Of course I would say the place to start is my own website – which in the spirit of MoneySaving is independent, free to use, plus ad free and sponsorship free. It is designed to complement the information in this book, by links to updated best-buys, and it allows people to chat to each other (and occasionally me) about new and better ways to save money.

2. Companies' own sites

The great thing about the internet is there is no shortage of space, so companies can include limitless information. This can mean the terms and conditions and specifications for every single product. It's a brilliant resource. So whenever you're thinking about a particular product, get on line to its parent website and read all about it. It will make your final decision much easier. Most companies now include their web address in TV, radio, newspaper and other adverts, so it shouldn't be too hard.

3. Search engines

Search engines are the internet's 'index'. By using them carefully you can find pretty much whatever you want. The one I use is www.google.co.uk. It's a powerful search engine because its criteria are set up in a different way to all the others. It sends out little computerised spiders that crawl all over the web and bring back results, which it updates roughly every couple of months.

To really use it properly take a little time to learn the advanced tips and tricks. Use double speech marks (" ") around a phrase to ensure it is matched exactly. This will narrow the field of your search. Articles, comparisons, past people's experiences, consumer reviews – all of these are available on the internet and will inform your decisions.

4. Shopping robots

Sometimes called 'shopbots', these are specialised sites that trawl around web retailers for you to find the cheapest prices. They're especially good for books, games, CDs, DVDs and electrical and computer goods. (For full explanation and a list of these, see 'Crash Diet', page 153.)

5. Financial price-comparison services

Similar to shopping robots, these services compare huge amounts of online info. Yet where shopping robots search many retailers for a single product, price comparison services compare many products that do similar things, to find the best rate. This could be savings accounts, cash ISAs or even airline flights.

On the whole these services will save you money, but do be careful. Though they are a great starting point for research, never rely completely on them. Don't ever think that just because a product comes top of a price-comparison engine it's automatically the best way to go. It should be seen as an information source, not an automated decision-maker. Above all, always remember price comparison services are virtually all profit-making enterprises, and want your cash. Potential problems are as follows:

They're biased! This is the most serious and – thankfully – the rarest problem. However, some price-comparison sites are run by companies which also own products included in the comparison. Funnily enough, when this happens, their own products tend to come top of the comparisons! This is either due to excluding cheaper competitors or skewing the comparison parameters.

A more difficult to spot problem is an inconsistent search

engine. This happens when although it provides a decent search for some goods, for others, often more complicated ones, such as health insurance or mortgage payment protection insurance, it takes the easy route and just links to a particular affiliated company, rather than searching right across the market. If ever a search engine site simply directs you to one company, avoid it.

They don't compare like with like. Sometimes just comparing prices isn't enough. There's often a huge variance in range, specifications and terms and conditions. For example, with home contents insurance, some policies are 'unlimited sum-insured', meaning it doesn't matter what your contents are worth, they're covered. Others may limit it to £20,000 of contents. With savings accounts, the pure rate ignores whether it's instant access or has a notice period, accessible via the internet or the phone, has transfer penalties or limited withdrawals. These factors affect your choice, so always make sure you know what you want and how to choose first.

They don't always give you all the information you need. Details can be scant and out of date. Once you've gleaned the info from a price-comparison engine, always then check products out directly on a provider's own website.

A question of commission. This is huge and hidden. With many money products, the company or adviser recommending or introducing it gets commission from the product provider. Price-comparison services are introducers, and usually make their money from this commission. Therefore, even though a price-comparison engine is searching the entire market's products for you, and finding the best possible rate, that doesn't guarantee it's the very cheapest. The same may be available elsewhere, with less commission paid. The only solution is to use a range of companies and price-comparison engines and compare the results.

Exclusivity. Many price-comparison services have exclusive deals arranged with providers. So search on one service and it won't include another's exclusives. There's also a problem that some direct sellers and companies only sell through their own direct agents. So you may need to look at these companies and providers separately.

They don't always rate the rate. Comparisons look at the main product price, yet they often miss the 'sidecar profit' products price (see page 92). In other words, just because it comes top of the table doesn't mean all the 'extras' like insurance and accessories are good value too.

Method 3: Newspapers and Magazines

This is much more familiar territory for most people. Although newspapers and magazines aren't as instantaneously up to date as the internet, often they do provide very useful information, both in articles and in best-buy tables.

If you want an easy way to find a good buy, then buy a Sunday paper, look through its money section and you will see lots of tables of 'Best Buys'. It's not the uber-best way, but it's a good starting point. However, most newspaper best-buy tables are compiled for the papers by information and comparison services and include some of the problems noted above.

Method 4: Shanks's Pony

There's nothing wrong with physically tripping from bank to bank, shop to shop. Actually picking up and feeling what you're going to buy is a great indication of whether you really want it. As long as you follow the golden rule 'Never shop in just one shop' it's a great idea. Plus if you're there in person you can haggle (see page 107).

Method 5: Professional Advice

Undoubtedly, professional financial advice may be worthwhile if you're scared, short of time and don't feel confident doing the research yourself. Yet the cost can outweigh the benefit. If you're going to get professional advice, always check it is an Independent Financial Adviser (IFA), as they can look across the entire range of the market, rather than a tied agent who can only sell you one company's product. This is a legal distinction – there are no halfway houses (though strangely there are plans to change this) – so ask the financial adviser, 'Are you an Independent Financial Adviser?' Don't accept any hedged answers.

When to use an IFA

Don't automatically flit to an IFA. It's a very common mistake to think they're experts on all money matters. They are not – their focus and training is in investments, pensions and protection products (life assurance and critical illness) and, to an extent, mortgages. They are *not* qualified in credit cards, loans, debts, savings and bank accounts, even though they can earn commission recommending them; never pay for 'unqualified advice' on these subjects.

Even if you do go to an adviser, remember *you're in charge*

– the decision is yours, not theirs. You don't *have* to do what they tell you. Read around their advice and ensure it's really right for you. When picking your IFA in the first place, always start by going to three and see who you prefer. Personal recommendations are another good way – though remember a good 'bedside manner' doesn't guarantee good advice. It's a tricky business.

If you are money savvy, my instincts would be to say avoid paying for professional advice even on the subjects IFAs are qualified on. Do the research and buy via a discount broker (see 'Crash Diet', page 190) and you will be much better off. Remember no one can predict the future and even IFAs' recommendations on what investments to go for are their best guess, not certain knowledge. However, especially with complex financial products, I understand people feel the need for help.

There are some areas where I think paying for advice is very useful. The three that immediately spring to mind are complex endowment or pension problems, and especially when getting an annuity. The reason for this is simple – when you retire, you use your pot of pension money to pay for an annuity, which then pays out to you every year until you die. Once you've got one, you can't change it. This means it's the biggest and most important financial decision you will ever make. And, if you find finance confusing, for the safety and security of knowing you're getting the very best annuity, I would suggest paying out a few hundred pounds for some good advice.

How to pay an IFA

IFAs are paid in two ways: either a flat hourly fee for their advice (this can be as much as £200 per hour) or by commission. Remember, though: advisers paid commission may seem like they're giving advice for free, but it's far from it – over the long run they tend to make more money this way than by charging a fee upfront.

Both payment methods have pros and cons. Pay a fee and you can be more sure the IFA doesn't bias their advice according to how much commission they make – as they should then pay any commission they earn straight to you (always ask and check this is happening). Pay no fee and let them take the commission, and you may end up with a better relationship as you'll feel free to seek advice regularly, because you won't need to stump up the cash upfront – leaving you with a retained adviser looking over your finances.

Other advisers

IFAs aren't the only ones who talk money. Tax accountants are often crucial and unavoidable if you're self-employed or have complicated tax affairs. Bank managers also talk money advice too – however, this is often just a way to flog you something from their own portfolio of products, and won't encompass the entire market. Be very careful of anything your bank advises you to do. If you're in serious debt, the free debt-counselling services are fantastic and I wholeheartedly recommend them (see 'Debt Crisis', page 335).

MOVING OUTSIDE YOUR COMFORT ZONE

'Reach out for info' and there's a massive boon – it should enable you to move outside your comfort zone, and this almost invariably results in your getting a better deal. Most people's comfort zones are familiar, omnipresent high-street shops and brands. Unfortunately, this enables those trusted patrons to price themselves higher on the grounds that they provide a sense of security.

Moving outside your comfort zone means shopping in places you've not heard of, buying on the internet and not always going for the straightforward option. It can be a little disconcerting, and occasionally you'll make the wrong decision, but more often you should benefit. And if you've done your research, comparison-shopped and are armed with information, the only real crisis is one of confidence. After all, wherever you shop in the UK you have the same statutory rights and protection (see 'Holler', page 117).

THE LIST OF TEN THINGS TO USE THE NET FOR EVEN WHEN YOU DON'T HAVE INTERNET ACCESS

The internet has re-divided society into 'haves' and 'have-nots'. Internet operators have low overheads – they've no expensive high-street premises, processes are automated and if necessary products can be posted or shipped cheaply. This usually makes them cheaper.

This list applies even if you don't have access to the net. Specifically where the discount is for applying online, and no further internet access is needed.

For those with the time and not the money, use a local library and take a quick course in getting online. However, if there's no time then ask web-savvy friends or family to do it with you.

Do remember, though, that as there's sometimes personal information involved you need to be very careful who you choose to help, and you must be sure you can trust them not to rip you off later. And always print out the terms and conditions, and receipts.

1. Savings accounts. These are simply places for money to sit, rarely touched, earning interest. Many of the top payers are internet-access-only accounts, yet if you set up the account on line initially, you can often call and operate it on the phone after that. Do check both that this is possible, and that there's no additional fee. Of course if you use a savings account to put money into and take money out of all of the time, it's a no go. (See page 156.)

2. Cash ISAs. After all, a cash ISA is just a tax-free savings account – so it's very similar. (See page 160.)

3. Flights. Whether it's long-haul through Expedia, E-Bookers or Travelocity, or a short-haul through Ryanair or EasyJet, booking is much cheaper on the internet. Once you've made your purchase that's usually it, and, if not, customer service tends to be phone-, not net-based. (See page 182.)

4. Credit-card balance transfers. Balance transfers are a long-term process. The best practice is to set up a direct debit to pay it off and put the card in a drawer without using it for anything else. So, if the best deal's online, it's worth considering. (See page 296.)

5. Personal loans. The cost difference between online and off-line loans can be enormous. Yet non-net-users will usually need to just take it out online then pay off a fixed amount each month by direct debit. (See page 322.)

6. Gas and electricity. Many top tariffs are online only. Yet some providers still send paper bills, so only the set-up needs to be online. If not, though, avoid. (See page 149.)

7. Big electrical goods. Get a friend to do a quick online search using a shopping robot to find the cheapest price for you, then either buy it, or print out the details and try for a price match in a high-street store. (See page 153.)

8. Term assurance. Use an online broker to find the cheapest; after that the actual product comes from a life assurance company and they tend to deal in paper. (See page 201.)

9. Travel insurance. Find the cheapest online, then when you make a claim it tends to be on the phone rather than on the internet. (See page 204.)

10. Car insurance. Using the internet to find it dramatically reduces the time it takes to get a good quote. (See page 218.)

seven

HAGGLE

There's no such thing as a fixed price. The ticket price is purely an indicator of what you need to pay. Legally they don't have to accept it, so you don't need to pay it!

CHUTZPAH

(hoot'spa) – n. effrontery, nerve [Yiddish]

Chutzpah is a powerful consumer weapon, especially when combined with talents not often evoked in the money world: 'seduction, a gentle patter and a twinkle in the eyes'. With these you can transform a twee UK high street into a stall-filled, hustling, bustling Turkish bazaar.

We British will banter and barter with the best if we're somewhere the flies need swatting. Yet on home turf we become complacent lily-livered cowards. Over the years UK shopkeepers have managed to hypnotise us into believing it's rude and impolite to haggle here and that prices are always fixed.

Haggling is neither difficult nor rude – it makes you a better consumer and the shops better retailers. And while I've used the word 'shop' so far, haggling needn't be reserved for shopping.

You can haggle for holidays, credit-card interest rates, new cars and hotel prices. At its most basic, haggling is just asking for a discount, yet with technique and cheek, it can become an art.

While haggling is easy in theory, doing it takes a deep breath and a conscious decision. I'll be honest, I don't always haggle – often the possible gain outweighs the time it'd take, or I'm just not in the right mood. However, over the years I've often been successful, though not every time.

For fun, while writing this, yesterday I decided to try the ultimate haggling challenge – a supermarket. In the main, I was pitiful; however, there was one triumph: I did manage to persuade the woman at the deli counter to give me a few extra ounces of cheese.

Usually, though, haggling is best reserved for bigger purchases than a pint of milk. To do it properly strategy and timing are crucial.

THE LIST OF TEN HEAVENLY HIGH-STREET HAGGLES

Even for the hard-core dedicated MoneySavers on www.moneysavingexpert.com, haggling is a tough one. Only 13% of them always try to barter, compared to 25% who never do. Most say they'll give it a go if it feels right, but the status quo is often easier. Yet, as encouragement, here are some of *their* tales, hints, tips and practical successes.

1. Finding a stitch in time saves. 'Look for the minutest of dents or scratches on electrical appliances, and marks on clothing. I once got money off a blouse with some kid's grubby handprints on it – the marks washed out. Just point out that they'll be unlikely to sell it to anyone else unless they pay for dry cleaning.'

2. *Turning the tables*. 'I am a sales manager in an unnamed big mobile retailer; we work on margin so if you get the right salesperson, you can save big pounds. The trick to haggling is to turn the tables on the salesperson. Make friends with them (I don't mean ask them out or anything like that ... just ask their opinion, build an obligation). The salesperson is more likely to sell/discount to someone they feel they like. The best time is the end of the month or end of the quarter, as the shops have to meet targets and need to make sales, so they're more likely to discount.'

3. *If you don't ask, you don't get*. 'We wanted a washing machine from Curry's. It was in heavy demand as it was £100 off. So we nipped round the corner to a local electrical store, which had the same machine actually in stock. After a bit of chat they agreed to give us the same discount as long as we paid in cash. No problem. A new washing machine at the cheap price, there and then.'

4. *Make it cheaper than interest-free*. 'When 0% interest-free credit is offered, I always ask what the cash price is, and usually find it's 5% cheaper. Until I started this I always thought interest-free was actually free; now I realise it's just one form of discount, so I ask for another instead!'

5. *Naughty but nice*. 'Bought a cooker and queried why it was £75 cheaper next door. The salesman went and checked, came back and agreed to sell it at the reduced price. Then I realised that although the cookers looked identical they were different models, and I ended up with the better spec. Result!'

6. Court Tottenham Court Road. 'Big electrical shop centres like the ones in London's Tottenham Court Road are haggling heaven for electricals. We went to about three different shops to get the lowest quote, then went back to the cheapest and pushed them to do it for even less. I got the laptop I wanted £250 cheaper than Dixons' advertised price at the time.'

7. It isn't always the end of the line. 'I managed to get £50 knocked off a stereo worth £300 because it was the last one in the shop and the display model. All that was wrong was that it was a bit dusty. Take advantage of the shops wanting to get rid of items like this so they can put the newer stuff in.'

8. Keen service means keen bargains. 'If you are pounced on by assistants, you know they're on commission – tell them you will come and find them in a while – they will be begging for that sale, and may be more likely to discount or throw in freebies.'

9. Seriously prepared to save. 'I bought a dishwasher and washing machine, and was told delivery would be £25. I asked for my card back and to cancel the sale. The saleswoman didn't believe me till I took the card out of her hand, then she agreed to free delivery.'

10. Cheeky flirting in shorts. 'In a surf shop sale last year I liked a pair of shorts priced £15 from £35 and a skirt priced £20 from £40. I managed to get both for £25 through a combination of haggling and cheeky flirting!'

Martin's Money Memories: Lewis v Lewis

One of the easiest and best haggles I've ever done was in the great high-street bastion, John Lewis. It's one of those stores people assume is unhagglable-with. Yet remember, its 'never knowingly undersold' price promise is effectively an open invitation. Even so, most people just walk in, get what they want, pay the set price and leave.

My purchase was a small wooden bathroom cabinet, original price £80, but on sale for £40. It was both the last one left, and the last sale item in that entire department. This, you should know by now, is a golden haggling opportunity as shops are keen to reclaim all their display space for new stock. My suspicion was if they didn't sell it that day, they'd chuck it out.

Having waited a couple of minutes, I spotted what looked like a senior departmental type walking past. Quickly I asked if I could have the cabinet for a discount. He was open to it straight away: 'How much?' My preamble was important – I wanted him to know I understood the issues, and I wanted to reinforce why he should give in. So, smiling, I said, 'Well, I'm sure you want to reclaim your display case, and I'm willing to remove this for you. So why don't I just give you a tenner for it and get out of here?' He tried to suggest £20 – already 50 per cent off! And he was half-hearted at that. 'Go on, a tenner and I'll just get it out of here.' Five minutes later I was out of the door with my £80 bathroom cabinet for £10 – and very nice it is too.

BRILLIANT BARTERING IN JUST 16 STEPS (BUT FOR YOU I'LL DO IT IN 15!)

1. The beginner's haggle – 'would ya throw in the ...' If you've never haggled before it is daunting. So, to start, rather than asking for a discount, just ask them to throw something in on top. Always try to get your batteries thrown in for free on electrical goods, extra shoe polish for new shoes. If there's an add-on extra, try not to pay for it.

2. Internet prices in real stores. Use the internet (see 'Crash Diet', page 153) to find the cheapest price available. Print the results and take it with you to the shops. Confronted with this kind of evidence, they will often price-match the net cost (though try to keep your fingers over the bit of paper that details any delivery costs).

3. Be polite, firm, non-competitive and maybe just a touch flirtatious. Being an aggressive or forceful haggler is usually a mistake; it often annoys the person you are dealing with – and your discount is at their discretion. If you are polite, charming yet firm and treat the whole process with humour, you'll get a bit further. In my experience this is especially true with male shopkeepers. Men tend to be extremely competitive (I struggle to stop racing people up the escalator as I get off the tube), and if it becomes a battle of wills they may be prepared to lose the sale just to keep some pride.

4. Seniority, yes. Head honcho, no. An assistant manager or supervisor is a good person to bargain with. They have more discretion than most of the shop staff, understand the retail game a little bit better, and are used to pleasing their customers. Go to the very top, though, and the person will be short of time, and not bothered about one small sale.

5. Reduced prices have extra flexibility. If the price is already reduced, for example in a sale or manager's clearance, etc, there is often more flexibility for bartering. As the boundaries have already flexed there's more room to play. Also the psychological loss for the person you are haggling with is reduced, as they have already given up the idea of getting full price.

6. *Don't commit to financing*. Don't talk about your payment method until it's necessary. Sellers prefer debit cards to credit cards. Certainly if you're going to pay by credit card, leave this until the end of the transaction. However, if they have their own financing options, it may be worth mooting you're interested, without committing, as there's often good commission on finance, so they'll be more disposed to give a bigger discount. One final thought – if they are offering interest-free finance this is already equivalent to a discount of 5% plus; see if instead of taking it you can get a discount for a debit card.

7. *Avoid busy bartering*. Try not to haggle when the shop is crammed with other customers. The last thing salespeople are interested in is reducing their margins when they can see lots of people willing to buy. Go during times of shopping serenity, like mid-week mid-mornings, when retailers are worrying about where the next penny will come from.

8. *Bulk bartering*. Discounts are often available for bulk buying. This may mean stocking up for a year, buying a combination of products, or even going with a group of friends who want to buy something similar. The advantage you have is you're going to hand over a lot more business, and you should secure a reduction of it.

9. Avoid seasonal products. The worst time to barter for a scooter, convertible car or air-conditioning unit is when the sun is beating down. And it's much easier to barter for a brolly when there's not a cloud in the sky; desperation isn't a good weapon.

10. Play them off against each other. Take quotes and prices from other sellers, and try to play providers off against each other. This has two advantages: it gives solid foundation to your request and it prods sellers' competitive instincts in your favour as they want to show they're better than the opposition.

11. End-of-month/year haggling holiday. Towards the end of their financial year, or monthly target, retailers and salespeople are often much more willing to haggle. At that point it's volume, rather than profit, that really counts, so they're willing to slice their margins down to a capriccio, just to make the sales. If in doubt when their financial month/year end is, assume it's the calendar month and the tax year.

12. Always ask for the sun and you may just get the moon. Do it with humour, do it with style, and there's no price or suggestion that's too outrageous.

13. Choose independents over chains. Bartering in independent retailers, where you can speak directly to the owner, is a better bet than a chain. There's more leeway. This doesn't mean chains won't barter (I've done it in Dixons, Comet and W.H. Smith to name a few). Yet with owner/retailer shops, the owner has complete discretion, so a smile and a hint that you'll become a regular shopper works wonders.

14. *Closing the deal.* If you are nearly ready to buy then start to use true sales negotiation language. Let them know the exact conditions they must meet in order to close the sale. But don't be afraid, even then, to walk away if they won't give you what you want – you can always try elsewhere.

15. *Don't settle unnecessarily.* Earlier in this book I mentioned one of the jobs I did in my year out before university – selling caravan awnings. As a salesman, I had full discretion to drop the price. Yet I routinely told customers I needed to check with my manager beyond a certain level. This both put a break in the negotiations if it wasn't going well for me, and allowed me to return and say, 'Sorry, it's not possible, I can only drop it so far' without looking like the bad guy. Often customers were fooled into settling at that point. Remember, even if the salesperson is telling the truth that they need a manager's permission, make them go back to the manager, or get them to bring the manager to you. All salespeople's facts are flexible when haggling.

TURNING 'ANNYULNEED' INTO 'ANNILLNEED'

There's a certain salacious joy to writing this bit. In 'Forget Loyalty', page 92, I detailed the *annyulneed* sales trick used to get customers to buy more goods. While I don't like that tactic, I do admire it. And by turning *annyulneed* into *annillneed* it becomes a weapon in our haggling arsenal.

It's a bonus haggle if you like. First push for the biggest discount on the main product, as that's where the biggest savings come from.

Then comes the time to use *annillneed* – once you've almost finished the haggle for the main item, but before they've closed the sale. Make it an almost instinctive reaction, act as if you're not really thinking about it and it's no big deal. Add-ons are the key, a floor mat with a tent, a scart lead with a DVD player, a better CD player in a new car. Simply say, '*Annillneed* that too.' The aim is to get them to throw it in for free, or at least try to get it for cost. Remember, if you've already been haggling, the door for discounts is open, so it's easier to swing it a bit further.

If they say no, hint it's a deal breaker or remind them how much you're about to spend: 'I'm about to pay you £12,000 for a new car and you won't throw in a nicer CD player?'

eight
HOLLER

You have rights, use them! Just because you buy cheap doesn't mean you can't expect good service. And just because you've been with a company for a long time doesn't mean you should let them take you for granted. If they do, move on!

NOT JUST RIGHTS, BUT EXPECTATIONS

Knowing your rights gives you power. Consumers aren't impotent – we've rafts of legal protection. Yet Money Dieters shouldn't have just rights, but also *expectations*. We live in a competitive world where many companies vie for our business. This means that even when we don't specifically have a legal right, there's nothing wrong with expecting top treatment.

Bad service, figures that don't add up, and being asked to pay for goods not received – these are all part of a consumer's year. Yet companies rely on their reputations, and even if they're not breaking the law, if their behaviour isn't what you want or expect, it's likely others wouldn't want or expect it either. So there's nothing wrong with complaining. Often it's only a matter of a simple letter or phone call to get the right result.

HOW TO HOLLER

I use the word 'holler' because it's nice and it's emotive. It evokes the all-important message – don't be downtrodden, run over or screwed by these companies. Stand up for yourself, claim your rights, and seek out what you deserve.

Yet though I want to pump you up, when it comes to making an actual complaint, cool, calm and rational is more likely to get results than an aggressive rant. It may make them want to get rid of you, but it's tough to argue coherently when your lungs are bellowing. The people we complain to are human too – usually it's not their personal money at issue, so win them onside, don't alienate them. Preparation and calm control work – after all, a company can deny your request even when you're right, and if they do the only ultimate recourse is going to court, and that massively increases the hassle factor.

Before complaining, sit down and work out exactly what your grounds are. If this is a substantive complaint, ensure you research your rights, how these rights are enforced, and what it is legitimate to ask for. Always know what you want and what you are willing to settle for. Do you want to exchange the goods? Do you want a full refund? Do you want compensation and, if so, what kind? What do you think is fair?

Run it past friends or relatives to see if they think it's reasonable or if they've had any experience of complaining in a similar way. Even better, if you know someone who works for a company similar to the one you're complaining about, ask them. All this information is useful ammunition, and once you're ready, if you're not feeling confident, try rehearsing, then holler to your heart's content and get a result.

YOUR RIGHTS

When all's said and done, though, the most powerful tool is knowing your legal strength.

Your agreement is with the retailer, not the manufacturer
If goods are faulty complain to the shop or company you bought them from. It's up to it to sort it out for you. If it tries to fob you off by saying go to the product's manufacturer, it's wrong. Stick to your guns.

Goods should be of satisfactory quality, as described, and fit for their intended purpose
Say you buy some hi-fi speakers and they don't work – then obviously they're not fit. However, if the speakers do work, but they don't fit your existing stereo system and this was something you specifically questioned, then they still aren't fit for the purpose specified. Of course, proving this is difficult without written evidence.

Time is of the essence
Examine anything you've bought as soon as you get it home and if there is a problem complain immediately. The amount of time legally allowed to check whether goods are faulty depends on what's reasonable for that product – it takes longer to check a speedboat than a kettle. However, as a rule of thumb, try and complain within a week. Do that and you are entitled to a full refund. Leave it longer and, even if the goods were faulty when you bought them, you may struggle to get a full refund, though even then you're still entitled to a replacement or a reduction.

Money Diet Quick Fact Snack: What is Reasonable?

Now there's a question lawyers have argued over for years. Reasonable is ... well ... reasonable. That's the point. So whenever that word is used in a legal context, it simply means what you or I or any normal person would consider to be reasonable.

Proving goods were faulty when you bought them

Take obviously faulty goods back to a shop and if it's within six months of the purchase, it is for the *shop* to prove they *were not* faulty when you bought them. However, after six months, the law changes, and *you* must prove they *were* faulty when you bought them. Yet if there is any disagreement over whether the goods are *currently* faulty, it's up to you to prove they are. And, it should be noted, if you know goods are faulty when you buy them, you don't have a right to return them.

Overall, you have up to six years to make a complaint, but this doesn't mean whatever you buy must last six years, it's just the maximum; they must last what most people would consider to be a 'reasonable' length of time. So if there is legitimate wear and tear that damages the product, the likelihood is you have no claim.

'No refunds' signs

Some shops display signs stating 'No refunds', designed to put customers off exercising their legal rights. These are illegal, and if you see one you should report it to your local Trading Standards office. Just log onto www.tradingstandards.gov.uk, or ring your local office.

Pay on a credit card

Pay for goods costing over £100 even partially (just a £1 deposit, for example) using a credit card (not a debit card – there's no protection there), then the credit card company is equally liable with the retailer, giving you a second bite at the complaining cherry. This protection is known as Section 75 as it comes from that part of the 1974 Consumer Credit Act.

You've actually more rights on the internet or by mail order

Under special rules called the distance-selling regulations, you have seven working days to cancel after receiving goods bought on the net or by mail order (this doesn't apply to fresh food, flowers, sealed audio equipment or travel for specific dates). You also have a right to clear information, written confirmation of the order, delivery details and information about how to cancel. If it's a service you've signed up to, the seven working days is the amount of time you have, after agreeing, to cancel. However, buy goods from firms based abroad and beware: UK laws won't cover you. So stick to countries where they have well-enforced legal systems, such

---

Money Diet Quick Fact Snack: Settling an Old Debate

You spot a can of beans in a shop mistakenly priced at 1p. Can you force the shop to sell it to you? No, sorry. If they're mispriced the shop can refuse to sell them, as until they accept your cash, you've no contract with them. However, you can report shops that are deliberately advertising misleading prices to the Trading Standards office, who can investigate and may prosecute. This does of course get tricky if it's online and the purchase is automated; however, even then they can argue, using what's known as 'the Law of Mistake', that the transaction wasn't finalised.

as the US or elsewhere in Europe – not that you'll ever pros-ecute, but problems are less likely

Is there a right to return expensive stuff?

There are a number of rights commonly assumed to exist that don't. You don't have a right to return goods if you spot them cheaper elsewhere (though if I ruled the world you would), change your mind or bought them for the wrong reason. However, though you don't have rights, this doesn't mean don't ask. Many shops would rather keep customers happy than be sticklers for these rules.

Enforcing Your Rights

You know you're right and your rights. You walk in, calmly holler and they wilt. Hoorah. Unfortunately, sometimes this doesn't happen. So what then? Well, the ultimate recourse is the courts – after all, that's where rights are enforced. Yet your local Trading Standards office and Citizens' Advice Bureau are quicker and easier routes; try them first.

YOUR EXPECTATIONS

Can You Really Expect Good Service at a Cheap Price?

The Money Diet is about cutting bills, cutting back, and look-ing for low-cost services. Some may argue that you can't then realistically expect top-quality or good customer service. Wrong! Cheap does not mean shoddy. Cheap does not mean poor service. The Money Diet is about value. Don't let ne'er-do-wells persuade you cheap can't be good – get it right and it just means the same product but less provider profits.

Even When You've No Rights, You're Not Wrong

There are many occasions when we don't get the service we expect or deserve yet legally don't have a leg to stand on. However, companies run on a combination of reputation, delivery and repeat business. Even though Money Dieters spit on loyalty, companies don't know that. They must consider all customers to be potentially regular consumers who will use their services or buy their products again and again. Therefore we as consumers need to twist their goodwill to get what we want.

For companies, complaining consumers are problem consumers. They may well tell other people, talk to journalists or television programmes about their bad experience, or even stand outside with a placard. Even though, legally, a company might not have done anything wrong, most people identify with other consumers, and sympathies are usually directed towards the little guy, not the big company. Use this to get compensation, a better product, or better treatment.

Face it. Companies Are Not Nice

Companies are not nice beasts. Some argue they have a social responsibility to make our lives better. Sounds wonderful. Ignore it! Whatever your beliefs, as a consumer you are better off considering that we live in an adversarial consumer society: a company's job is simply to screw every possible penny out of you – to maximise profits and create value for shareholders.

This concept brings clarity.

Of course, if companies' products and service were clearly and transparently appalling, nobody would ever use them and they'd go bust – so they have to have a balance. Firms may say, 'Our customers are the most important thing, we want to

Money Diet Quick Fact Snack: Cut the Cost of Complaining

There's nothing more annoying than having to pay to complain. Yet many customer service lines are sneakily charging a fortune. Many companies charge 'non-geographic' local-rate 0845, or, even worse, national-rate 0870 numbers when you call. While these don't sound expensive, they can cost up to 8p a minute for daytime calls.

So when they leave you on hold, sadly all too common, it quickly adds up. Even worse, often the company you're complaining to gets a cut of this call cost.

A sneaky tip to defeat them. Many companies list special numbers to call to contact them when you're overseas. These tend just to be standard numbers, which are much cheaper to call. Yet these numbers put you through to the same system, so dial the number for overseas customers (leaving out the GB code) when in the UK and save. Check out www.djbnet.co.uk/tel for a list of the numbers.

give them the best.' That is a pile of pants. They want to make money. Part of making money is a bright, smiley, customer-focused public face to attract customers.

Yet servicing customers is never an end in itself: it is purely a means to make money. Some product-providers will focus on customer service – they make it their edge, their unique selling point. But it's not for the greater good, it's because it builds their business. Plus, those who spout about it most are often the ones not willing to compete on cost.

There is no right or wrong here. This is a practical, not a political standpoint. Once you take this on board, dealing with product-providers becomes easier. If they turn you down for a loan, you know you had no right to be lent it. If they give you poor service, well, it's only understandable. Our reactions must be geared towards this, so do say, 'You haven't given me good service. Either sort it or I will do my best to make sure I'll hit you where it hurts – in your pockets.'

THE LIST OF FIVE SPECIFIC RIGHTS

1. Holidays

Should be as described. The holiday should reasonably match the description you had beforehand. It is a criminal offence if descriptions aren't truthful and accurate. 'A minute from the beach' is by foot or by taxi, not supersonic jet; accommodation should not be overbooked; photos shouldn't mislead either. Plus, under package-holiday regulations, you've a right to compensation for any negatively misleading descriptions too.

Changes before you go. There's an automatic right to cancel, but if they substantially change the holiday terms, you've a right to a full refund. If you still want the holiday, but aren't happy, write and tell them that you will assess the impact the changes actually have on the trip.

Problems while you're there. If things go wrong during the holiday, ask for a complaint form there and then, otherwise you may lose the right to any compensation. You must give them the opportunity to put it right. Take video or photo evidence and notes from other holiday-makers if there is a problem. Keep details of who, what, where, when, how and why things went wrong, and receipts of any extra costs incurred.

If the tour operator won't do anything, either take them to court or go to the ABTA tribunal service.

2. Dry cleaning

Check the cleaners belong to the TSA. The Textiles Services Association does quality checks, so it's well worth checking your dry cleaner belongs to it.

Problems with dry cleaning. Always give them as much information as possible about the goods. If a re-clean doesn't solve it, you are entitled to reclaim the product's value when it was cleaned (not 'as new').

3. Second-hand goods

You still have rights. Second-hand goods and sales goods bought from shops follow the same rules: if they're faulty, you can return them. Like other goods, they must be of satisfactory quality – but after the price is taken into account. If you buy a laptop for a fiver, you can't really expect it to run normally. And if you are made aware of any faults when you buy, you can't return it later because of those.

With private sellers it's 'buyer beware'. Buy second-hand goods from private sellers, and then it's *caveat emptor* or 'let the buyer beware'. If the seller doesn't say anything and you buy it, then even if it doesn't do what *you* thought it might, you were not mis-sold. The only restriction is that the product should be correctly described and the owner has the right to sell it.

4. Second-hand cars from dealers

Same as all main goods, but a car should be fit to use on the road, be in a condition that reflects its age and price, and be reasonably reliable. 'Sold as seen' has no basis in law; your Sale of Goods Act rights still apply.

Note: Private sales of cars work like all second-hand private sales (see above); however, unless stated, you have a right to expect it will pass an MOT.

5. *Restaurants*
Prices. All pubs and restaurants should clearly display their prices.

Quality. Food should be of 'satisfactory' quality; this includes being hot when it's meant to be. If it isn't, claim a full or partial refund depending on the problem. You may want to report the restaurant to your local Environmental Health Department, as improperly cooked food or food served at the incorrect temperature may pose a health risk.

The food should be as described. If it says 'home-made' on the menu, it should be home-made – if not, it's a breach of criminal law under the Trade Description Act and a breach of contract. This means that you could fairly deduct the value of the difference between home-made and manufactured cost from the food price.

Service charges. There's no requirement to pay extra for 'service' and if the service charge is included in the price, you are legally entitled to deduct a reasonable amount if it wasn't as expected – say 10 to 15%. Also, be careful not to pay a service charge twice – some restaurants encourage this by leaving a blank space on the bill or credit-card slip, even when it is already included.

What if they say 'Pay or we'll call the police'?
If you are reducing the price as you don't think it is reasonable, always explain why. If you feel forced into paying, then pay 'under protest' and then dispute the cost and/or make a claim later; after all, it's never worth a fist in the face. If you do pay a

reduced amount, give the trader your name and address, and invite them to sue you in the County Court. If you're in the right then they won't usually bother.

A LONG-TERM COMPLAINT

During a radio phone-in programme about bank accounts, one caller complained, 'I've been with my bank 19 years and it's always been appalling, the service is terrible, they never do what I ask, it's one mistake after another, and they pay me virtually no interest. I want everybody to know how useless they are.'

Martin's Money Memories: Trains, Complaints and Automatic Discounts

I'm actually hastily scribbling the notes for this *memory* as I sit on a train – one nearly two hours late leaving the station. No big surprise there!

While waiting I popped into the station bookshop. There were signs plastered everywhere saying, 'Two books for £10 on ALL non-fiction paperbacks' and then, in small print underneath, 'under £7.99'. So I grabbed two, to read during the wait. At the till I'm told Jeffrey Archer's *Prison Diary*, at £6.99, isn't included. The reason – 'Only the books at the front of the store count.'

Now, the sign said 'ALL' and it was everywhere – front of store, side of store, back of store and directly above the section where this book was. So I decided to 'holler' – politely and calmly, but taking my time so a queue formed behind me at the till. It wasn't long before I had the two for a tenner.

Now, it isn't much cash, but it's important we speak up when we're right. It teaches companies to deliver on their promises, or they will lose custom and it will cost them.

Oh, and by the way, as the train was two hours late I've already got my form out to get my partial refund on the fare, too.

To be honest, I laughed. 'Why on earth do you come on here complaining about your bank, telling us about its awfulness, and yet you've been with them for 19 years?' I asked. 'Have you never thought of switching, never thought of changing to someone better, never thought of trying a different option?'

While hollering is useful, rarely is the remedy better than picking a good provider in the first place.

nine
THINK THROUGH THEIR LOGIC

Shopping around isn't enough – you may just get the best of a bad bunch. To really see through their charades, ask, 'How do companies make money from me?' and 'How much do they make?'

'Shop around' is oft-quoted advice, and while it's not wrong, for more advanced Money Dieting, it is bland. More important is adding, 'How are they making money out of me?' The answer allows us to start to work out how to cut their profits and reduce our costs. I'm not pretending this is easy, and there are no fixed rules, but let me show you through a couple of practical examples.

LOGICAL SAVING 1:
WHEN FREE ISN'T REALLY FREE

Though it sounds complicated, level-term life assurance is a simple issue. It pays out a fixed lump sum if you die within a set amount of time. As whether you die or not isn't open to

---

Martin's Money Memories: Utilising Logic

Thinking through the logic is a powerful weapon. After some nagging by an overly persistent press officer, I agreed to have lunch with the Chief Executive of a new small gas and electricity price comparison service (see 'Crash Diet', page 149).

While eating she asked me, 'What would it take to get you to recommend us as the best service?' The obvious answer was 'Nothing!' but then I had a flippant thought. *Why not try and cut its profits*. Price-comparison services make money because, if someone switches via their service, providers pay them to do the back office functions. So I said, 'If you want me to recommend you, give customers a cut of the cash.' I was a little surprised when she said she'd try, and more so when one week later she e-mailed me to say they'd crunched the numbers and could do it. And for two months, it both found customers the cheapest provider, and paid £10 per switch on top. Other companies have since followed the lead, and the marketplace has changed for the customer's benefit.

---

debate, and the amount paid out is fixed, it simply boils down to 'the cheaper, the better', providing the company you get it with is reliable.

Most people buy this product straight from their bank. Almost always a bad idea: a) it costs a fortune; b) it doesn't involve shopping around; and c) banks take every extra penny they possibly can.

Some people at least try a few providers. A few, especially following newspaper advice, find themselves at the doors of a life-assurance broker. These companies promise to shop around the entire market to find the cheapest price for you. This route usually cuts the cost by 20 to 40%.

Sounds good? But this is only 'shop around' not 'think through the logic'. At this point ask yourself, 'Why does this broker do this for me?' The answer, of course, is commission. This then leads to, 'Will anybody else do exactly the same for less?' In the life-assurance market the answer is a definite yes.

Many brokers, often smaller firms, will rebate some or even most of their commission. As commission makes up a huge part of the life-assurance cost, this cuts another 20% or 30% off the price. (See 'Crash Diet', page 190.)

LOGICAL SAVING 2: THE WRONG PRODUCT FOR THE RIGHT THING

It's possible to use some products in ways other than they're designed for. This may sound slightly bizarre but, to quote an old comedy phrase, 'That's exactly what they *want* you to think.' Shopping around limits you to one set of products, but by looking at what else could do the same job, you widen the choice and can take advantage of a greater marketplace.

The classic example is my old favourite, personal loans – where prices range between 7% and 15% interest. The wrong product is a credit card, as while there are no interest-free personal loans, there are many interest-free cards. So bend a credit card to work like a personal loan, then you've cracked it and can cut the cost. (I explain the mechanics in 'Healthy Eating', page 330.)

This works across a range of different areas. Don't think within the boxes they create for us – think around the issues. Ask, 'What would solve my problem?' and seek it out. There are no limits to this – it could be using level-term insurance to cover your mortgage, white vinegar as a household cleaner, 'all-risks' household-insurance cover to protect your mobile phone, or a draughts board to play chess on.

Martin's Money Memories: Taking a Different Route

Cheap flights don't necessarily mean outside toilets on the plane. My friend was tripping to Sri Lanka with her mother to visit family there. The only flights available cost around £600 per person on a scheduled airline. She gave me a quick call and asked if I could help. I checked the usual sources, and didn't come up trumps. Most annoying! I hate not to be able to beat a deal. But in a moment's inspiration I decided to check chartered package-holiday offers, and found dozens of specials to Sri Lanka at a much, much cheaper price. One self-catering holiday flying only a day apart from the scheduled flights was around £400 – so I called her back. 'We're staying with relatives, though, why get a package?' The wrong product, the right thing – just because you get a hotel room, you don't need to use it. It's the £200 saving that counts.

If It Sounds Too Good to Be True, It Probably Is

Every time something looks too good to be true, rack your brain to think it through. Could it simply be a loss-leader to envelop your custom? Could there be a cunning undercurrent to how they make money? Could it be a special trick to make you pay more in an entirely different way?

Find the answer and you will be one of the very few who knows. You're then in a position of power. Think through the logic, then work out how you can turn their tactics to your advantage.

THE LIST OF THREE REASONS TO USE STORE CARDS

Store cards are the devil's debt. They make me more angry than any other financial product. Specifically, these are the special cards usable in just one store or group of stores. You will know the type I'm talking about – Debenhams, Selfridges, Top Shop … those cards.

The applications sit near the till, and are sold based on joining inducements.

The interest rates are usurious, often 30% or more; that means spend £500 on a store card without paying it off and by the end of the year, you'll owe it £650 – an extra £150 for nothing. (If you have debt on one, zip to 'Healthy Eating', page 231.)

Yet think through the logic and there are three decent reasons for having store cards.

1. *A feeling of belonging*. They often provide membership rights, special offers, storecard-holder-only evenings, privileged access to new collections, etc. There's nothing wrong with this. Just never, ever, ever use it for borrowing.

2. *Extra discounts for shopping with friends*. Sign up for a store card and they often tempt you with discounts of 10% or even 20% off your first purchase. Grab them and repay in full: nothing wrong with that. Yet Money Dieters can push this further. Never sign up for, and use, a card on your own – rather, go shopping with friends, sign up and then pay for everyone's purchases on the card, this way everybody benefits from your discount. Of course, ensure your friends give you the money and be sure to pay the card off in full so there's no interest charge. Then a few weeks or months later, go back with your friends and let one of them sign up for a new card and its discount, and likewise allow all to shop on it. You can do this again and again and again. But never, ever, ever use it for borrowing.

3. *A handy tool*. If it's late at night, it's dark and you're locked out of your house, waggle the store card correctly in the lock on your door, and you might just be able to persuade it to open. But remember: never, ever, ever use it for borrowing.

PRICE PROMISES HAVE THEIR FINGERS CROSSED

Price promises are devious, misleading devils – whether it's 'we're never beaten on price', 'never knowingly undersold' or 'find it anywhere else and we'll refund the difference'.

All, surprisingly, favour the retailer more than the consumer. They're a clever psychological ploy. They offer reassurance that you're getting the best price, but without delivering anything of the kind.

Just because something has a price promise doesn't actually make it the cheapest. All it means is the price *may* be dropped, if you're prepared to do the work. However, people allow themselves to feel it's a good deal just because the store has a price promise and therefore don't bother looking to beat the price. Price promises are worth nothing unless you put them to the test.

Stores offering price promises can set prices at any level they choose, knowing that at the worst they'll just have to lower them to the same level as another shop.

To put this in context I popped to Comet's website. One of its main special offers was an all-in-one printer/scanner/copier for £69.99 including delivery. Flashing at the top of the web page was the price-promising phrase: 'We always check others' prices online – then we lower ours.' Quickly I clicked across to the internet shopping robot 'pricerunner' … the same printer was available online for less at five other retailers. The cheapest was £54.99 – £15 less.

£ten

FIND THE LOOPHOLES

They make money out of you. So always ask, 'Can I make money out of them?' Companies assume everyone is lazy and apathetic. If you're not, you can surf a wave of offers to make money. Go on – twist their terms and conditions.

This is the hardcore circuit-training section of the Money Diet, beyond 'what's the best possible product?', beyond even 'how are they making money out of me?', and onto 'let's do it to them before they do it to us'. It's about how to find, spot, activate and use legal loopholes, breaks and gaps in the system to benefit in ways product-providers haven't expected or planned for. But it is not for everyone. If you have any doubts STOP! Do not read on. It plays on the margins of finance – get it slightly wrong and it can all go pear-shaped.

The primary targets are financial service providers, simply because they complicate terms and conditions in a way nobody else does. Yet it's not exclusively them – in the past others have all been my targets, too: including online casinos' intro offers, gas and electricity companies, car salesrooms and shops.

IT'S CONSUMER REVENGE

Loophole-spotting isn't for everybody. Even if you have the inclination you may not have the time. It's not as easy or as straightforward as other Money Diet techniques, and takes much longer. 'Consumer Revenge' teaches companies they can't expect to take advantage of apathy any more, and if they do we will snatch their pounds and put them in our pockets.

Spotting loopholes is not an integral part of the Money Diet. It's more like the icing on the cake. It's for people who like playing games and finding a better way to do things. It can be really rewarding.

THE FOUR CORNERSTONES OF SCREWING THE SYSTEM

Hmmm – how to explain spotting a loophole? After mulling long and hard, I think there are four cornerstones, four thought processes to build on. Each has a slightly different methodology and the best results come when more than one is available. Most people are apathetic; most people don't learn how products work; most people don't study the instructions; most people stick with what they've got – companies expect this. Be different and you gain.

Cornerstone 1: TLC for Ts and Cs

I'll say it once, I'll say it loud, and I'll say it proud: *I love terms and conditions.* Some people can see a sheet of music and hear the notes; I look at a list of terms and conditions and start dreaming loopholes. The legalese, the rigid way of working, is designed by teams of lawyers and marketeers attempting to try and stop us doing things they don't want. But to err is human, and they make mistakes. It's often possible to use products in ways providers have never dreamed of.

So look carefully at those terms and conditions. What is it you'd like to do? Is it possible? It's rare, but spot a gap in the Ts and Cs and the big bucks are possible.

An example – the great Barclaycard 0% for life loophole

My guess is the most expensive loophole I've spotted (expensive for them, not us) was one which will perhaps cost Barclaycard millions of pounds over the next few years.

It was all based around a new promotion that sang '0% for life on your balance transfers'. An amazing deal! Yet of course there's a catch. Here it was: 'providing you spend on the card'.

As I will explain in Healthy Eating (page 299), credit-card companies allocate repayments to pay off all cheap debt before touching the expensive debt – leaving it sitting there hastily and heavily accruing interest.

The clever thing about this Barclaycard deal was it forced you to spend in order to get the 0% balance transfer. Digging into the Ts and Cs, though, the 'new' spending only needed be £1 a month.

This was again a clever idea; it takes into account that actually spending £1, no less, not much more, every month for years is a difficult thing to do.

As always the solution seemed simple – after I'd found it. Set up a direct debit (technically on a credit card it's a continuous payment authority) for £1 a month to go to, say, a charity – and thereby automatically fulfil Barclaycard's terms and conditions. The charity gains, you gain, Barclaycard loses. Even at an ultra-conservative estimate, thousands of people followed exactly this system, all denying Barclaycard millions in profits over the next few years and instead pocketing it themselves.

Perhaps the most pleasing and disappointing moment then came when I saw Barclaycard announce it was closing the deal just a few weeks later. A couple of articles even named and shamed me and this loophole as the reason why (though, believe me, I was anything but ashamed).

The replacement scheme looked similar, except with a minimum £50 spend per month. No way round this particular offer, unfortunately, so best avoided. Still, it was great while it lasted!

THE KEY QUESTIONS

- Have you read all the terms and conditions?
- Can you think of any way you can manipulate the product?
- Is there any term that they've missed or wrongly drafted that allows you to do so?
- Is it legal?

Cornerstone 2: Riding the Waves

Introductory offers are gold dust for the loophole-spotter. Companies, especially new ones, are desperate to build their market share and suck in new customers with market-beating introductory offers.

They hope people will get the intro offer, and then not be bothered to move, so gradually the companies can claw the savings back by pushing up prices. Yet, milk the system, move from offer to offer, riding the waves of intro bonuses, and you will always be one step ahead.

Without doubt this is the easiest type of system playing.

An example – 'suck, slap and flog'

'Suck, slap and flog' is my name for a common trick played by savings-account providers. They suck you in with high interest rates, slap the rates down while you're (presumably) not looking, and then flog a new account with a very similar name, so you think you're still getting the best deal. Yet monitor and repeatedly move and *you* flog *them*.

Always have an easy escape route – easy transferability is the key to riding the wave. Do this and you can consistently earn more than the base rate. Keep track of all products and surf to continually be a 'new customer'.

THE KEY QUESTIONS

■ How long does an offer last?
■ How much of it can you have?
■ When should you move?
■ Can you escape?

Cornerstone 3: Cut the Commission

If you've ever had advice from an Independent Financial Adviser and didn't pay a fee, often part of the money you pay each month for the products pays this adviser's commission. And, scandalously, if you bought a product direct from a financial services firm that could've been bought via an adviser, this firm keeps the commission itself, so you're paying for advice you never received. This happens on a vast range of products – critical illness cover, income protection, life assurance, unit trusts, stocks and shares ISAs, pensions – right across the board.

However, there are specialist execution-only companies, 'discount brokers', whose offer is 'Get it through us and we don't give you advice, so we will rebate some of this commission, so your plan is either cheaper, grows more quickly, or you get cash back.'

Of course, the best thing to do is buy it this way in the first place, if you don't need advice. But even if you have a plan running at the moment, it's often possible to jump ship and shift your nominated adviser to become a discount broker. In many cases this means some of the commission will be rebated either to you or to your plan, so that you gain. (For a detailed example of this see 'Repensioning', page 196.) So always ask, 'Am I paying for advice I'm not getting?' If so, move.

THE KEY QUESTIONS
- Are there hidden costs for commission?
- Would these hidden costs be cheaper anywhere else?
- Is it possible to move? Are there any moving costs?
- When do you pay them?
- Is the same advice available for free?

Cornerstone 4: Precision Products

Most product-providers like to sell us multi-use and multi-function financial products, as the more things you use a product for, the more money the company makes, because more cash flows through it. This is one of the reasons offset and current account mortgages are coming onto the market – after all, if you've got a mortgage that's also a bank account, savings account and personal loan, this company now has your custom for four products for the price of one.

The next attempt to create 'chic customised products' is in the credit-card market. A few create-your-own cards have already come out, with patter promising the card can morph with your usage. Yet they continue to milk you for profits as you use it in different ways.

However, the loophole-spotting Money Dieter can utilise 'multi-tasking'. To sell a product, companies advertise their strongest, sharpest and cheapest point. It may be it's the cheapest credit card for spending abroad; it may be it's the loan with the lowest interest rate; it may be it's the mortgage that allows you to overpay the most each month – anything.

As in physics, for every action there's an equal and opposite reaction. With money, for every positive element there's an equal and opposite negative one. Providers make sure that where we gain with one hand, they profit with the other – *if* you use all the multi-functions. Instead loophole-spotting says, 'I will only use it when it's good, and use something else to fill in the gaps.'

'Precision Plastic' ('Healthy Eating', page 283), is the epitome of this. Only ever use products for their very, very best feature. This is simple, effective, and works across the board. For example, many mobile phones offer free 'cross-network' minutes – so you can call landlines or mobiles with your free minutes. As calls to mobiles cost more than landlines, use your mobile to make as many expensive to-mobile calls as possible, even when at home, and your landline for calling landlines as often as possible, and you skew the provider's equation, leaving you spending less.

THE KEY QUESTIONS
- How does it work?
- Who is it targeted at?
- Can you gain by using it accurately?

THE LIST OF THIRTEEN WAYS TO SCREW THE SYSTEM

1. Free cash. Credit cards give you cash back when you spend and may lend you money at 0% at the same time. By making all spending on the card, you can earn cash back and save your unspent wages. This way you earn interest on money they've lent you for nothing. (See 'Healthy Eating', page 311.)

2. Flex an inflexible mortgage. Good bog-standard old-fashioned mortgages charge less interest than flexible ones. By, amongst other things, manipulating the length of your mortgage term you can recreate many of a flexible mortgage's features, without paying the high rates. (See 'Healthy Eating', page 268.)

3. Less-than-no-commission life assurance. The cheapest life assurers on the market charge you a fee but don't take any commission. However, a range of other brokers who normally try and suck loads of commission out try and make themselves look competitive by offering 'price-beater' policies. So go to the cheapest life assurance company on the market, get a quote, then take it to the price-beating brokers and ask them to give you exactly the same deal without a commission and without the fee. (See 'Crash Diet', page 198.)

4. Free mortgage advice. The big mortgage brokers all charge you a fee except for London & Country. So seek three of the big brokers, get them to give you their best advice – and as you only actually pay for the advice when you complete the mortgage, process it through London & Country, and you won't pay a fee, but will have ensured you got the best advice possible. (See 'Crash Diet', page 207.)

5. *Healthcare cashback schemes – be sure you claim*. These pay cash back on your spending on dental, optical, osteopathic and similar treatments. The reason they can give you really good rates is that most people simply forget to claim small payments. If you do claim you beat their pricing policy, and can claim back up to six times what you pay. (See 'Crash Diet', page 179.)

6. *Repensioning*. If you are no longer receiving advice from your pension adviser, or you bought direct, then 'repensioning' is my invention to make you more money. You simply move your existing pension to a discount pension provider. This means with exactly the same pension you get more growth. (See page 196.)

7. *Override your mobile network*. It's possible to use one of a few special providers to bypass your mobile phone network's charges. You dial a freephone number to access the service, and then make your calls on this secondary network. This means you have landline call costs off your mobile. (See 'Crash Diet', page 172.)

8. *Half-price plastic personal loans*. The best credit cards are cheaper than personal loans – manipulate your credit card into becoming a loan. Create a debt on your current credit card and transfer it to a new card using the special balance-transfer rate. (See 'Healthy Eating', page 330.)

9. *Make the networks cross*. Push the override provider system above a little further. Take out an Orange phone which has cross-network calls – free calls to other mobiles or land-

---

Martin's Money Memories: You Always Remember Your First Time

Sorry, no salacious gossip here. Actually, I mean the first time I spotted a really big loophole was for my *Deal of the Day* programme, my first TV job at Sky channel *Simply Money*. The then newly launched internet bank Cahoot offered an incentive to join: shift a balance from another card and you get 5% of the debt back as cash. Hidden within its Ts&Cs was the fact it allowed two balance transfers onto this card, paying 5% each time. Therefore this money could be moved to the Cahoot card, back to your original credit card, and returned to Cahoot to get 5% on the same debt twice, leaving you with almost 10% less debt overall (nerdy note: it's almost 10%, as the second time you are only getting 5% of 95% of the original debt, leaving you with 90.25% of the original money). Not only that, but using a technique similar to 'Free Cash' (on page 311) you didn't even need to have debts to do this. With a £5,000 credit limit, it was possible to make nearly £1,000 in cash at no risk in just a few weeks. Beautiful.

---

lines – then use the override number to call landlines and only use the free minutes to call other mobiles. This leaves all your free minutes as mobile-to-mobile calls, the most expensive type, leaving you riding roughshod over Orange's plan that the cheap mobile-to-landline calls will offset their expensive mobile-to-other-mobile costs. (See 'Crash Diet', page 172.)

10. Cash ISA fixed rate? Unlike fixed-rate savings accounts, where you really can't withdraw money early, government regulations require cash ISA providers to allow you to. This means that you can fix your rate over a long period but with a cheap get-out clause if rates change and there's better on offer elsewhere. (See 'Crash Diet', page 165.)

11. Stick it to store cards. One final dig at these horrors. Store cards charge hideous rates of interest, so sign up for the card when they have introductory discounts and buy all the shopping for you and your mates on it. Your friends pay you back, and you pay the card off in full. Next time you shop there, another one of you signs up for the discount and you all save again. (See page 133.)

12. Perfect phone tariffs. Sign up for a phone provider, and they expect you to make all your calls via them, but there's absolutely no need to do so. Other providers can be accessed via a special code, so you can connect to their services at no cost, and so pick the cheapest tariff for each type of call. (See 'Crash Diet', page 225.)

13. Christmas presents at January sales prices. Barclaycard and RBS have price-beater policies – find anything cheaper afterwards and they will refund you the difference. When you're shopping at Christmas, use these credit cards. Then, when prices are reduced in the January sales, you can simply send off and get a refund on the difference in price. And hey presto! Christmas presents at January sales prices! Ho! Ho! Ho! (See 'Healthy Eating', page 310.)

PART 2

THE CRASH DIET

Want to save money quickly? Simply look down the Money Diet Calorie Counter on page xiv to the products you have or need. Turn to the page and make the saving. This section is not an exhaustive list of every possible product, but a wide selection of ways to save money. If something you're looking for isn't included, read 'Financial Fitness for Life' on how to get the best deals on anything and everything, as well as money-saving hints, tips and tricks.

CRASH DIET TOPICS

Each topic is divided up into the following:

THE MENU
The hoped-for result and how and why you can save.

CHOOSING YOUR DISH
How to find the cheapest and best.

CALORIE COUNT
The scale of savings. Examples are taken from real-life situations at the time of writing. They are for guidance only and, of course, the scale of savings will vary vastly with personal circumstances.

SUGGESTED INGREDIENTS
Where to find the cheapest and the best.

(News) means Sunday papers, which carry best-buy tables for the product, but always check for traps pointed out. (MSE) indicates my website www.moneysavingexpert.com, which is specially designed to accompany *The Money Diet*, and has updated best-buys links and articles.

This is followed by a list of providers. These have been picked as they are traditionally good payers and players. Do remember, though, things change quickly in the money world, so they may not remain the best; newcomers may be better. See the ingredients as the first port of call to set a benchmark standard, but don't be shy of checking others. Always follow the logic of the main article to establish their worth, though.

ADDED SPICE

Special hints and tips to customise the recipe to your special tastes.

GAS & ELECTRICITY BILLS

NUTRITIONAL INFORMATION

Typical Saving: £150 per year.
Time Taken: 10 minutes.
Difficulty Level: Easy.

THE MENU

Perhaps the easiest dish on the Money Diet menu. If you've never changed supplier you could be paying up to 25% too much. Even if you have switched, up to 15% is possible.

Shifting supplier is not a big deal: you keep the same pipes, circuits and wires, the only difference is the customer service and billing. The new supplier will perform the switch – all you need do is sign the right forms and take a meter reading.

CHOOSING YOUR DISH

Unless you're a slide-rule Jedi, forget doing the comparisons yourself. A range of phone and internet comparison services do the work for you. Simply plug in your details. It's best to compare using the kilowatt-hours amount detailed on your bill. If you haven't got your bill cost, even an educated guess will do. Some comparison companies will even estimate your energy usage for you, based on house size and heating supply, etc if you don't know the figures. Even with these services there are a number of things to watch for:

- **Dual fuel isn't cheaper.** It's a marketing myth that getting gas and electricity from the same supplier makes it cheaper. Sometimes using the cheapest stand-alone suppliers wins. Always check this option.

- **Direct debit is cheaper.** This isn't a myth. Save up to 10% through paying by fixed monthly direct debit from your bank account. If you've overpaid you will be refunded at the end of the year. If you've underpaid extra will be due. The reason it is cheaper is suppliers are sure you won't default, plus they can earn extra interest on your money where there are overpayments.

- **Missed providers.** Due to some technicalities, some price comparison companies omit certain tariffs. If you have time, do the same comparison on a couple, to be doubly sure of the best deal.

Whichever supplier you choose remember to take regular meter readings, so you don't overpay. As tariffs change regularly, it's worth redoing a price comparison once a year to check you're still with the best. Also, the government's Energy Saving Trust has some great booklets on how to cut energy use and therefore cut bills.

CALORIE COUNT

A family spending £700 a year using their regional electricity company and British Gas's standard policy could save around

15% by switching to the cheapest providers, or 25% by using direct debit.

Switch to save Manchester family spending £700				
	Gas	Electricity	Total	Saving
Current (bills)	£250	£450	£700	–
Switch to cheapest				
Dual fuels (bills)	–	–	£586	£114
Stand-alone (bills)	£191	£371	£562	£138
Dual fuels (direct debit)	–	–	£549	£151
Stand-alone (direct debit)	£175	£360	£535	£165

SUGGESTED INGREDIENTS (MSE)

Price comparison companies: www.buy.co.uk; www.saveon
yourbills.co.uk, 0800 083 0808; Simply Energy, 0800 093 9884;
www.ukpower.co.uk; www.uswitch.co.uk, 0845 601 2856;
www.switchandgive.com, 0870 922 0353; www.energyhelpline.
co.uk; www.energylinx.co.uk.
Other: www.staywarm.co.uk, 0800 1694 694.

ADDED SPICE

- *Over 60s special:* If there is someone over 60 living in your
house, one energy supplier, StayWarm, provides a special flat-
fee service. You must get both gas and electricity from it, and
then, rather than paying a charge depending on energy usage,
you simply pay depending on the number of people and
rooms in your house. The big advantage is the security of
knowing how much you'll pay, and it's great for anyone who
wants to turn the heat up but is worried about cost. It's not
cheaper for everyone, though, so compare it to the best result
from the price comparison services. As a rule of thumb,
unless StayWarm is more than 5% costlier, choose it.

- *Green energy.* Some companies offer special tariffs, which promote environmentally friendly energy sources. It is more expensive, but you can still use the price comparison engines to find the cheapest greens for you.

- *Cashback.* As you'll have read on page 131, one comparison service once gave cash back to anyone who switched via it. Similar incentives are becoming commonplace – it's worth trying a few comparison services to see what current offers they have.

Martin's Money Memories: How to Knock Knockers

An added bonus – follow this tip and you'll have the confidence to firmly close the door in the face of all the energy touts knocking at it.

When someone disturbs my peace, I often try and have a little fun. I always remember one chap who mistakenly arrived on my doorstep touting gas and electricity and promising, 'Did you know you can save a fortune if you switch to us?'

'No,' I say. 'I didn't know.'

'Oh yes,' says he. 'Move to us and you can save up to 15%.'

'No,' I say again. His 'I've found another punter' smile was short-lived. I didn't know he could save me money, because he couldn't. His offer was 5% more expensive than my current provider.

As I pointed this out, his lips turned down. So I thought I'd try and cheer him up.

'Where do you live?' I say.

'Eh?' says he.

'Where do you live?'

'Round the corner.'

'Who do you use for your utilities?' I asked.

Within ten minutes I'd written out which suppliers he should switch to on his clipboard, and I added his cheapest phone supplier while I was at it. Better than commission any day, surely? Then again he was lucky. Most of the time I feel confident in saying, 'I'm fine thanks' and close the door.

BOOKS, CDS, DVDS, VIDEO GAMES AND ELECTRICAL GOODS

NUTRITIONAL INFORMATION

Typical Saving: £250 per year.
Time Taken: 10 minutes a time.
Difficulty Level: Easy.

THE MENU

Internet shopping robots (shopbots) scan internet retailers to find the cheapest price. Simply enter what you want, press compare and the results are displayed in order of cost, including extras like delivery, which should also be broken out and listed separately.

CHOOSING YOUR DISH

Each shopbot searches a slightly different range of retailers, so it's always worth trying two or three. For more specialised goods, such as computer parts or fridges, you'll find some dedicated shopbots.

These sites make cash via advertising, or retailers' commission for sales links. There's nothing wrong with this providing there are no unfair promotions for higher-commission goods and the price is unaffected. Always keep an eye out for this. (See price comparisons, 'Financial Fitness for Life', page 98).

Also remember that price-comparison services note the delivery costs of an individual product. However, buy three or four goods at a time, and the delivery costs per product may change, in which case compare using the main product price not delivery price.

CALORIE COUNT

By just using two price comparison services for a range of goods, I saved 35% over using an individual online retailer – and that was already cheaper than most high-street shops. Over a year this makes a massive difference, especially if you buy big goods such as a fridge or TV.

Shopbot savings	Chart CD	New Chart Hardback Book	New Chart DVD	New Playstation 2 Game	Delivery	Total	Saving
Standard online retailer	£11	£17	£20	£40	£4	£92	N/A
Shopbots (includes delivery)	£8	£10	£15	£33	Inc.	£66	£26

SUGGESTED INGREDIENTS

www.kelkoo.co.uk; www.pricerunner.co.uk;
www.easyvalue.com; www.onlinepriceguide.co.uk;
www.checkaprice.com; www.priceguideuk.com;
www.dealtime.co.uk; www.comparisonmagic.co.uk.

WATER BILLS

NUTRITIONAL INFORMATION

Typical Saving: £100.
Time Taken: 10 minutes (internet) or 25 minutes (otherwise).
Difficulty Level: Easy (internet), Mid (otherwise).

THE MENU

The choice is simple, as the market isn't open to competition – either fit a water meter or stick to the old-style bills.

It's all about choosing the right way to be charged. The traditional bill depends on the 'rateable value' of your home, regardless of how much water you use. This very roughly means the more your home can be rented out for, the more you pay for water.

The alternative is a meter, which measures water usage. Many product providers have accused me of talking excrement in the past. This time it's true, as what comes in usually goes out, so water meters also calculate your sewerage bill. Meters must be fitted free of charge, unless it's justifiably impractical. If you switch to a water meter you have a right to switch back within either 12 months, or a month of getting your second measured bill, whichever is later. However, move into a home which already has a meter and you can't switch back.

CHOOSING YOUR DISH

Whether to fit a meter or not depends on the water company's area and your usage. Those with access to the internet can use www.buy.co.uk, which asks questions about your water usage, and quickly calculates whether a meter will cut the cost.

For those without internet access, as a very rough rule of thumb, if there are the same number or fewer people living in your house than there are bedrooms, check out fitting a meter. Just contact your water company, which should send a table to work it out. If the saving looks to be minimal don't fit a meter, as the security of knowing exactly what you will pay regardless of usage is worthwhile.

CALORIE COUNT

The table below shows the savings in three water areas in late 2003. It's for a four-bedroom home for residents with average water use. The savings from switching to a meter can be over £200.

Waste not, want not: traditional bill £360 per year										
	1 person		2 people		3 people		4 people		5 people	
	Cost	Saving	Cost	Saving	Cost	Saving	Cost	Saving	Cost	Saving
United Utilities	£154	£206	£211	£149	£269	£91	£341	£19	£398	£38 more
Thames Water	£113	£247	£156	£204	£199	£161	£253	£107	£295	£65
Northumbrian Water	£125	£235	£172	£188	£219	£141	£278	£82	£326	£34

SUGGESTED INGREDIENTS (MSE)

www.buy.co.uk or your water company.

SAVINGS ACCOUNTS

NUTRITIONAL INFORMATION

Typical Gain: £150 a year.
Time Taken: 20 minutes.
Difficulty Level: Easy.

THE MENU

Savings accounts are bank accounts which pay more interest, but have less functionality. Yet the first place to put your cash, if you can, is a tax-free cash ISA (see page 160). Then look at a regular savings account (see page 158). Only after that consider a standard savings account.

CHOOSING YOUR DISH

The prime consideration is the interest rate, yet even with this simple product there are a few things to watch out for.

- **Access.** How quickly do you need the money? Notice accounts mean you need to wait to withdraw it. And since these days 'instant access' (just go into a branch and withdraw) and 'no-notice' (the money is available instantly, but as it's via electronic transfer or post it takes about three days) don't pay much less than notice accounts they're often a better pick.

- **Short-term interest rate bonuses.** These temporary rate hikes mean providers can advertise higher rates to attract custom, but the rates soon shrink. There's nothing wrong with going for these if they pay the best rate, providing you're prepared to switch account as soon as the rate drops. If not, stick to non-bonus accounts.

- **Tax.** The interest on savings accounts is automatically taxed at the basic savings tax rate, currently 20%. This means basic-rate taxpayers needn't do anything, but higher-rate taxpayers must declare on the self-assessment form the interest and will pay a total of 40% of it. Non-taxpayers can get a R85 form, so that all interest will be paid tax-free. One final note – if your spouse is a lower-rate taxpayer than you, this makes it worthwhile putting the savings in their name to reduce the tax bill.

- **Rates are variable.** Savings accounts interest rates are variable and move both when the Bank of England Base Rate moves (see page 262) and when the product provider changes the rate for its own competitive reasons. This means it's important to monitor the interest rate you receive. If it drops, just withdraw the money and put it in a better account. If that's too much of a hassle then look for a tracker, where the rate follows the Bank of England Base Rate. (Also see the 'Suck, slap and flog' technique, page 140.)

CALORIE COUNT

Many people leave their savings languishing in accounts paying pitiful rates. In real terms you're losing money as the after-tax interest is often lower than inflation.

Interest on £5,000 in a savings account before tax				
		1 year	3 years	Gain over 3 years
Pitiful Bank	0.5%	£25	£75	–
Top Payer	4%	£200	£620	£545

SUGGESTED INGREDIENTS (NEWS, MSE)

www.INGDirect.com; www.egg.com; Birmingham Midshires, 0800 1691543; Abbey National, 0800 100801; Nationwide, 0800 302010; Northern Rock, 0845 6006767; Coventry Building Society, 0845 766 5522; www.cahoot.com; your local building society (some have special rates for local people).

REGULAR SAVINGS ACCOUNTS

NUTRITIONAL INFORMATION

Typical Gain: £120.
Time Taken: 30 minutes.
Difficulty Level: Mid.

THE MENU

Regular savings accounts are an oft-unused breed, yet usually they beat even the market-leading standard savings. They are marketed as enforcing saving discipline as they require a payment to be made every month, but there's a sneaky trick to enable lump-sum investments too.

CHOOSING YOUR DISH

The interest rate is crucial, but also check the following:

- **Monthly payment required.** Different minimums and maximums apply – usually £20 to £250. Some accounts require a fixed payment each month, but it's preferable if they just require you to deposit 'at least' the minimum.

- **Qualifying for a bonus.** These accounts work by paying a bonus, which boosts the interest each year, providing you've made all the required payments. The qualifying rules vary. Some limit withdrawals, others accept one missed payment; pick one that suits your habits.

- **Variable rates.** Just like ordinary savings accounts, these rates are variable. If they drop the rate below competitive levels, wait until you've been paid the bonus, then withdraw your money immediately and open an account elsewhere.

CALORIE COUNT

Regular Savings Accounts beat Standard Savers			
Save £200 per month for three years	Interest rate	Interest earned (basic-rate taxpayer)	Increase in interest
Poor Savings Account	0.2%	£20	–
Top Savings Account	4.3%	£370	£350
Top Regular Savings Account	5%	£440	£420

SUGGESTED INGREDIENTS (MSE)

Ipswich Building Society, 01473 211021; Leeds & Holbeck BS, 0113 2257777; Furness BS, 0800 220568; Birmingham Midshires, 0800 169 1543; Halifax, 0845 7263646; Monmouthshire BS, 01633 844402; your local building society (some have special rates for local people).

ADDED SPICE

To invest a lump sum. To invest a lump sum using these schemes, put the money first in the highest-paying standard savings account. Then set up monthly payments from it to the regular savings account, at the maximum level in the first months to get the cash in quickly. However, always ensure there's enough left to keep up the minimum payments over the year. This way your money trickles across and you always meet the terms and conditions.

MINI CASH ISAS

NUTRITIONAL INFORMATION

Typical Gain: £80 per year.
Time Taken: 20 minutes.
Difficulty Level: Easy/Mid.

Note: For a full, easy guide to how ISAs work, first read page 169.

THE MENU

Mini cash Individual Savings Accounts (ISAs) are simply savings accounts you don't pay income tax on. This means there's an extra 25% interest for basic-rate and 66% for higher-rate taxpayers. Each tax year (6 April to 5 April) everyone aged 16 or older gets a new ISA allowance.

If you've got savings, and don't need to utilise an ISA for shares, then you should get a mini cash ISA. Even non-taxpayers often benefit as the best cash ISA rates usually beat the best savings account rates.

Each tax year you can currently save another £3,000 of cash in an ISA. Money can be withdrawn at any time without losing tax benefits, but it can't then be returned to the cash ISA. (See page 169 for full explanation.)

CHOOSING YOUR DISH

The higher the interest rate the better, though watch for the following:

- **Short-term interest rate bonuses.** These temporary rate hikes allow providers to advertise higher rates to attract your custom, but they soon disappear. There's nothing wrong with going for them if they pay the best rate, providing you're prepared to transfer the cash ISA as soon as the rates drop. Otherwise, stick to non-bonus accounts.

- **Transfer penalties.** You are allowed to change ISA provider (see page 162) and it should be easy. Yet some providers levy a fine when you leave them, which can outweigh any gain made by moving. These may effectively trap you if they drop their rate. Try to avoid these.

The only way to guarantee the rate won't drop is using a fixed-rate mini cash ISA (see page 165). Yet this means your money is partially locked away.

CALORIE COUNT

Interest on £3,000 saved over 3 years	Rate	Basic-rate taxpayer	Higher-rate taxpayer	Gain
Pitiful Savings Account (there are many)	0.1%	£7	£5	None
Top Savings Account	4.5%	£335	£250	£245
Worst-Paying Cash ISA	3.5%	£330	£330	£325
Top Cash ISA	4.5%	£425	£425	£420

SUGGESTED INGREDIENTS (NEWS, MSE)

Kent Reliance Building Society, 08451 220022; Portman BS, 01202 560560; Northern Rock, 0845 6006767; Abbey National, 0800 100801; Nationwide, 0800 302010; Safeway (store), 0800 995995; Halifax, 0845 7263646; your local building society (some have special rates for local people).

EXISTING CASH ISAS: IMPROVING THE RETURNS

NUTRITIONAL INFORMATION

Typical Saving: £100 per year.
Time Taken: 20 minutes.
Difficulty Level: Mid.

Note: First read 'Mini Cash ISAs', page 160, and 'How an ISA Works', page 169.

THE MENU

Cash ISA providers smugly smile when you open an account, as they assume they have your business for life, regardless of whether they pay decent interest. Prove them wrong.

There are three reasons to consider switching a cash ISA – to up the interest; fix the interest; or to link the returns to the stock market. ISA transfers must be like for like, so a mini cash ISA must stay a mini cash ISA. If you're moving the current year's ISA, it must be moved whole, but a previous year's ISA can be moved and split between different providers.

However, don't just withdraw the cash to switch your account, or you'll immediately lose the ISA tax benefits. Instead, talk to the the new provider and ask about their transfer process.

Before moving, check if your current provider has any transfer penalties – roughly one in three do. Small penalties, like 30 days' interest, aren't a problem. Yet the few with higher fines (up to about £50) may scupper the gains.

CHOOSING YOUR DISH

Follow 'Mini Cash ISAs' (page 160) for the basics. There are a couple of additional transfer factors too.

Not all cash ISA providers accept transfers in, but it's easy to find out – just ask. Also, with some providers you could get paid more if you transfer the combined value of a number of years' cash ISAs.

One further option, to up the risk of your cash ISA, is to use Guaranteed Equity Bond mini cash ISAs. Offered by many banks, these usually last for around five years, and your money is locked away during that time. The returns are linked to the performance of one or more, usually a combination of, stock markets. For example, you may receive approximately 70% of the growth of a stock market index such as the FTSE-100. If the market does well, they will outperform standard cash ISAs, if it does badly you will just get your original cash back. This means that the worst-case scenario is you miss out on the interest from a normal cash ISA.

CALORIE COUNT

Upping cash ISA interest alone can make a big difference. It's easily possible to have a combined £15,000 in cash ISAs from this and past years. By shifting this amount, you could gain over £200 a year.

Possible transfer benefits	Rate	Interest			Gain
		1 year	2 years	3 years	3 years
Poor Cash ISA	3%	£450	£915	£1,390	–
Top Cash ISA	4.5%	£675	£1,380	£2,100	£710

SUGGESTED INGREDIENTS (NEWS, MSE)

Main providers: see 'Mini cash ISAs', page 160. Guaranteed Equity Bond ISA providers: Bristol & West, 0800 1811111; Birmingham Midshires, 0800 1691543; Norwich Union, 0845 3000009; Britannia BS, 0800 132304; National Savings & Investments, 0845 9645000; Northern Rock, 0845 6004466.

FIXED-RATE CASH ISAS

NUTRITIONAL INFORMATION

Typical Gain: £100 per year.
Time Taken: 30 minutes.
Difficulty Level: Mid/Hard.
Note: First read 'Mini Cash ISAs' (page 160) or 'Existing Cash ISAs: Improving the Returns' (page 162).

THE MENU

There's a loophole in the mini cash ISA regulations that benefits savers. Unlike normal savings accounts, it's possible to fix a high rate on your tax-free cash ISA, protecting it from interest rate cuts, but without needing to lock the money away.

This is because years after ISAs were launched, the Inland Revenue Service finally told providers who mandated a lock-in that even though the rate was fixed, they had to give people reasonable access to their cash. Of course it isn't quite that simple – providers may still snatch back some interest via early withdrawal penalties.

CHOOSING YOUR DISH

Most cash ISAs are variable-rate, yet the few that are fixed tend to be very competitive – not a bad start. All in all, this means you can take advantage of guaranteed earnings if interest rates are dropping, yet have a way out if they start to rise and better deals are therefore available elsewhere.

Incidentally, those whose fixed-rate mini cash ISAs were taken out before the rule change are now able to withdraw money under these conditions too.

There are three elements to consider:

- *The rate.* As always, the higher the better.
- *The length of the fix.* They usually last one to five years. It'll always be better to stick to the full term of the fix, rather than withdrawing early and taking the penalty. Therefore a shorter fix is safer, as rates should move less.
- *The withdrawal penalty.* Penalties are usually measured by a set number of days' worth of interest, e.g. 45, 90 or 180 days' worth. The shorter the penalty, the more escapable the ISA.

These three elements can't be looked at in isolation – a long-term fix isn't so bad with a short withdrawal penalty, as you can escape. A long withdrawal penalty isn't so bad with a short-term fix, as it's likely you'll stick to the full term anyway.

CALORIE COUNT

The table below indicates the impact of withdrawal penalties on the interest rate. For example, take a two-year fixed rate at 4%, withdraw the cash after a year and a half, and you'd still have earned the equivalent interest of 3.4% over that time.

Fixed rate mini cash ISAs	Full rate	Interest penalty on withdrawal	Equivalent interest rate if money withdrawn							
			1yr	1½yrs	2yrs	3yrs	3½yrs	4yrs	4½yrs	5yrs
Two-year fix	4%	90 days	3%	3.4%	4%	–	–	–	–	–
Four-year fix	4.1%	180 days	2.1%	2.8%	3.1%	3.4%	3.5%	4.1%	–	–
Five-year fix	4.35%	180 days	2.1%	2.9%	3.2%	3.6%	3.7%	3.8%	3.9%	4.35%

SUGGESTED INGREDIENTS (MSE)

Portman Building Society, 01202 560560; Abbey, 0800 100801; Halifax, 0845 7263646; Julian Hodge Bank, 0800 0283746; Kent Reliance BS, 08451 220022; your local building society (some have special rates for local people).

TOISAS: WHAT TO DO WITH YOUR MATURED TESSA

■NUTRITIONAL INFORMATION

Typical Gain: £150 per year.
Time Taken: 30 minutes.
Difficulty Level: Easy/Mid.

■THE MENU

If your Tessa has just matured, or even matured years ago, there's a simple process to increase the interest earned. Tessas were tax-free cash savings products that lasted five years, sales of which ended when ISAs were introduced in April 1999.

■ *Maturing Tessas.* If your Tessa has just matured watch out – fail to act and it may have automatically been shifted into a non-tax-free account sometimes paying as little as 1%. The solution is in the form of a special tax-free product called a Tessa-only ISA, tongue-twistingly known as a Toisa.

These allow an amount equal to the original Tessa investment to be deposited, although you can't include any interest that's accrued. To set one up, obtain a maturity certificate from your Tessa provider, but be quick – they're only valid for six months: miss this and miss out. Though your Tessa provider may moot otherwise there's nothing requiring you to stick with it for your Toisa. Toisas don't affect your annual ISA allowance (see ISAs guide, page 169): they're completely separate.

Unlike Tessas, money may be withdrawn from Toisas at any time without losing the tax benefits, though any money you withdraw can't then be replaced in the Toisa. This is very useful as even those who want to spend their matured

Tessa cash soon can just deposit it in a tax-free Toisa for the meantime.

■ *Existing Toisas.* If you already have a Toisa, there is nothing stopping you transferring it to earn more interest. Don't simply withdraw the cash, though – then you lose the tax-free status. Just ask your chosen new provider for its procedure and it should guide you through.

CHOOSING YOUR DISH

This works the same way as mini cash ISAs (see page 160). (It is also possible to up the risk while keeping it tax-free – see Existing Cash ISAs: Improving the Returns, page 162.)

CALORIE COUNT

£9,000 over three years dunked in a 1% interest-paying holding account earns a basic-rate taxpayer a pitiful £215. A Tessa in an ISA is way more than twice as nice.

Increase your £9,000 matured Tessa returns over 3 years*				
	Interest rate	Interest (basic-rate taxpayer)	Interest (higher-rate taxpayer)	Increased return (higher rate)
Holding account	1%	£215	£160	N/A
Top Toisa	4.5%	£1,270	£1,270	£1,110
*assumes rates are static for ease of illustration				

SUGGESTED INGREDIENTS (MSE)

Merrill Lynch HSBC; Northern Rock; Abbey; Nationwide; Lloyds TSB; Halifax; your local building society (some have special rates for local people).

Money Diet Quick Fact Snacks: How an ISA Works

What is an ISA? An Individual Savings Account isn't a financial product in its own right – it's just a tax-free wrapper you can place either cash, shares or insurance-based investments in.

Imagine a cake with many different ingredients: chocolate (cash), strawberry (shares) and lemon (life insurance). Usually the taxman comes along, picks up a slice and takes a bite from it. But each year you're given a tax-free wrapper, like cling film, which you can put around some of the cake as you choose. Once inside the cling film, the nature of the cake hasn't changed, the chocolate's still chocolate, the lemon's still lemon, the strawberry's still strawberry, but as it's wrapped up the taxman can no longer take a bite.

How much can be invested? Each tax year (starts 6 April) everyone over the age of 16 receives an ISA allowance with a limit of £7,000. Any savings or investments must be opened and made by the next 5 April. Though investments stay within that year's ISA wrapper after the end of the tax year, nothing more can then be put in. However, this still means it's possible to have substantial amounts invested within ISA wrappers – a maximum £7,000 plus gains for each tax year since they started in 1999. It should be noted that government plans for ISAs may change in the next couple of years, including dropping the limit to £5,000.

What can be put inside an ISA?

■ **Cash:** Cash ISAs are simply savings accounts where the interest isn't taxed (see page 160).

■ **Shares:** Share-based investments in various forms are ISA-able. Self-select ISAs allow you to pick your own shares. However, a more common use is for collective investment vehicles like unit or investment trusts, where fund managers pick a basket of shares and returns depend on the average performance, (see 'Discount Brokers', page 190). Placing these investments inside an ISA wrapper provides two tax advantages. First, any profits made from share price increases aren't eligible for capital gains tax, and second, it enables all the tax on bonds to be reclaimed.

■ **Insurance:** This isn't household or motor insurance but insurance-based investments, like with-profits funds. It's often thought these aren't taxed, as tax is usually deducted within the investment, so returns feel like they're tax-free. Yet within an ISA there genuinely is no tax. However, insurance investments are out of favour and the limits are small, so for most people they're probably best left unused.

What's all this Mini and Maxi stuff? Unfortunately the ISA rules are unnecessarily complicated and each year anyone opening an ISA must pick whether to go for one of two types of ISA container, either mini or a maxi

■ *To MAXIMISE your share-based investments go for a MAXI:* A maxi is a suitcase-type container, as everything has to be bundled together and bought from just one provider. You can have up to £3,000 in cash, £1,000 in life assurance, and whatever you don't use up in shares. This means it's possible to have up to the full £7,000 in share-based investments. Usually maxi ISAs are therefore bought from investment companies, and they pay relatively poor cash returns, so maxis are best used for shares ISAs.

■ *For the best CASH returns MINIMISE your share-based investments with a MINI:* If maxis are suitcases, minis are like three handbags. Each can be bought from a different company and must carry something different. The limits are £3,000 in the cash bag, £1,000 in the life-assurance bag, but only £3,000 in the shares bag. As cash ISAs can therefore be bought from specialists, minis provide the best cash returns.

The rules strictly prevent the opening of a mini and a maxi ISA in the same tax year. Do this and you are potentially invalidating any tax gains.

Therefore think before opening any ISA: even if you open a mini cash ISA with just a pound at the start of the tax year, there's no going back – you're on the mini route. And if you later decide you want to invest the maximum £7,000 in shares that year, you'll find £4,000 of the allowance is lost. This is very important if you have a direct debit on a current account. If that automatically carries over into the next tax year, the choice is then made for you. Be careful.

How can money be withdrawn? ISAs don't need to be held for a set length of time. Money can be withdrawn at any time without losing any tax benefits – providing the rules of that individual product allow it. The confusing thing is the limits are only affected by the cash or shares on the way into the ISA. Some examples should clarify this:

■ *Mr Rich Devil invests £7,000 in a shares ISA at the beginning of the tax year.* Options: he may sell the investment at any time without tax implications, but no more may be put inside that year's ISA wrapper. However, he can still buy and sell shares within the wrapper based on the proceeds of the original investment.

■ *Ms Irma Indecisive invests £2,000 in a mini cash ISA at the start of the tax year.* Options: she may invest a further £1,000 in the mini cash ISA plus £3,000 in a mini shares ISA and a further £1,000 in a life insurance ISA with another different provider before the end of the tax year.

■ *Irma then decides she needs to withdraw £1,000 of this cash.* Options: the fact that she has withdrawn the cash doesn't impact her allowance at all – she can still only put £1,000 more in the mini cash ISA, £3,000 in the mini shares ISA and £1,000 in a life assurance ISA.

Can I switch provider once I've set up an ISA? There's nothing stopping you switching provider for cash, shares or life insurance ISAs. However, don't simply withdraw the cash or investment as you'll lose the tax benefits. Instead, ask the new provider about its procedures for moving the money.

MOBILE CALLS AT LANDLINE PRICES

NUTRITIONAL INFORMATION

Typical Gain: £350 per year.
Time Taken: 45 minutes.
Difficulty Level: Mid/Hard.

THE MENU

If you don't want to invest in a ten-mile-long cable, there's another way to sneakily make mobile calls at landline prices.

Some override providers work by utilising freephone numbers from home phones to access their networks (see 'Calling Overseas', page 222 for a full explanation). Mobile networks usually kibosh this working on their phones, but there are a limited number of override providers who work round the system.

CHOOSING YOUR DISH

■ *Orange contract customers (must be on an Orange tariff).* Calls to freephone numbers are usually free (always check). Therefore you should be able to dial the override number and connect to it at no charge. However, usually Orange simply detect it and add a charge.

There are a few companies, however, who play a 'mobile override number' cat-and-mouse game. They offer freephone numbers, which really are free on Orange; then at some stage Orange catches them and issues a charge. When this happens, call and you will hear the dulcet female tones that characterise such messages announce, 'All calls to this calling card service are now at a standard rate.' At this point the override providers slap back by issuing a new freephone access number that is still free – all customers need do is call them to find this new number out. This cycle normally takes about ten weeks.

The whole thing is a legal grey area: override providers aren't breaking any rules by issuing freephone numbers; equally the network may legitimately block them to protect its investment. There is a chance calling an override may breach your mobile contract, so do check, but the network's usual reaction is to target numbers not customers.

To really push these savings see 'Make the networks cross', page 144.

■ *Other networks' customers.* Other networks charge for calls to freephones, usually at the same rate as normal calls to landlines. However, this still means savings are possible on calls to mobiles and overseas. As there's no cat-and-mouse game here, most override providers can be used (see 'Calling Overseas', page 222).

CALORIE COUNT

The possible savings here are really huge, with mobile calls to landlines at just 2p/min or calls to the USA on your mobile for just 3p/min. The size of saving varies hugely depending on which network you are on, which package, and which override provider. Yet it is possible to cut a mobile bill by up to 80% with this system.

SUGGESTED INGREDIENTS (MSE)

Orange overrides: www.onetel.net, 0800 9570700; Connaught Telecom, www.ctelecom.co.uk, 0800 074 0111.

For non-Orange override providers see 'Calling Overseas', page 222.

CURRENT ACCOUNTS

Typical Gain: £125 per year.

Time Taken: 30 minutes.

Difficulty Level: Easy/Mid.

Note: See 'Healthy Eating', page 240, for more info on over-draft cost cutting.

THE MENU

Current accounts are the standard day-to-day bank accounts we all use. Most people are still with the big four high-street banking mafia – Barclays, HSBC, Lloyds TSB and NatWest. These four tend to pay a pitiful 0.1% standard interest in credit. Worse still, their overdrafts cost between 14% and 18%. Admittedly, pay at least £50 a year for a premier account, or bank on the internet, and they may provide better rates, but usually better is available elsewhere for free.

Switching accounts is substantially easier than it used to be. New banks now automatically move standing orders and direct debits for you, but you must always notify your employer and others who regularly pay money in yourself. Plus for safety, keep a sum of money in the old account until you're happy the transfer is completed.

CHOOSING YOUR DISH

Look at your account first, and determine whether you are usually in credit or overdrawn. Depending on the result either focus on the highest interest in credit, usually 2% to 4%, or the lowest cost overdraft, usually 7% to 10%. There are other things to watch for, though.

- **_Minimum monthly funding._** The bank requires you to pay in a set amount each month. In practice it's a way of setting a minimum salary requirement to qualify for better accounts. For example, the requirement to deposit £1,000 a month is the same as saying someone who earns £15,000 a year (roughly £1,000 a month after tax) must pay their salary in. This doesn't mean you can't spend the money or be overdrawn, just that a regular payment must be deposited each month.

- **_Introductory overdraft offers._** A new trend is for 0% overdrafts when you switch accounts. Especially useful if, as some promise, they'll match your existing overdraft. If you're regularly overdrawn, forget in-credit interest rates and look at overdraft rates.

- **_Overdraft charges._** Never go beyond your overdraft limit. Do this and fines, charges and increased interest cost a fortune. Always call the lender and try and arrange a temporary extension first.

- **_Branch, phone or internet._** Branch banking is expensive to provide, which is why phone and especially internet-only accounts usually pay more. To bank online, it's very important to be able to access the internet whenever you want, usually with both work and home access; otherwise stick with phone or branch. If internet banking does tempt you, it's actually often easier and more convenient than going to a branch: you manage your balance on screen and move money electronically. To pay cash and cheques in, do it at a post office, for added security using a specially receipted envelope; and to withdraw money, just do it via any bank's cash machine.

CALORIE COUNT

Switching pays. Someone with a £25,000 salary starting in credit could earn just £8 over three years with a Big Four bank account, but up to £310 with the best payer. For someone starting £2,000 overdrawn it'd cost £780 with the Big Four, but just £170 moving to the cheapest overdraft.

Banking interest and costs for someone on £25,000 salary over 3 years						
	In Credit			Authorised Overdraft		
	Rate	Interest after tax (1)	Extra interest	Rate	Interest cost (2)	Saving
Standard Big Four bank	0.1%	£8	–	17.8%	£780	–
Best Overdraft bank (2)	2.1%	£210	£208	0%/6.9%	£170	£610
Best In-Credit (1)	3.15%	£310	£302	7%	£280	£500

(1) & (2) salary paid in monthly after tax, but spent in full over the month, no interest spent or repaid (1) initial £2,500 credit (2) initial authorised overdraft £2,000

SUGGESTED INGREDIENTS (MSE)

www.cahoot.com; Abbey; Alliance & Leicester; www.smile.com; Intelligent Finance; Halifax; Bank of Scotland; Lloyds TSB (for internet-using higher earners only).

INTERNET ACCESS

NUTRITIONAL INFORMATION

Typical Gain: £150 per year.
Time Taken: 45 minutes.
Difficulty Level: Mid.

THE MENU

Nearly 70% of users get onto the internet on a computer that dials up via the home phone. The word most commonly used in internet service provider (ISP) adverts is 'free', yet the one thing that it never means is 'no cost'. It can be 'free access, but calls cost', 'free calls, but access costs' and 'free calls and access, but for a fee'.

CHOOSING YOUR DISH

Whatever the price, the quality of the connection is crucial. It's worth asking what the 'contention ratio' – the number of users per line – is. This is a useful though not infallible guide. An average ratio is between 10:1 and 15:1. Business users paying for high quality will want around 5:1, low-quality connections go up to 40:1.

When it comes to cost, before you even start, watch for technical support phone line charges, especially for net newcomers, as a £1 per minute charge soon eats up any cheap service benefits.

The other main sales ploy is advertising unique content and child protection software – yet inevitably similar stuff is available elsewhere on the net. However, if you are a complete newcomer, it may be wise to start with one of the bigger providers until you get used to the internet, then start the money-saving shopping around.

- *Heavy use.* Unmetered internet access means you pay a fixed monthly amount for unlimited net access with no call or other costs. The big three providers, AOL, BT and Freeserve, tend to dominate this market, and all offer similar prices. Yet many smaller ISPs offer the same thing for around half the price.

Admittedly, cheap, unmetered access is hit and miss. Because of this, always ensure no notice is needed to cancel if the service deteriorates.

■ *Low to mid use.* For anyone using the net for less than roughly 15 hours a month, there's no point signing up for 'unmetered access'. The alternatives are 'free' internet service providers, where accessing the service is free but the calls you need to make aren't (providers get a cut of the phone call cost). Most make you dial via 0845 local call rates, which cost a lot more than you'd think – usually 4p/min daytime, 1.5p evenings and 1p weekends, meaning an hour during the day costs £2.40.

Yet some providers do exactly the same thing, but at just 1p a minute at all times. Plus there's also a new range of 'prepaid internet access cards' recently launched, with a start price of 0.5p a minute – for low users a much better deal.

CALORIE COUNT

Using the wrong service provider can cost a fortune. Even someone using just eight hours a week can pay nearly £1,000 a year using the wrong provider.

Use: Per week:	Monthly Cost				Annual Cost
	Very Low 1hr	Low 3hr	Mid 8hr	Heavy 20hr	Mid
Local calls access (1)	£2.60 to £10.40	£7.80 to £31.20	£20.80 to £83.20	£52 to £208	£250 to £998
Mainstream unmetered	£16	£16	£16	£16	£192
1p/min calls access	**£2.60**	**£7.80**	£20.80	£52	£250
Cheapest unmetered	£8	£8	**£8**	**£8**	**£96**

Cheapest in bold (1) 0845 calls. The range of prices reflects when calls are charged – daytime is most expensive, weekends and evenings cheaper.

SUGGESTED INGREDIENTS (MSE)

www.myinternetpass.co.uk; www.onetel.net, 0800 9570700; www.fast4.net, 0870 2251055; www.free24-7.net, 0870 4429600.

ADDED SPICE

- **E-mail lock-in.** One final weapon in ISPs' arsenals is allocating you one of their own e-mail addresses. It mightn't sound bad, but it means that switching ISP requires losing this, which can be such a hassle it substantially disincentives a move. Using universal addresses like Hotmail or Yahoo or auto-forwarding services solves the problem, and provides flexibility.

- **Broadband.** The pricing model for super-fast broadband internet is rapidly developing along the lines described above. The first providers all offered 'unmetered' access, but some cheaper 'pay-as-you-go' operators are now launching. However, set-up costs are also common for broadband, so carefully check these too.

HEALTHCARE CASHBACK PLANS

NUTRITIONAL INFORMATION

Typical Gain: £350 per year.
Time Taken: 30 minutes.
Difficulty Level: Mid.

THE MENU

These clever little policies can pay back over six times their cost, tax-free, every year, and cover a family's NHS and private medical bills. They're very different to and much cheaper than private medical insurance. The best known example is HSA, though smaller providers normally offer better returns.

Each month you pay a fixed amount, from £3 to £150. Cashback plans don't provide treatment; instead when (either NHS or privately) you go to the dentist's, optician's, have a specialist consultation or the like, simply submit the receipt to claim the cash back. Most plans repay only a proportion of the costs and the maximum amounts differ with each treatment, e.g. 75% of optical bills up to £100. The higher your monthly contribution, the higher the maximum cashback limit.

A big plus is that age and gender don't affect the cost, though with some plans you must join by the age of 65. Many providers are non-profit organisations founded in pre-NHS times to facilitate affordable healthcare for ordinary people.

Commonly Covered Treatments
- Dental treatments and check-ups
- Optical treatments and check-ups
- Complementary health – osteopathy, chiropractics, acupuncture, etc.
- NHS prescriptions
- Maternity payments
- Chiropody
- Physiotherapy
- Hospital in-patient cash payment
- Special consultation fee

CHOOSING YOUR DISH

Plans are available for individuals or couples; and children are often covered for free. As well as the payout level, look for:
- **Return compared to cost.** Compare the payout to the policy cost. It doesn't have to repay all your bills, it's more important that it pays back at least what you pay in every year, if not more.

- **Check the percentage return.** The percentage payback is often more important than the maximum cashback, e.g. 100% of costs up to £90 makes it easier to get your money back than 50% of costs up to £100.
- **Guaranteed costs.** If you always go to the dentist twice a year, and wear glasses or contact lenses, then these are guaranteed costs. Look at how much each plan pays for these specific treatments. This provides the security of knowing how much you can claim back before other treatments.
- **Likely treatments.** If you think you're likely to use the osteopath a lot, focus on plans with the highest limit for that.
- **Pre-existing conditions.** Most plans don't require a medical, but may exclude claims on pre-existing conditions for the first year or so. Worth checking.
- **Immediate claims.** No plans allow immediate claims, there's always a delay of a few months to stop people signing up to claim for a current problem. And you must be a member for over nine months for maternity benefits.

As payouts here can be huge, the obvious question is how can they afford it? The answer is simple ... they don't. Just because people can claim doesn't mean they do. Many people forget to send in claim forms after the first year, yet the direct debits still drip from their bank accounts. To test yourself, sign up at a low level to start, to see if it suits. If you're not claiming, cancel, though better still, remember and be quids in.

CALORIE COUNT

Using cash plans can make you money. Just look at the table below; if you had a wide range of treatments, the 'Return' indicates how many times you get your money back – the best is seven times what you pay in. Most people won't be claiming this much, but anyone having dental or optical costs should get back at least what they paid in and have the security of knowing that if anything goes wrong there's help available.

Healthcare cashback returns (for a heavy range of treatments) (A)						
	Single Adult			Family		
	Cost/ month	Payout/ year	Return (B)	Cost/ month	Payout	Return (B)
Worst Choice (C)	£11.70	£400	2.9	£19.10	£970	4.2
Best Choice	£10.00	£625	5.2	£18.45	£1,530	6.9

(A) Each adult's bills are £120 dental, £120 optical, £150 consultation with a specialist, £350 osteopathy and 1 night in hospital for a year; each child is 1 night in hospital and £150 consultation. (B) The annual payout divided by the annual cost (the number of times you get your money back). (C) Using the individual policy for one adult and the family policy for the others.

SUGGESTED INGREDIENTS (MSE)

Foresters Cash4Health plan, www.foresters.co.uk, 0800 0730303, has come top in every comparison I've ever done. Use it as a benchmark and then compare Westfield Health, www.westfield-health.org.uk, 0114 2502000; Premier Health, 01924 373552; Healthsure, 0800 854721; Norwich Union (good for the over-60s), 0800 0150221.

PACKAGE HOLIDAYS

NUTRITIONAL INFORMATION

Typical Gain: £150 off bargain price, £600 off brochure price.
Time Taken: 2 hours.
Difficulty Level: Mid.

THE MENU

Travel agents make you think their prices are as fixed as their smiles, but this simply isn't true. I've a special technique to cut holiday costs.

To start, it's worth establishing the difference between travel agents and tour operators. Travel agents sell holidays and tour operators make them. This means one tour operator's holidays may be stocked by a range of travel agents, and this is crucial. It means you can find the identical holiday cheaper elsewhere.

CHOOSING YOUR DISH

When it comes to booking a package holiday, the later the better. Yet if you need a specific destination or defined services, like children's facilities, then there's a risk that what you need mightn't be available. In that case forget late – early booking discounts aren't as big, but they're still a saving, so book at least nine months ahead and compare a number of travel agents' prices for the trip.

For those who can wait, the best bargains come from picking the right holiday and bartering for a better price.

■ *Picking the holiday.* Location and timing are crucial. Take a holiday when others can't, such as outside the school holidays in May and June, especially to family destinations like Florida, and you'll find prices are cheaper. Alternatively, venture to once in-vogue destinations, now off the boil, where there's lots of empty hotels and value's available.

■ *Martin's bartering technique.* Once you've a basic idea of what you want, immediately go to Teletext, simply because it's a big list of late bargain travel agents in one place.

1. Search. Scan the pages to find the destination, type and rough price of holiday you are looking for.

2. Choose. Pick an advertised holiday, call the travel agent, discuss what's available. If one suits, take down as many details as possible and find out the price and what's included. Often airport transfers, meals on the plane and credit card booking fees are separate, so ensure you find the total cost. (For example, £692 per person for a fortnight all-inclusive in the Dominican Republic.) (For the cheapest travel insurance, see page 204.)

3. Find competitor agents. Note the phone numbers of all the Teletext travel agents specialising in that destination. Pick one, call it and describe the holiday you've been quoted on – date of travel, airport, and flight times. This way you're certain both of you are talking about exactly the same holiday.

4. Sneakily shave prices down. Take the quote you've got and – now for a bit of subterfuge – ask the agent to beat the price, but shave just a little bit off the quote you were given: it speeds the whole process up (for example, tell them £660 per person for this fortnight in the Dominican Republic). They should match it. Also try to ask the agent to write off the extras such as transfers and in-flight meals – this is worth a further £30 per person.

5. Start to play. Play companies off against each other by continuing the gradual bartering process to get the price down as low as possible (e.g. £630 per person). You'll need to talk to a few agents to do this. Always talk per person price not 'total holiday' cost as it makes the amount it is discounting seem smaller.

6. Try price-beater agents. Once it looks like the price

won't drop any more, go to the specialist agents on Teletext who offer to beat any price – they may be able to cut a last few pounds off (e.g. final price down to £615 per person).

7. ***Book with the cheapest agent.*** Remember it's exactly the same holiday you originally fancied, just at a reduced price.

CALORIE COUNT

The example prices above are real, done as part of my appearance on ITV1's *Package Holiday Undercover*. The brochure start price was around £900 per person, the original Teletext discount price £692. It took an hour and a half to get it to £615 per person. The holiday was for a couple, so the total saving was £154.

SUGGESTED INGREDIENTS

Teletext travel agents.

ADDED SPICE

For booking scheduled or 'no frills' flights, the rule is simple: book as early as possible, as there's more predictability in the scheduled flights market so bargain offers are better managed and quickly consumed. There are also two online price-comparison services that compare both direct and broker flight prices: www.travelsupermarket.com and www.traveljungle.co.uk. They're not always accurate, but are useful for benchmarking. Also go direct to the cheap flight brokers. The main ones are ebookers.com, Travelocity and Expedia. The main no-frills carriers are Ryanair, BMI Baby, EasyJet and Mytravelite.

CONTACT LENSES

NUTRITIONAL INFORMATION

Typical Gain: £100 per year.
Time Taken: 30 minutes.
Difficulty Level: Easy.

THE MENU

Now here's a sight for sore eyes. There is a range of specialist phone and internet direct contact lens delivery firms. You send them the prescription and they provide the lenses the optician has recommended. The cheapness isn't due to the fact the lenses are substandard – it's because these companies bulk-buy direct from the manufacturers, sell from warehouses, not retail premises, and have limited staff as they're purely fulfilment operations – so they're not paying expensive opticians.

CHOOSING YOUR DISH

In truth, there are only a few lens manufacturers. Opticians' 'own brand' lenses are usually identical lenses to the big name lenses, but with different packaging. The discounters will tell you who makes what brand. As the lenses are identical, it's simply a case of the cheaper, the better.

For daily disposables, the bigger supply you buy, the cheaper they are. If you've got spare cash, it's worth shelling out for a year's lenses all in one go. With monthly disposables, factor in the cost of solutions, however buy these with the lenses.

It's easy to be sceptical – after all, it's your eyes we're talking about – but reputable discounters will only supply lenses if your optician's confirmed you've had an eye test and aftercare within the last year. And, by law, if you have already been fitted with contact lenses, the optician is obliged to issue you with your prescription and information without further charge.

CALORIE COUNT

For daily disposables, you can save up to £125. It should be pointed out that this does not include an eye test and after-care, but that by no means makes up for the price difference.

Daily disposables 1 year	Lenses	Solutions	Total (inc. delivery)	Saving
High-street optician*	£30 x 12 months	N/A	£360	–
Cheapest discounter	£235	N/A	£235	£125
Monthly disposables 1 year				
High-street optician*	£15 x 12 months	Included	£180	–
Cheapest discounter	£59	£55	£99 **	£80
*Includes eye test and aftercare				
**Includes £15 discount for buying solution and lenses together				

SUGGESTED INGREDIENTS

www.postoptics.co.uk, 0800 0383333; www.spectacles.gb.com; www.net-optics.co.uk, 01858 545892; www.cluboptique.com.

DVD PLAYERS

NUTRITIONAL INFORMATION

Typical Gain: £60.

Time Taken: 45 minutes.

Difficulty Level: Easy.

THE MENU

DVD players, once cutting-edge home cinema technology, are becoming *de rigueur* in most homes. Yet many high-street machines are overpriced and underfunction.

CHOOSING YOUR DISH

■ *Avoid hidden restrictions.* DVD's high-tech nature generates its own problem. It allows Hollywood to clench an iron grip on worldwide distribution. This is because every disc and player is allocated a region code, and unless the codes match, the disc won't play. The UK, as part of Europe, is Region 2. However Region 1, the USA, has a wider range of films, usually available earlier, with more functions, and easily accessible via the internet or on holiday often at a cheaper price than here in the UK.

Multi-region machines play all discs available, yet they're rarely spotted on the high street. It's mooted this is because retailers come under pressure from film distributors to stock only single-region machines so as not to sour their relationships. Even so, multi-regioning isn't illegal, as it's only Hollywood studios not the law you'll be upsetting. However, UK shops aren't allowed to sell US discs as they are not approved by the British Board of Film Censors, but importing them yourself is fine.

- *Look for a cheap warranty.* There's no need to spend more than £40 on the cheapest multi-region DVD player; most sub-£100 players are pretty much the same thing inside different boxes. Yet there are a couple of other things to watch out for. The first is check for a cheap extended warranty. You may be shocked at this, as such warranties are a notorious rip-off, but I'm not advocating getting one, it's just that the fact a company offers a cheap warranty is often indicative that the player itself should last.

- *Not for technophiles.* Of course, for a technology junkie, a low-end spec won't match their hi-end expectations or their £10,000 plasma screen. Yet for anyone just wanting plug and play, go for cheap, easy and multi-region.

CALORIE COUNT

The funny thing is, buy a multi-region player and you should still undercut the single-region machines offered by the big high-street technology retailers – and the warranty will be just a fraction of the standard price.

DVD Player	Multi-region?	Player cost	3-year warranty cost	Total w/warranty
Cheapest multi-region	Yes	£30	£10	£40
Cheapest from high street	No	£70	£45	£115

SUGGESTED INGREDIENTS

Richer Sounds; Asda; Tesco; plus use shopbots (see page 153) to check internet prices.

DISCOUNT BROKERS: HOW TO BUY INVESTMENTS FOR LESS

NUTRITIONAL INFORMATION

Typical Gain: £250.

Time Taken: 15 minutes.

Difficulty Level: Easy.

THE MENU

How many fund-management companies does it take to screw in a light bulb? None – fund-management companies screw us. Okay, maybe not funny, but, hopefully, illuminating. Never buy a fund unit trust or ISA direct from a fund manager – do that and up to 6% of your investment pays for advice you haven't been given.

Unit trusts are collective investment funds, where the price depends on the value of a group of shares or bonds picked by a professional manager following a theme (like the investment type or industry) such as smaller Japanese companies. As the combined value of these shares rises or falls, the funds move proportionately. It is possible to invest in a unit trust within an ISA wrapper (see page 169).

A unit trust's performance is eaten away by two types of charges.

- *Initial charge.* An upfront chomp off the investment of up to 6%, mostly used to pay commission.
- *Annual charge.* A smaller snack taken every year of up to 1.5%; of which 0.5% may be commission.

The commission is designated to pay Independent Financial Advisers for their advice. No problem, if you use one, but make your decision and buy direct from the fund manager, and, outrageously, you pay without getting the advice.

The charges are clever: you don't pay them directly, you just receive proportionately less investment – e.g., invest £5,000 in a fund with a 5% upfront charge and only £4,750 buys the investment. This means you don't feel the cost, but it's still there.

If you're buying without advice, use a discount broker. They're bulk-buy fund specialists and as you just tell them what you want, they can rebate most of their commission, so you receive more, making them cheaper than buying direct.

CHOOSING YOUR DISH

- *It's the charge not the commission rebate that counts.* Not all discount brokers are equal. To start with, some charge fees. More confusingly, though, many advertise zero initial *commission*, yet this doesn't mean the initial *charge* is zero, as each broker may have different commission arrangements with fund managers. Therefore, it's important to compare exactly what the initial charge is on the fund.

- *Look for annual charge discounts too.* A few discounters also rebate a small proportion of the annual commission as well as the initial commission. This helps your plan grow even faster and is well worth going for. The only time not to pick this is if it's possible to get a much lower initial charge elsewhere.

CALORIE COUNT

Take a selection of four funds and invest £7,000. Pay full commission and if the funds all grow by, for example, 7% a year, the ISA would grow by £1,690. However, buy them via the top discounter rebating both initial and annual commission, and you'd have total returns of £2,215 for the same thing. It's important to note that you may lose money investing in shares, but even if the markets drop you'll lose less buying via a discounter rather than direct, due to lower charges.

£7,000 invested in 4 identical funds (assumes 7% annual growth over 5 years)					
Discount broker	Ave. initial charge	Return	Annual rebate	Total return	Increase
Full commission	5.13%	£1,690	None	£1690	–
Top discounter	0.56%	£2,110	£105	£2,215	£525

SUGGESTED INGREDIENTS (MSE)

www.wiseup.com, 0113 3684080; www.chartwell-investment. co.uk, 01225 446556; www.bestinvest.co.uk, 0800 0930700; www.hargreaveslansdown.co.uk, 0117 9009000; www.chelseafs. co.uk, 0800 0713333; www.tqonline.co.uk, 0800 072 3186.

ADDED SPICE

Buy a unit trust inside a tax-free ISA wrapper and there's another advantage to using a discounter. Most operate fund supermarkets, which bypass the ISA rules dictating only one provider's funds are allowed in any ISA, as the fund supermarket itself counts as the provider, allowing investors to pick 'n' mix fund managers. (See page 169 for ISA rules.)

GETTING A PENSION

Typical Gain: £9,000 on pension fund.
Time Taken: 60 minutes.
Difficulty Level: Mid/Hard.

▰▰▰THE MENU

Stakeholder pensions are marketed as the low-charge pension solution; even so you can take a further slice off the charges, increasing the fund performance, just by buying it a different way.

A pension isn't an investment; it's just a tax-free wrapper where the cash is locked away until retirement. People often misunderstand this, but it's important, as its performance depends on what you choose to invest in (from shares for higher risk to cash funds for safety), not the pension itself. The big advantage is all contributions go in before income tax is paid, meaning that for a basic-rate taxpayer to invest £100 it costs them only £78 off their take-home salary.

Stakeholder pension charges are capped, currently at 1% of the fund each year. This includes the cost of paying commission to Independent Financial Advisers for their guidance. There's nothing wrong with this, as hopefully it pays for good advice, but, ridiculously, buy direct from a pension provider, as many people do with stakeholders, and the charges are identical even though there's no IFA advice.

There is a way to beat the system. A limited number of specialist discounters sell pensions without advice, and rebate some of the commission earned back into your fund. While this is only fractions of a percentage point, with the effect of compounding over the years it can add up to thousands.

To go it alone with a stakeholder, it's necessary to choose your contribution level, provider and funds. As a rule of thumb, to retire on two-thirds of final salary, invest half your age as a percentage when starting a pension and continue this until the age of 65 (i.e. if you start at 30 you need to put in 15% of your salary each year). This obviously means the earlier you start the better.

There aren't actually that many providers so choice isn't too difficult – look at the range of funds offered and read the brochures. When it comes to choosing funds, very general rule of thumb is the younger you are, the higher risk fund you should be in.

CHOOSING YOUR DISH

When choosing a discounter, simply ask for an illustration. The most important thing is how much commission it rebates. Some also charge fees and this needs keeping to a minimum too – however, the sheer scale of the savings over the long run means you should concentrate on the commission rebate first. As there aren't many companies offering this service, it is quite easy to pick.

CALORIE COUNT

Using a discounter isn't for everyone; advice is sometimes crucial, especially with complicated affairs. However, buy without advice and discounters will increase the amount in your pension fund whether it grows or shrinks.

The table below shows the impact. Put £150 a month into a Norwich Union stakeholder pension (for example) over 30 years, and if there was growth of 5%, it'd grow by £9,000 more if it were bought via a discounter.

Invest £150/month with *Norwich Union* for 30 years at 5% growth			
Bought via	Fee	Fund final value	Increase in fund
Direct	None	£105,000	–
Cheapest discounter	£25	£114,000	£9,000
Based on an illustration in summer 2003			

SUGGESTED INGREDIENTS

www.cavendishonline.co.uk, 01225 471912; Torquil Clarke, www.tqonline.co.uk, 0800 0561836; www.bestinvest.co.uk, 0800 0370100.

ADDED SPICE

What happens at retirement? The rules currently state that at retirement, 25% of your pension fund may be taken as a tax-free lump sum. The rest must be used to buy an annuity by the age of 75. An annuity is a payment each year for life until you die, but once you die it's gone. The payout is taxed as income.

There's a lot of disquiet about this system, and of course if you're currently many years from retirement, there's no guarantee it will still exist when you do retire. Many people have shied away from pensions, but if you remember a pension is just a tax-free wrapper and you choose the investment, I believe it's worth using a pension for part, though not all, of your retirement planning (if you want a safe investment, many pensions offer a cash fund, for example).

If you are buying an annuity, then remember, you've a right to buy it from the open market, not just from your pension provider. As you can't change your mind, it is inexcusable not to shop around. (See 'Financial Fitness for Life', page 13.)

REPENSIONING: IMPROVING THE RETURNS ON STAKEHOLDER PENSIONS

NUTRITIONAL INFORMATION

Typical Gain: £4,500 on final fund.
Time Taken: 2 hours.
Difficulty Level: Hard/Very hard.

THE MENU

While remortgaging is common, repensioning doesn't exist – or hasn't until now. It's my invention to increase the returns on existing personal or stakeholder pensions by over 4%. This could mean an extra £4,700 on your fund over 25 years without changing plans.

It sounds impossible, but the concept behind it is quite simple. If you bought a pension via an Independent Financial Adviser it reaps the commission over many years. Alternatively, buy direct and the pension company keeps this cash itself. There's nothing wrong with continually paying for advice, providing you continue to receive it – but otherwise you're doling out cash for nothing.

Unfortunately, tell the pension company 'Stop paying my former adviser commission' and it just keeps the money itself. Yet using a special discount broker who rebates some of their commission back into the plan (see 'Getting a Pension', page 193) can reduce the pension's annual charge to about 0.7% from 1%. Repensioning takes advantage of this – simply move your existing pension to a discounter.

The discounter should manage the process, but remember 'repensioning' isn't something advertised, it's my idea, so you may need to explain, check and monitor it.

- ■ *Stakeholder pensions.* As stakeholder pension providers aren't allowed to impose transfer penalties, just transfer your current plan to an absolutely identical one set up by the discounter, effectively keeping your existing plan but at a new lower charge.
- ■ *Personal pensions.* It's much trickier with personal pensions as there are transfer penalties, so it's only for those who understand their finances in detail. The gain is greatest if you are substantially increasing your pension payments, something especially common in the years building up to retirement – e.g. you were paying £50/month and now it's £100/month.

  This is because it's likely the existing provider has already received commission for your planned contribution – so it's only the commission on the new amount that's up for grabs. The easiest method is to ask the discounter to become your 'adviser' so it 're-assigns' the plan and any commission to itself, rebating some to you. Still, be careful.

CHOOSING YOUR DISH

Follow 'Getting a Pension', page 193. (It's also worth comparing the best illustration with an illustration from your existing set-up.)

CALORIE COUNT

Repensioning can improve your position, whether the market rises or falls, at little or no cost. The table below illustrates the gains for a 35-year-old who started a £100/month stakeholder pension three years ago, and is increasing the contributions by 5% annually until the age of 60. At 5% annual growth, the fund would end up at £114,000 – however, repension and it'd grow by a further £4,700, even though it's exactly the same pension as before.

Stakeholder fund size assuming 5% annual growth paying £100/month increased by 5% a year		
	Fund size	Extra growth
Full commission/Direct	£114,000	(–)
Repension after 3 years via top discounter	£118,700	£4,700
Investment starts age 32, continues to age 60, in managed fund		

SUGGESTED INGREDIENTS

www.cavendishonline.co.uk, 01225 471912; Torquil Clarke, www.tqonline.co.uk, 0800 0561836; www.bestinvest.co.uk, 0800 0370100.

LEVEL-TERM ASSURANCE: PROTECTING YOUR FAMILY IF THE WORST HAPPENS

NUTRITIONAL INFORMATION

Typical Gain: £240 per year.
Time Taken: 20 minutes.
Difficulty Level: Easy.

THE MENU

Roughly one in twenty adults die whilst they have a dependent child. The devastation is added to by potentially dire financial consequences. Level-term life assurance is the one policy you hope is never used. It protects your family's income if the worst happens. Whether you're looking for a new policy or already have it, you can cut your costs by half.

It guarantees a fixed lump sum payout upon death within a set time. Don't confuse it with either mortgage decreasing term assurance (see page 201) or whole-of-life insurance – an investment-based policy used mainly for inheritance-tax planning.

There's no investment element with level-term assurance because the payout is fixed, and there's no argument over whether someone is dead, so providing the assurer is reputable it's simply a case of the cheaper the better. However, do ensure the premiums are fixed, meaning they never rise, rather than reviewable.

■ *How much cover?* The cost increases with the size of the lump-sum payout – you need enough to pay off outstanding debts and provide your family with a reasonable standard of living. Cover should also be taken out for a non-working spouse, especially when children are young, because if they die, the main earner may need to stop working. A rough rule of thumb for either parent is ten times the highest earner's income.

The cost also increases with the likelihood of death within the term – age, health, being a smoker, having a risky occupation, or undertaking dangerous sports can increase the price. So if you're an 88-year-old tobacco-chewing sword swallower with a penchant for freefall aerobics, don't boast about it to the life-assurance company.

■ *How long should the policy last?* If the cover is to protect children, it should last until they finish full-time education. If it's for a partner, cover until the earner reaches pension-able age. The shorter the term the cheaper the policy. There's no need to stick to a round number of years – a 17-year term, for example, is fine.

■ *Switching your existing policy.* If you already have level-term assurance, there's no problem changing. Just stop your existing policy and start a new one for the remaining time, though a quick check of the terms and conditions never goes amiss – and never cancel the old policy until you've started the new one. Existing policyholders who bought policies a long time ago or have experienced health problems mightn't find the cost decreases significantly – or perhaps no saving is possible at all, as these impact the risk pricing of a policy.

It is, however, always worth getting a quote as term assurance prices have dropped rapidly over the last few years. Anyone who's quit smoking should save a lot. (See the 'No Butts Guide to Smoking', page 62.)

CHOOSING YOUR DISH

Life-assurance brokers trawl all the non-direct-sales insurance companies to find the cheapest policies. They will cut the cost, but don't think all brokers are equal. They make money by taking commission from policy providers. Most keep all this commission, and sell themselves as 'searching for the cheapest provider'. However, some brokers both shop around and rebate some or all of this commission to make your policy cheaper (those rebating all commission charge a fee). As the commission is massive, this cuts the cost hugely.

Yet, when getting assurance is complicated – if you've got health issues or inheritance-tax issues – then the very cheapest brokers won't help, but there are still some who provide advice and rebate commission.

CALORIE COUNT

The savings are huge. A 40-year-old male smoker getting

a policy direct from a bank would pay £68 a month. Use a standard broker and this could be down to £48, but with the cheapest broker it drops to £32 a month. Over 25 years that's a saving on the policy of over £10,000.

£150,000 level-term policy over 25 years						
	Go to the bank direct		Full-commission broker		Cheapest broker		Saving
	Per month	25 years	Per month	25 years	Per month	25 years	25 years
M30 Non Smoker	£14	£4,200	£11	£3,300	£9	£2,700	£1,500
F30 Smoker	£18	£5,400	£15	£4,400	£11	£3,300	£2,100
M40 Smoker	£68	£20,400	£48	£14,400	£32	£9,600	£10,800
F40 Non Smoker	£22	£6,600	£19	£5,700	£13	£3,900	£2,700
Joint 40 Smoker	£110	£33,000	£82	£24,600	£54	£16,200	£16,800

SUGGESTED INGREDIENTS (MSE)

www.cavendishonline.co.uk, 01225 471912; www.money world-ifa.co.uk, 01494 443806; www.theidol.com, 015395 61663; www.tqonline.co.uk, 0800 0561836 (advisory).

MORTGAGE LIFE ASSURANCE

NUTRITIONAL INFORMATION

Typical Gain: £200 per year.
Time Taken: 20 minutes.
Difficulty Level: Easy.

THE MENU

Mortgage decreasing term life assurance (MDLA), to give it its correct name, pays a lump sum to cover the mortgage debt if you die during the term. It's 'decreasing' because the mortgage debt, and therefore the potential payout, decreases over time. It ensures your dependants needn't worry about paying off the mortgage. Unfortunately many people are automatically sold over-expensive policies when getting a mortgage, yet it's possible to cut these costs in half.

For the rest of the recipe and suggested ingredients simply follow 'Level-Term Assurance' on page 198, as the rationale and providers are identical.

One final thought. If you're looking to cover your mortgage, check out using a level-term policy instead. If the cost isn't much more, it's worth plumping for as the payout is fixed rather than decreasing; if you move to a larger house, it may automatically provide the extra cover.

MORTGAGE PAYMENT PROTECTION INSURANCE

NUTRITIONAL INFORMATION

Typical Gain: £240 per year.
Time Taken: 30 minutes.
Difficulty Level: Easy.

THE MENU

Accident, sickness, and unemployment can devastate your finances. State help is limited, especially for anyone who took out a mortgage after 1995 – it only kicks in after nine months and it just pays the interest; and this only for those with limited savings and a partner who doesn't work full time.

Mortgage Payment Protection Insurance (MPPI) ensures your mortgage repayments, and possibly other related expenditure (e.g. buildings insurance), will be met if any of these circumstances occur. Most MPPI policies are bought with mortgages, and though a few building societies offer low-price policies, lenders usually charge way over the odds.

Policies start to pay out 30 or 60 days after you become unable to work. They last for a limited term, usually 12 months, though after that state help should start. Those with savings that can cover this period probably don't need MPPI.

It is possible to opt out of the 'unemployment' element of MPPI cover – worthwhile if you're self-employed and the policy wouldn't pay out anyway.

CHOOSING YOUR DISH

Getting a policy from a specialist provider rather than the mortgage lender is normally much cheaper.

The price of MPPI surprisingly depends simply on the mortgage payment size rather than the usual risk factors like age, sex and health. There are a rare few age-related policies, and these are well worth having if you're under 35.

The only reason not to change is many policies operate initial exclusions so you can't claim within a set period, usually three to six months, after switching. Some policies don't pay out to anyone where there was foreseeability of unemployment or with pre-existing medical conditions when the policy was taken out – so don't switch if you're likely to be in these categories.

CALORIE COUNT

To cover a £1,000 monthly mortgage repayment a standard mortgage lender's policy could cost £60 a month, £720 a year, but with a typical specialist provider it is £30, just £360 a year.

SUGGESTED INGREDIENTS

www.helpupay.co.uk, 08000 350292; www.moneysupermarket.
co.uk; Paymentshield, 0870 7594010.

TRAVEL INSURANCE

NUTRITIONAL INFORMATION

Typical Gain: £150 per year.
Time Taken: 30 minutes.
Difficulty Level: Easy.

THE MENU

The travel insurance Green Cross Code is 'stop after you book,
don't listen!' Buy a holiday at a travel agent's and the insurance they then try to flog you can cost four times as much as
is necessary.

There are two cost-cutting options:

- *Annual multi-trip.* This covers all travel during a year for
  a one-off fee. The number of days away is limited, usually
  to 30, 45 or 60. Travel is defined as the moment you leave
  home until you return, on any travel overseas, even a day
  trip, and possibly more than two consecutive nights away
  in the UK at prepaid accommodation. If you go away more
  than twice a year, it is worth considering.

- *Single trip.* This is what travel agents sell you: the cover is
  specific for the journey. Single-trip cover is fine if you're
  only going away once a year – just usually not through
  travel agents, as it's often available for a fraction of the cost
  elsewhere.

CHOOSING YOUR DISH

While many supermarkets now sell 'off the peg' travel insurance for substantially less than most travel agents, going through specialist cheap travel insurers is even cheaper.

- *Check what's covered.* The big areas are usually standard; medical expenses are the most important and should be at least £2 million, also ensure policies include personal liability and cancellation and curtailment insurance. Plus, if you will do winter or dangerous sports, check that such activities are included.

- *Don't over-cover.* Getting £25 million rather than £5 million medical cover is pointless as claims over that amount are negligible. One insurer with half a million policies told me it hasn't received a claim over £200,000 in the last two years, yet insurers aren't shy about pushing expensive 'gold cover' with soothing but completely irrelevant maximums.

- *Where possible use a couple or family policy.* These are cheaper as providers assume you're usually travelling together, and some risks depend on the trip not the people, so increasing the size of the party doesn't increase all risks. However, if you do travel independently, check the cover still applies.

- *Excesses.* Most policies require you to pay an excess of, for example, £35 on each claim. If you are willing to pay a higher amount you should be able to cut the costs.

- *Get an E111 form.* These forms, available from the post office, mean you're signed up to the reciprocal health agreements between European Union countries, so you can use their state health services. It's not an alternative to insurance, but it may save you having to pay an excess.

- *Baggage, personal possessions.* Often it's optional, and if you're not taking much of value with you, exclude it.
- *Check credit-card cover.* Some cards may offer free travel insurance if you buy the holiday on the card, though the actual cover tends to be limited, so check what's on offer before assuming you're covered. (See 'Healthy Eating', page 309.)
- *Stick with Europe-only cover.* When you choose an annual policy, you can choose between European cover and worldwide. Unless you know you're going outside Europe during the year, stick with European cover as it's much cheaper. If necessary, you can upgrade the policy or get a standalone policy for a specific trip.

CALORIE COUNT

Buying the right travel insurance will save you serious cash. For a family of four taking a fortnight in the USA and a week in Europe using a tour operator's single-trip insurance the total would be around £200, yet the cheapest annual family policy would be just £55 for the year. A saving of £145 – maybe enough for a quick break in Paris, which of course would be covered too.

Travel insurance for a family of four				
	Fortnight USA	Week Europe	Annual total	Annual saving
Bought with holiday*	£120	£80	£200	–
Cheapest annual policy	–	–	£55	£145
*Typical cost from high-street travel agent				

www.direct-travel.co.uk, 01903 812345; www.insureandgo.co.uk, 0870 901 3674; www.moneysupermarket.co.uk (travel insurance comparison engine); James Hampden, 01530 41639; Matthew Gerard, 01483 730900; Travel Plan Direct, 0800 018 8737; Travel Protection Group, 020 8424 7777.

GET MORTGAGE ADVICE FOR FREE

■NUTRITIONAL INFORMATION

Typical Gain: £750.

Time Taken: 20 minutes.

Difficulty Level: Easy.

Note: Read the 'Healthy Eating Guide' to remortgages/mortgages (page 252) first.

■THE MENU

Picking the wrong mortgage or remortgage costs a fortune. Getting someone to do it for you, ensuring you find the best deal, can be costly – but there is a way to do it without paying a penny.

A good mortgage broker searches the market for you, advises on the best deals, carries more clout with lenders and puts you ahead of the game. Statutory regulation is scheduled to start in October 2004; until then there's always the possibility of overpriced and dodgy dealings – like pushing mortgages that make them more, not save you cash.

Brokers make their money in two ways. They get 'procuration fees' from lenders when you take out a mortgage; these average from 0.25% of the mortgage value for standard mortgages to 1% for those with credit problems. So on an £80,000 mortgage this is a not insubstantial £200 to £800.

Most also charge customers a fee on top: 0.5% of the mortgage value is common, but it increases with complexity. The most you should ever pay is 1%, but some disreputable brokers target those with poor credit histories and charge up to a scandalous 10% – and the advice isn't good. Use a mainstream broker.

CHOOSING YOUR DISH

In the mortgage-broker world bigger is often better, as big brokers have more influence and research resources and more solid reputations. Of the four biggest brokers, three – Savills, Charcol and Chase de Vere Mortgages – primarily operate face to face and earn both commission and a fee. However, London & Country is phone only, so it operates on a cut-price basis, doesn't charge customers a fee, just takes commission.

You can go straight to London & Country. Yet there's another sneaky potential tactic – I'll leave you to decide the ethics. As mortgage advice is only paid for when you complete the mortgage, a broker simply telling you its pick doesn't incur a fee. As best practice is always to get more than one opinion, speak to three of these four brokers, then complete via L&C. This way there's best advice and no fee at all. Another alternative is go straight to the lender – but it's always better through a broker if it's no extra charge due to the additional benefit of a broker's influence.

Doing this has two potential stumbling blocks. Some brokers will reveal the mortgage rate without naming the lender. To get round this just use the internet or another broker to find out who offers that rate.

More significant is the fact that the big brokers often have their own specific competitive exclusive deals. If these are better, then factor in the cost of the broker fee and compare. This is especially common with the UK's biggest broker Charcol, which tends to have many good exclusives. If it's one of these you want process the mortgage via its website even after one-on-one advice and there's no fee to pay there either.

CALORIE COUNT

The saving in fees alone, never mind the mortgage, are huge. On a £100,000 mortgage, broker fees are usually around £500. On a £200,000 mortgage with complicated credit issues it could be £2,000. Yet here it's free.

SUGGESTED INGREDIENTS (MSE)

London & Country, 0800 9530304; www.charcolonline.co.uk, 0800 718191; FPD Savills, 0870 9007762; Chase de Vere Mortgages, 0800 3585533.

GIVING TO CHARITY

NUTRITIONAL INFORMATION

Typical Gain: £80 per year.
Time Taken: 15 minutes.
Difficulty Level: Easy.

THE MENU

The Money Diet isn't about being tight. Frankly I'd love it if everyone gave 5% of what it saves them to charity. And it's possible to donate up to 80% more at no extra cost by forcing the tax system to help.

Any charity registered with the Charity Commission (it'll have 'registered charity' on its literature) can take advantage.

CHOOSING YOUR DISH

The simplest way to give is via 'gift aid'. This allows charities to claw back on either one-off or regular donations. There's no minimum contribution, so even on a pound tax is reclaimable. All the charity needs is your name and address and a declaration that you're a UK taxpayer: as this can be verbal, it can even be done over the phone.

Charities reclaim the tax you have paid at the basic 22% rate, which actually means they get around 28% more than you donate. People paying higher-rate tax are able to reclaim the extra 18% tax they've paid for themselves. Though the tax self-assessment form includes a note of charity gifts so higher-rate taxpayers may choose to keep this extra tax money or automatically have it donated too.

To give even more there is a special system called 'payroll giving' where you donate a regular amount before tax is deducted direct from your salary, via your firm's payroll. Then the charity receives the 22% for basic-rate taxpayers, and automatically the whole 40% tax benefit from higher-rate taxpayers. Even better, until April 2004 it is guaranteed the government will add an extra 10% on top, and, at the time of writing, the hope is this will be extended.

To do this your employer must have a scheme in place. Ask if your firm runs a scheme; if not, try to encourage it, as it's a simple process just run through an automated payroll.

CALORIE COUNT

Donate £20 a month to charity using payroll-giving and it only costs you £15.60 if you're a basic-rate taxpayer or £12 if you're a higher-rate taxpayer – yet the charity receives £22. Over a year this means a higher-rate taxpayer would give £264, while it'd only cost them £144 – a massive difference.

Give more than you pay for: the cost of donating £20 a month to charity							
	Monthly				Annually		
	Basic-rate taxpayer pays	Higher-rate taxpayer pays	Government adds	Charity receives	Basic-rate taxpayer pays	Higher-rate taxpayer pays	Charity receives
Gift Aid	£15.60	£12	–	£20(1)	£187	£144	£240
Payroll-giving	£15.60	£12	£2	£22	£187	£144	£264
(1) Assumes higher-rate taxpayer donates all tax gains to the charity							

ADDED SPICE

Easy giving. The Charities Aid foundation (www.allaboutgiving.org, 0800 993311) runs a special Charity Account. Pay money in through either gift aid or payroll giving, and it automatically collects the tax and the state bonus and adds it to your account. After this use its special card or chequebook to donate to a charity of your choice. The big advantage is you can donate tax efficiently on impulse, even putting the special cheques in collection tins so the charity gains the maximum amount.

STUDENT BANK ACCOUNTS

NUTRITIONAL INFORMATION

Typical Gain: £150 over the course.
Time Taken: 20 minutes.
Difficulty Level: Easy.

THE MENU

Students get the best bank accounts in the business, though each bank's definition of 'student' varies. Even so, whether you're on a BTEC, three-year degree or post-grad, you should be able to find one.

CHOOSING YOUR DISH

All banks' customers have access to all other banks' cash machines to withdraw money, so differences of proximity and service aren't too relevant. Students are offered freebies to open accounts, but the big gift is the interest-free overdraft. This is the decision-making bedrock: quite simply pick the bank offering the biggest 0% borrowing.

Interest-free debt isn't just important, as most students graduate over £10,000 in the red. Those in credit should also opt for the biggest 0% debt, and use a budgeting trick I call 'deficit banking'. To do this keep as big a negative balance as possible, but always stay within your interest-free overdraft limit. Put most of the money in an easy-access high-interest savings account (which for most students should be tax-free) – and gradually move it back into the bank account as it's needed. This means you earn interest on the money the bank is lending for free. And, remember, if you are currently a student there's nothing stopping you switching.

To compare interest-free overdrafts, factor in the limits for each year, not just the first year. An easy way to do this is simply add up the limits over the course length and compare – the bigger the better. For example, on a three-year course, £1,000 Year One, £1,200 Year Two, £1,400 Year Three is a £3,600 total.

CALORIE COUNT

Student accounts massively outrank even the best normal accounts. However, even within the 'student account world' there's a big variance: choosing the right one could easily save a student over £160 over the course length.

Student bank account: Cost of an approved overdraft(1)

Bank	Year 1 debt is £1,400 (2)		Year 2 debt is £1,600 (2)		Year 3 debt is £1,800 (2)		Total cost	Saving
	Rate	Cost	Rate	Cost	Rate	Cost		
Top normal account	6.7%	£95	6.7%	£105	6.7%	£120	£320	–
Poor student account	0% to £1k, 14.6% above £1k	£60	0% to £1,250, 14.6% above	£50	0% to £1,500, 14.6% above	£45	£155	£165
Top student account	All authorised debt interest-free	£0	All authorised debt interest-free	£0	All authorised debt interest-free	£0	£0	£320

(1) All debt is assumed to be pre-approved and therefore at the authorised overdraft rate.

(2) Debt is assumed to be fixed at this level. For ease of illustration, the interest isn't compounded.

SUGGESTED INGREDIENTS

NatWest; Co-Op; HSBC; Halifax; Lloyds and Barclays. Bizarrely, for once the big banks are the ingredients. The reason being, as an old statistic quotes, 'You're more likely to get divorced than change your bank account.' Students are young, potential high earners, so the banks should get many years' custom if they can attract you early. The Money Diet counter-move is grab the best benefits you can as a student and graduate, but as soon as you're switched to its standard account then shift. (See page 174 for current accounts.)

ADDED SPICE

There's one further sneaky question oft asked by students: 'Can I open another student account at a different bank?' Surprisingly, the answer is usually yes – few accounts have terms and conditions prohibiting it. So more freebies should definitely be possible, though a second interest-free overdraft is trickier. Providers often require students' loans to be paid into their accounts to get one and they also say they'd be reluctant to offer an overdraft to students already with one elsewhere. Plus, all applicants are credit-scored, and the access to interest-free credit elsewhere won't count positively.

GRADUATE BANK ACCOUNTS

NUTRITIONAL INFORMATION

Typical Gain: £200 over a three-year account.
Time Taken: 20 minutes.
Difficulty Level: Easy.

THE MENU

There's a special prize awaiting every recent graduate, yet many don't take it – but anyone who's left university in the last three years can still benefit by getting the top graduate account.

Most students simply allow their banks to shift them out of a student account when they leave university. This can be a big mistake – some banks don't offer special terms, and so graduates miss out on the free money available.

Even a year or more after graduation you can move to another bank to get its graduate account. Only those who didn't complete or pass their course shouldn't switch, as banks automatically transfer students to graduate accounts on the expected date of course completion, whereas a new bank will check if you have graduated.

For the rest of choosing the menu, and suggested ingredients, follow the logic of 'Student Bank Accounts' on page 212.

LOAN INSURANCE

■NUTRITIONAL INFORMATION

Typical Gain: £200 per year.
Time Taken: 30 minutes.
Difficulty Level: Mid.
Note: see 'Healthy Eating', page 322, for a full guide to personal loans.

■THE MENU

Whether it's a big dodgy bloke called Ron or a high-street bank, beware the 'protection business'. Financial services providers push customers borrowing money to get their (usually expensive) loan insurance. Yet it's possible to slash the cost, both for new and existing loans.

Payment protection insurance (PPI) is a welcome comfort

for some people. It ensures your repayments are made, usually for a year, if you're unable to work due to accidents, involuntary unemployment or sickness; some also include full repayment if you die.

Lenders usually add PPI straight into a loan. However, it is possible to get a loan from one company and PPI from another. These stand-alone PPI policies tend to be much cheaper than a lender's own policies.

CHOOSING YOUR DISH

First decide whether you actually need PPI. Those with small debts or anyone who could cover their repayments using savings, relatives' help, or other financial protection policies may be better off without the huge expense of PPI. For the self-employed, the unemployment element is often useless, as most policies' self-employment benefits are poor.

While most policies are pretty similar, whether the PPI is with the loan or stand-alone, it's always important to check policy terms for personal suitability – bizarre clauses are common; for example, some policies exclude motorbike riders or extreme sports enthusiasts from accident cover.

The only time it may be worth not using a stand-alone policy is with a flexible loan, as in this case the insurance cost is only for the outstanding amount of the loan. Stand-alone PPI policies don't have such flexibility.

- *Switching PPI on existing loans.* Some, though not all, lenders will permit PPI cancellation while keeping the loan, though watch for redemption costs. If this is the case it's possible to switch PPI to a stand-alone provider without changing the loan. Lenders mightn't make it easy, though, and getting illustrations to see the benefits are never easy.

Yet it is possible, and worth a go.

The only time not to try it is if your circumstances have changed – a 'foreseeability of redundancy' or 'pre-existing conditions' when you take a new policy out usually invalidate claiming. Switching if this applies to you could mean you lose cover.

CALORIE COUNT

For a £5,000 high-street loan, the insurance alone would add an extra £29 a month, so together with the interest, the total cost over five years is £3,800. Even with the cheapest insured loan on the market, the total cost would be just £1,705. Yet use the cheapest uninsured loan, coupled with a stand-alone PPI policy, and the cost is just £1,270, beating all else.

£5,000 loan over 5 years	Monthly loan cost	Insurance cost	Monthly total	Total 5-year interest & insurance cost	Saving
High-street loan	£119	£29	£148	£3,820	None
Cheapest loan with insurance	£102	£10	£112	£1,720	£2,100
Cheapest uninsured loan and stand-alone PPI	£98	£6	£104	£1,240	£2,580

SUGGESTED INGREDIENTS

www.freeinsuranceuk.com; www.goodinsurance.co.uk, 0870 2403946; www.moneysupermarket.co.uk.

CAR INSURANCE

NUTRITIONAL INFORMATION
Typical Gain: £300 per year.
Time Taken: 1 hour.
Difficulty Level: Easy/Mid.

THE MENU

Car insurance is inescapable, compulsory and expensive, and finding the cheapest can be hell. There is never simply one cheapest provider, as there are too many variables – location, driving history, who drives the car, whether it is used for commuting and of course its make and model. However, I've got a strategy …

CHOOSING YOUR DISH

To find the cheapest insurer takes work. The only way to guarantee the cheapest is to get a quote from every one of the many hundreds of insurers and brokers. Yet my drop, shop, double and haggle system should cut both time and costs.

■ *Step 1: Drop – Lower the price regardless of policy.* Ensure you're the lowest risk possible. If possible fit an alarm or an immobiliser; don't overestimate the annual mileage you tell them; keep your car off the street and in a drive, or better a garage overnight. Choose whether you really need to pay extra for a policy with a courtesy car. Decide how much you're willing to pay towards any claims – the higher this 'excess', the less you'll pay. The final choice is comprehensive or third-party insurance: here, weigh up the cost of repair versus the increased cost of comprehensive insurance; those driving old bangers are often best sticking to third party.

■ *Step 2: Shop – Have your shopping around done automatically.* The aim is to cover as many underwriters as possible. These are the companies who assess the risk of covering any individual, yet they all do it differently. These assessments are then supplied to the insurers themselves – yet even with providers using the same underwriter the price can differ due to how competitive they wish to be in various market sectors.

1. If you're on the internet: To do this quickly and easily involves using two internet sites. These aren't brokers – they work off a limited panel of insurers and have their own pricing and supply arrangements with insurers – they are effectively car insurance search engines. You fill in your details and they submit your claim to a large number of providers and brokers and feed you back the results. In return, they are given a small commission if you get a policy via their search.

Think of it like this. A broker is like a shop; it sells 15 loaves of bread that it prices accordingly. These two sites simply wander round checking the price of loaves in all of them. A much more efficient system. The two sites are www.confused.com, which provides a detailed and accurate search, and www.insuresupermarket.com, which provides a quicker search of more providers, but is less accurate, especially for drivers who've had an accident or motoring conviction in the last few years, in which case the quoted price can be way off. Insurance supermarkets can also charge a few pounds on occasion for displaying some insurers' details; if that's the case, compare with confused first.

2. If you're not on the internet: If you're not on the net, you are severely disadvantaged. The sheer speed and power of the internet means it is worth asking a friend who does have it to help. However, if that is not possible, the insurers I would suggest you get phone quotes from first are in 'Suggested ingredients' below.

- ■ **Step 3: Double – Double-check and get the discounts.** Once you have the search results, note which providers come top of both. It's not just the prices that are important here, it's the order, as that shows you their attitude to your risk. Pick the top three from each site and go separately to their websites. This way you may be eligible for further direct sales discounts on top of the quotes.
- ■ **Step 4: Haggle.** The car insurance market is very competitive and haggling is possible as companies aim to retain business. Once you've found the cheapest quote, take it to your existing insurer or a broker to see if they will beat it.

CALORIE COUNT

For a young couple, going direct to an insurer, the quote was £750. Using a broker the price quoted was £703. However, following Drop, Shop and Double, the best price found was £565 (incidentally the highest quote found was £940) and that's before Haggle.

SUGGESTED INGREDIENTS

Search sites: www.insuresupermarket.com; www.confused.com. Insurers themselves: Direct Line; Direct Choice; Esure; Tesco; Sainsbury; Budget and Co-Op Insurance; Diamond; Endsleigh and Elephant.

ADDED SPICE

Further tricks and tactics include these:

- *New may be better than renewal.* Applying to your existing insurer as a new customer often produces a cheaper price than its renewal quote.

- *Add a second person.* Adding a second driver with a good record, even if they won't use the car, will, surprisingly – sometimes but not always – reduce the premium as it smooths out the average risk. It's worth a quote.

- *Don't pay insurance interest.* Most policies either allow you to pay per month or per year. Pay by the month and they effectively loan you the lump sum, so you pay instalments with interest at up to 20% on top. If you can, pay it as a lump sum. If not and there's cheaper borrowing available elsewhere, use that to pay the lump sum instead.

- *Younger drivers – check out free insurance with a new car.* Some cars include free insurance, worth only a few hundred a year to an experienced driver, but to a young car owner it could be worth thousands.

- *Gender specific isn't always best.* Don't fall for the 'we know women drivers are a lower risk, so we specialise in them' hype. Yes, women are a lower risk, so all insurers factor this in to their pricing structures. Gender-specific policies aren't automatically cheaper than unisex.

- *No-claims discounts don't necessarily reduce the premium.* Each year you don't claim you get a discount, which makes a substantial difference to the overall cost. If you do claim, two years is usually taken off this discount; this is deliberate to discourage claims. You can also get a 'protected no-claims discount', so that claims don't impact it. Remember, though, if you have an accident, while not claiming protects the discount, the actual price of the policy may still rise, just because you may be assessed as being at higher risk of future claims.

CALLING OVERSEAS

■ **NUTRITIONAL INFORMATION**
Typical Gain: £300.
Time Taken: 45 minutes.
Difficulty Level: Easy.

■ **THE MENU**
Cunning calls can mean it's cheaper to call Alaska than Altrincham, Singapore than Swindon, Argentina than Aberdeen.

To do this, use one of the specialist 'override' providers – so-called because after dialling a number on your home phone, you're connected to another network, thus 'overriding' the normal provider. There are two different types.

■ *Billed providers (BP).* Dial a freephone number or a short four- or five-digit prefix number to access their system. Then simply dial the number you want to call. As call to access their network is free, the only cost is the override provider's own charge. Some providers are prepay, others set up accounts and bill by direct debit at the end of each month.

■ *Call charge providers (CCP).* Dial a special number to connect to their network rather than a freephone number. These numbers are usually what are called 'non-geographic numbers' such as an 0845 local-rate or 09XX premium-rate number. The more expensive the destination, the higher this charge. Thus the access call is billed via your home phone provider's bill. That's the only cost; the override provider never bills you itself, it makes its money by receiving a proportion of the income from the initial access calls. In other words:

- With BPs you pay nothing to access the network, and are then billed per call.
- With CCPs you pay to access their network, but aren't billed per call.

CCPs' advantage is that they're much easier to use, especially for one-off calls, as there's no need to set up an account. However, with CCPs you are billed as soon as you dial whether the final call is connected or not. This can be expensive.

CHOOSING YOUR DISH

If calling overseas is a substantial part of your expenditure, it's likely you call just one or two destinations. This means it's worth spending the time to locate the cheapest provider for those specific locations. Yet, because a company is the cheapest for calling a specific country, it doesn't mean it's necessarily cheapest for calling that country's mobile phones. Always consider these as separate destinations.

Override providers' line-quality and connection ability vary, as they often underbuy capacity to keep costs low. Bigger providers can't risk it, so they must overbuy. Differences in routeing technology can also diminish call quality with override providers, but for most non-business calls, they should be fine.

CALORIE COUNT

Calling China on BT standard can cost over £1 a minute, and

it isn't that much cheaper on BT's discount tariff. However, it is possible to make the call for as little as a penny a minute. A huge saving.

Cost savings on a 15min call each week over a year (late 2003 BT prices)						
	BT Standard		Cheapest override		Saving over BT	% saving
Destination	Per min	Year	Per min	Year	Year	Year
USA	22p	£170	1p	£8	£162	95%
India	60p	£465	10p	£80	£385	83%
China	103p	£800	1p	£8	£792	99%
Venezuelan mobile	131p	£1,020	15p	£120	£900	88%
TOTAL	–	£2,665	–	£216	£2,450	92%

SUGGESTED INGREDIENTS (MSE)

www.18866.com (BP); www.superline.com (BP); www.planet-talk.co.uk, 0800 0362195 (BP); www.onetel.net, 0800 957 0700 (BP); www.Just-Dial.com, 0870 7940000 (CCP); www.tele discount.co.uk, 0845 3510045 (CCP); www.telestunt.co.uk (CCP).

ADDED SPICE

When travelling abroad it's also possible to cut the costs of calling home (or anywhere else). Websites www.1st4phone cards.com and www.zaptel.com offer search engines showing the cheapest price of a range of phonecards – simply enter the country you're calling from and calling to.

However, remember to check:

■ *Is the access number a freephone?* Is the initial number you dial a freephone number or a paid-for line number? If paid for, add up the phonecard call cost and the access call cost to find the total charge.

- *Does the card expire?* Most phonecards have an expiry date; it's usually 90 days, but it is worth checking before you buy.
- *Does it have a service charge?* Some cards have a service charge of around 1p per day. This means the value of the card drips away slowly over time.

HOME PHONES

NUTRITIONAL INFORMATION

Typical Gain: £300 per year.
Time Taken: 60 minutes.
Difficulty Level: Mid.

THE MENU

This is my nightmare. Finding my recommendations for the cheapest home phone provider usually takes me five days and a ream of spreadsheets. There are hundreds of providers, each with three or four plans, all with hundreds of different prices, which change rapidly. Luckily the paradox is that heavy competition means cutting your bill substantially is easy; it's only finessing the very best that's a problem.

- *Your line provider and call provider needn't be the same.* There are only three major UK line providers: BT, NTL and Telewest, but hundreds of call providers. Most people use a BT line, and BT is obliged to allow other call providers to operate via its lines.

    NTL or Telewest line customers, on the other hand, must use them for calls as well. While these can be competitive for mixing TV and phone packages, there are often high hidden call costs, such as for phoning mobiles, which can actually make them more expensive even than BT.

■ *How to use a different call provider from line provider.* Carrier Pre-Selection (CPS) is fast becoming standard practice. This means that while using a BT line, all the calls are automatically routed through your chosen call provider without you needing to do anything. If you use it, make sure you only pay BT its very basic line rental.

■ *The internet.* Best practice is to treat the net as a separate issue: see page 176.

CHOOSING YOUR DISH

Finding the cheapest involves a combination of four main factors:

■ *Calling landlines.* Using a home phone is the cheapest way to call landlines. Providers know this and therefore focus their ads this way. Unless you make a great many calls during the day, the cost isn't too heavy.

Most companies now offer a range of different price packages. For a higher monthly fee 'free' calls are usually offered at certain times. The correct term is actually 'unlimited' (not free, as you're paying extra to get these calls), as the length and number of calls isn't monitored. However, for most providers even this is a lie, since calls are only 'unlimited' for the first hour and are then charged by the minute. To get round this, just put the phone down before that time is up and redial, and it's 'unlimited' all over again.

Most tariffs fall roughly into one of three categories, so I've indicated who should use what. Once you know which tariff you are on, first switch to the right tariff with your existing provider (this alone can cut the bill by 30%), then compare others to see if it can be beaten (remembering you will still pay the BT line rental).

1. Basic option. Daytime calls are a few pence a minute while evening and weekend costs are either charged by the minute or fixed for an hour (e.g. 6p). This tends to be a free or a small additional monthly cost option.

Who's it for? Those who make very few daytime calls and only moderate numbers (e.g. about 20) of off-peak calls a week.

2. Unlimited evening and weekend calls. Daytime calls are still charged per minute, but there are unlimited UK calls evenings and weekends. Normally it is necessary to pay £5 or £6 extra a month for this.

Who's it for? Someone using not more than a couple of hours' worth of daytime calls a week.

3. Unlimited UK calls 24 hours. All calls to UK landlines at all times are unlimited – this will usually add around £10 to the monthly fee.

Who's it for? Only worthwhile for those with heavy daytime landline use.

■ *Calling Mobiles.* While we usually call mobiles less than landlines, the per minute cost is massively more. So they make up an increasingly large proportion of our bill. This price is rarely mentioned in home phone providers' advertising, yet it is often the most important factor, as there can be huge discrepancies.

Unfortunately, comparisons aren't simple, as the cost varies for calling each network days, evenings and weekends. An easy method is to pick three options, e.g. calling Vodafone days, O2 evenings and Orange weekends, and

10min daytime call to Vodafone from landline	
NTL	£2.42
BT Standard Rate	£1.99
BT Together Options	£1.89
TalkTalk	£1.70
188661 Telestunt	£1.00
For illustration only, early 2004	

compare those prices, for a quick indication of a tariff's overall mobile pricing policy. However, there are other ways to save (apart from waiting until your friends are home to call them, that is).

1. Override providers. Some cheap override providers (see 'Calling Overseas', page 222) can also offer cheaper calls to mobiles. Especially those that tend to offer a fixed tariff – e.g. call any UK mobile any time for 10p a minute – whereas normal providers will be roughly 19p days, 11p evenings and 5p weekends. These override providers are therefore much cheaper during the day and much more expensive at other times – so just use them during the day.

2. Use your mobile. It's often cheaper to call a mobile from a mobile, both because calling the same network is reduced, and, more important, because many mobile contracts include calls to any mobile in the free minutes. If you have these minutes, use your mobile to call mobiles even while at home, and your landline only to call landlines. By focusing this way, it defeats all costing assumptions and shifts the odds and savings in your favour.

■ *International calls.* It's almost not worth considering your main providers' prices. Inevitably they will be much, much more expensive than the best override providers', so just turn to page 222.

■ *Minimum call charge.* Minimum call charges are sneaky little devils, with huge impact. The majority of phone calls are very short. Some companies take advantage of this by promoting cheap call prices, but with a high minimum or connection charge – if the minimum call charge is above 6p steer clear.

CALORIE COUNT

The overall solution is pick a main provider based on a combination of correct landline tariff and mobile costs. Yet, if possible, use a separate provider for international calls and possibly some mobile calls, to really save.

How it adds up – calls savings for a heavy phone user								
	PER MONTH						ANNUAL	
	Line rental	Landlines	Mobiles	Total UK calls & line rental	International	TOTAL	TOTAL	Saving
BT Basic	£9.50/ £10.50	£67	£61	£138	£32	£170	£2,040	–
Cheapest stand alone provider	£26.50	£0	£50	£77	£15	£92	£1,100	£940
Three provider solution*	£23.49	£0	£41	£64	£1	£65	£780	£1,260

*Uses cheapest stand alone provider for landline calls and calls to mobiles at weekends, and separate providers for calling mobiles midweek and for all international calls.

SUGGESTED INGREDIENTS (MSE)

Main providers: Carphone Warehouse, www.talktalk.co.uk, 0845 4565599; www.onetel.co.uk., 0800 9570700; www.power gen.co.uk, 0800 0152662; www.tiscali.co.uk/smarttalk, 0800

9542223; www.tesco.com; www.tele2uk.com, 0800 2795333; www.justdialsaver.com.

To mobiles and overseas: see 'Calling Overseas', page 222.

ADDED SPICE

The one call type missed out above is the 'non-geographic' call – 0845 and 0870 numbers – now common when you contact companies. There is a way to cut the cost of these calls, though (see 'Cut the Cost of Complaining', page 124).

PART 3

HEALTHY EATING

DEBT ISN'T BAD ...

What? Shock! Horror! Think you misread it? Well, let me say it again. *Debt is not bad*. There is nothing wrong with rationally deciding to pay more, to get something now you would otherwise have to wait for. Governments borrow, companies borrow and individuals borrow; it's a financial necessity.

In our funny world, half the time the cause-célèbre is 'over-indebtedness', the rest it's disenfranchisement from credit. There's verbal dexterity here – debt is bad; credit is good – yet they're almost identical.

Get debt right and you profit, or at least have easy access to cheap money. 'Healthy Eating' is about how to do just that.

... But There Are Bad Debts

Before you smile lovingly at credit cards, loans, mortgages and HP agreements – while debt isn't bad, this doesn't mean all debt is good. Overly expensive debts, ill-thought-out debts and, worst of all, debts you can't afford to repay are hideous.

Get debts wrong and it's a nightmare. In a worst-case scenario, you will become financially crippled. Home, cars, families and lives have been lost due to debts.

While 'Healthy Eating' is about prevention more than cure

– how to do it right in the first place – I have also included a special section on what to do if you're in Debt Crisis.

Why 'Healthy Eating'?

For many people, borrowing, like eating, is necessary. Even some who consider themselves debt-free actually have a mortgage, often the biggest loan of all. Do it right and you'll be healthy and fit, get it wrong and you'll be obese and ill. The reason I wanted to dedicate an entire section to debt is that you're paying for money itself, rather than any intrinsic goods, so reducing its price is MoneySaving purity.

one

WHEN TO EAT WHAT

I want to cover two main areas in this chapter:

How Debt Works

Ten years ago mortgages, credit cards and personal loans were different beasts – now they merge into one. Before looking at the different types, it's necessary to choose what's right for you.

How They Decide Whether to Lend You Money

Beneath all debt is the murky world of credit scoring. A secret scheme lenders use to decide if they want to lend you cash. Knowing how they decide, and what you can do about it, is laying the table for healthy eating.

So without further ado ...

THE FIVE CRUCIAL COMPONENTS OF ANY DEBT

Debt is simply any type of borrowing. The reason it causes problems is that, unlike a newspaper subscription or gym membership, when times are tough, you can't simply cancel it and stop repaying. Once you know you need to borrow and why, whatever type of debt you incur, there are five questions to consider.

1. How much is needed? The more you borrow, the more you will repay.

2. What is the interest rate? The higher the interest rate, the more you will repay.

3. How long will you borrow the money for? The longer you borrow, the more you will repay. Debt costs rely on length of time as well as rate. This is a commonly forgotten fact. While a mortgage at 5% looks cheaper than a personal loan at 10% – don't forget the time factor.

Repay £1,000 at 10% over five years and it costs £260 in interest. Repay £1,000 at just 5% over a 25-year mortgage term and it costs £740 in interest.

Admittedly, the impact of inflation diminishes the difference

---

Quick Wealth Warning: Secured v Unsecured

'Don't worry, your loan is "secured", they tell you. Doesn't that sound good – far better than a risky old 'unsecured loan'. Noooooooooo! Don't fall for it. It's not you it provides security to – it's the lender. A secured debt is one where the loan is secured on your home (or some other potential valuable asset). This means if you can't pay off the debt, ultimately they can throw you out of your house. Admittedly, fail to pay off an unsecured loan and after substantial legal process your home could ultimately still be at risk, but it is much less clear cut – if other things are equal, stick with 'unsecured'.

slightly. Even so, always remember the longer you borrow, the more it costs.

4. *Are there any fees or other charges?* Watch for annual fees, insurance costs, penalties tying you in and administration costs. Financial services is a creative industry, especially when lenders are thinking up new ways to charge us.

5. *How much flexibility do you have?* Pay something off more quickly, and you pay less interest on it. Ensuring you have access to borrow more when necessary means you can avoid penalties or fines for going over the limit, or ruining your credit score. Flexibility pays.

AN INTERESTING TALE

Interest is the cost of borrowing money. Unfortunately there are more ways to express it than positions in the Kama Sutra. To help, we have the wonderful term 'APR – Annual Percentage Rate' to guide us. The APR is a great idea, it nets together all the costs of borrowing money over the full term of a loan. Unfortunately, the reason I say it 'nets' is because APRs are full of holes, and therefore are often misleading, irrelevant, confused or all three. So let's ignore APRs and go …

Back to Basics

An interest rate of 5% over a year means borrow £100 and by the end of the year you will need to repay £105 on it. If only it was always this simple:

Interest compounds: Borrow over a longer time and you need to pay interest on the interest that's already been charged. An example. Borrow £100 over 3 years at 10% a year and:

- After year 1, the total interest is £10
- After year 2, the total interest is £21 (£10 from year 1, £10 from year 2, plus £1 – the interest on the interest from year 1)
- After year 3, the total interest is £33.10 (£21 from years 1 and 2, another £10 for year 3, plus the interest on the £21 – £2.10)

This little piece of maths means debts don't just get bigger if they're not repaid, they get bigger more and more quickly.

Fees: To make interest look cheaper, lenders charge fees on top instead. Don't be fooled.

Flat interest: Can you spot what's wrong with this sales patter, common in the car trade? 'It's a really cheap loan. Look, you borrow £5,000 off us over three years, with 36 monthly payments of around £160. That means you'll be paying us £5,750 in total. Which is a total of 15 per cent over three years or about 5 per cent a year.'

This all sounds perfectly reasonable and cheap. Yet it's dodgy, dodgy, dodgy. Did you spot the problem? It's not the figures – they're roughly right. It's the entire concept.

Borrow £5,000 over three years and repay a lump sum at the end of £5,750, then indeed it is roughly equivalent to an annual interest rate of 5% a year. Yet you aren't borrowing £5,000 over the whole three years, as you're paying it off as you go. Halfway through the loan period nearly half the loan is cleared so you should only pay interest on around £2,500. In fact the annual interest rate on this loan is roughly 10% not 5%. Watch out.

Money Diet Wealth Warning: Be a Round Peg in a Square Hole

The debt industry is damn clever. It's aware people don't understand it, and to 'help' has developed different products for different circumstances: a mortgage for your home, a secured loan to consolidate debts, a credit card for spending, a personal loan for a lump sum, overdrafts to extend the monthly pay packet. This is its way of boxing you in and charging you more. Don't fall for it.

There's no reason not to use a credit card rather than a loan to buy your new kitchen, if it's cheaper. There's no need to get a 'secured' consolidation loan for your debts, when a mortgage is the same thing at a much lower rate. A 'car loan' for a car isn't the only choice. If you know what you're doing, choose the product that means you pay less.

A Simple Solution?

After all these complications, the solution is actually quite simple. One question beats all these tricks. When you get a loan just ask, 'What is the total cost of borrowing this money over the time period, including all fees and charges?' And compare the answer.

FLIPPING THE TWO-SIDED MONEY COIN

I've said it before, and I'll say it again: debt and savings are two sides of the same coin. Both are paying a set amount out of your salary each month. Except that debt pays for something you've already had, while saving is for something you will have. The big difference is: with savings they pay you a little interest; with debt *you* pay *them* a lot of interest. Therefore to flip the coin in your favour, pay off the debts with the savings.

In even the best savings account on the market, £1,000, after tax, will probably earn you only around £40 a year in interest.

On a typical high-street credit card, £1,000 debt will cost you around £170 a year in interest.

So pay off the credit card with your savings and you'll be roughly £130 a year better off. It staggers me that many people have both debts and savings.

Of course it's always important to have some cash available for emergencies. Yet to be sophisticated, remember a paid-off credit card can provide an emergency facility too. So pay off your credit-card debts with your savings and you're better off. If in the future you need emergency cash and have to use the card for it, you are no worse off than you were in the first place, yet in the meantime you have had a good few months paying less interest, leaving you overall in ruder financial health.

Freak Interest – Occasionally Debt is Better than Savings

'Damn you. I'd just understood that. Now you're changing your mind!' Okay. I'm aware of the contradiction, but in some *very specific circumstances* the aim is borrow as much as you can and save it. Those circumstances are the rare occasions when the after-tax interest earned on savings is higher than the cost of borrowing.

This may sound like madness, but it happens. Interest-free credit is a common enticement to borrow, so why not earn interest on money they're lending you for nothing by saving it in a high-interest instant savings account? This 'freak interest' situation predominantly happens in five areas, four of which are covered elsewhere – student bank accounts (see page 212), graduate bank accounts (see page 214), and introductory credit card and overdraft offers (see 'Free Cash', page 311). The only one left is student loans.

To do this with student loans. The student loan interest rate is set at the rate of inflation. Usually this is lower than the best savings account rates, though once tax is taken into account it can be close. While it may not always be worth playing the game, it does mean there's very little point in paying student loans off early as, effectively, the real cost stays the same. It's much cheaper debt than pretty much anything else, so there's not too much harm leaving it over a long period. Plus, it may mean you don't have to get other expensive commercial loans out to replace it.

Cheap Debt is Better than Expensive Debt

I know this is obvious. Yet you'd be amazed how many people get this wrong (not you, of course, but why not read this bit, just to tell your friends). The classic mistake is with overdrafts, as people often don't see this as debt. Yet it is, and it's often expensive. Of course, the first step should be move to a better bank account (see 'Crash Diet', page 174). Next is never use overdrafts when other cheaper borrowing is available.

Let me give you a scenario:

Ms Irma Spender
Take-home salary: £1,500 per month after tax

Credit Card: Moreballs Misercard
Rate: 0% for six months, then 13.9%
Current balance: £1,500
Credit limit: £3,000

Overdraft: Barstools Bank Account
Rate: 17.9% authorised
Current overdraft: £1,300
Overdraft limit: £2,000

Irma has debts on both her credit card and her overdraft. However, the overdraft debt is substantially more expensive, even after the credit card interest-free period is over. Irma would pay around £200 a year in interest in this scenario. There are some sophisticated ways to move debts from a current account to a credit card (see 'Super Balance Transfers', page 297), but for the moment let's take the easy route.

If Irma spends on her credit card rather than from her bank account, her wages will start to pay off the overdraft. Even without actually paying any debt off, after a couple of months she'd be in the following situation:

Credit Card: Moreballs Misercard
Rate: 0% for four months (all that remains of the 0% period), then 13.9%
Current balance: £2,800
Credit limit: £3,000

Overdraft: Barstools Bank Account
Rate: 17.9% authorised
Current overdraft: £0
Overdraft limit: £2,000

She's now borrowing the same, £2,800, but not paying any interest on it. Even when the credit card reverts to its standard rate, it is 4% cheaper than the overdraft borrowing, so Irma should keep her debts there, rather than going overdrawn to feed it. Of course, it still needs repaying, but that will be quicker as there's less interest accruing.

WHERE IT ALL BEGINS — CREDIT SCORING

How They Decide Whether to Lend You Money

Let me start with a pet peeve. There are two commonly used terms that simply don't exist. Newspapers use them, and people use them in conversation. To make my point properly I'm going to use very big letters.

YOU DON'T HAVE A CREDIT RATING
There is *no* central list anywhere which says whether you should be lent money.

THERE'S NO SUCH THING AS A CREDIT BLACKLIST
Equally, there's *no* list of 'no-go people'.

Try to borrow money or get a credit agreement and the credit company tries to work out how you measure up against its 'wish list'. To make this decision they use a secretive technique known as credit scoring. Every lender uses its own bespoke system. This affects not just whether you get a loan, but sometimes the actual rate you get.

Now, I didn't say they weigh you up to decide whether you're a good or bad 'risk'. Actually they weigh you up to decide whether they can make a profit out of you. This is so important, let me shout again:

IF THEY THINK YOU'LL MAKE 'EM PROFITS, THEY'LL LEND YOU CASH

This is the basis of the decision. Remember, lenders have absolutely no obligation to give us their money. This does not mean risk isn't a factor at all. Giving money to someone who isn't a good bet to pay it back is not a potentially profitable transaction, and this is where the idea of a blacklist comes from. Those with a poor credit history will score badly on most credit-scoring systems, and will usually be turned down.

However, the blacklist concept is dangerous. Assuming that if one company turns you down they all will is wrong. Of course, if your credit history makes Nick Leeson look solvent, then most mainstream lenders will turn you down. But for those who are middling, it's worth considering that some lenders' scoring policies are more forgiving than others.

Who Will Lend to those with a Poor History?

I just used the phrase 'mainstream lenders', and this is important. There are also 'sub-prime' or 'adverse credit' lenders, who target people who have had problems. For these companies, a poor risk makes them salivate with the thought of huge profit, so they score them high. Their business models are built on the fact that they can lend money to people who can't get it elsewhere, and at inflated rates. What is profitable for one isn't profitable for another – that's why there's no such thing as a credit rating, just a different score with each and every lender.

Does Credit Scoring Impact Tarts?

For super tarts like me, who serially rotate 0% cards (see page 296), the 'profitability clause' also causes problems. There's no

---

Money Diet Quick Fact Snack: Info for Tarts

The risk that tarting will impact your credit score isn't always because a lender can see 'they've got loads of 0% debt – they're trying to scam us'. Often they don't know what rate you're paying or who with. Actually it tends to be a symptom of some other factors.

- **Over-indebtedness:** If you are holding £50,000 on 0% cards, all a lender sees is you have £50,000 debt. This in itself may be a reason for rejection. Tarts with lower balances are less likely to be rejected.

- **Lots of credit searches:** If you apply for many cards in a short space of time it'll be a problem – try and keep card applications as far apart as possible.

- **The sheer number of cards:** If you have many outstanding cards with debt on them you will again be likely to score more lowly.

Most credit scoring systems are not currently sophisticated to score out 'tarts' specifically. However, this is changing and their aim is to do so, so be careful.

---

fixed rule on how many times you can rotate debts before lenders get wise. Yet few people have problems until they've had 10 cards in a row (especially if they cancel the unused old ones). Still this means be careful about applying for cards willy-nilly. A free camera may sound a good freebie, yet if it's the straw that breaks the credit-scoring camel's back, and you then can't apply for any more cards, you may have wasted access to £6,000 of interest-free credit for a quick snap.

This may all seem tremendously unfair, reminiscent of the 'I am not a number' cry of the Prisoner.

However, it works well for the credit industry. Of course, they make mistakes, but why should they care? Applications are aggregated into millions, so the mistakes cancel each other out. And, overall, credit scoring is easier, cheaper and crucially more profitable than either lending everyone money willy-nilly or doing a manual personalised assessment.

THE PRACTICAL PROCESS

Credit scoring is a number-crunching attempt to predict your potential behaviour from the vast range of data they have. The actual scoring systems are never published and differ from lender to lender and product to product.

What They Know About You

Their info is gleaned from three primary sources:

1. The application form. Fill it out precisely as it's the primary source: salary, family size, reason for the loan and whether you're a home-owner. Many people don't get credit because of filling in forms incorrectly. Adding an extra '0' to your salary would probably leave you rejected for security reasons. Be careful.

2. Past relationships with the lender. Any previous dealings you've had with a lender will help inform them. For those with a poor credit history but better recent behaviour, this can mean existing providers are a better bet than complete unknowns.

3. Credit reference agency files. Three companies, Equifax, Experian and Callcredit, compile data from three sources:
a. Electoral roll information: contains people's address details and the details of who lives with whom.
b. County Court Judgements (CCJs) and bankruptcies: used to indicate if you have a history of debt problems.

c. Financial data from banks, building societies and others, compiled from all payments and transactions. Around 200 million records a month are tracked.

While there is no credit rating, Experian often produces an indebtedness score based on your information, which it supplies to some lenders. It is never used in isolation but is often used to form the basis for their own individual socring system.

Credit Reference File Errors

Before worrying about a poor score, there's a possible chink in the armour. It could just be they've scored you incorrectly due to a data error. Lenders should recommend you check your credit reference file upon rejection. It's very important at this point not to apply for other credit until you know, as if there is a hideous error, and you keep applying, it's likely most lenders will turn you down, so you'll have pointless applications on your file, which won't help your score even once the errors are fixed.

You have a legal right (to be technical, but only in brackets so it's not too bad, this right is currently contained in the Data Protection Act 1998) to see your credit reference files. The three agencies, Equifax, Experian and Callcredit, all allow this. The quickest method is online or by phone but you can also write – it should cost around £2, which can be paid using a debit or credit card. You will need to tell them details of your six previous addresses and postcodes. Even if you're not applying for new products it's worth checking your file for errors every 18 months or so.

Things to check include your present and past address and your family details. (I once lived in Cardiff – not a good thing for your credit score when your name is Lewis. One of the agencies decided that I was the son of some Lewis who'd lived there four years before, and linked our files. This Lewis had a CCJ: I was rejected for credit. Thankfully, the rules allowing this linking have now changed.)

If you disagree with anything on your file, contact the agency and ask that it be changed. The entry will be marked 'disputed' and the agency will contact the organisation that provided the information. If it's agreed it's wrong, the file will be amended, though always check this is actually done. Sometimes it'll be necessary to talk directly to the organisation that supplied the incorrect information to the agency in the first place. Normally, however, this will be done for you. Unfortunately, at times the information provider may disagree with you and be unwilling to allow the credit reference agency to amend your file. If this happens, unless you take them to court, or try to kick up a stink, your only option is to add your own comments to the file to explain your side. Do this carefully keep your entry concise and factual.

CREDIT REFERENCE AGENCY DETAILS
Experian: www.experian.co.uk, PO Box 8000, Nottingham N61 5GX; **Equifax:** www.equifax.co.uk, PO Box 3001, Glasgow G81 2DT; **Callcredit:** www.callcredit.co.uk, Callcredit plc, One Park Lane, Leeds LS3 1EP.

How to Improve Your Credit Score

If you've just scanned down the page to this bit – the exciting bit – then, sorry, but before you read it, please go back and read the above on how credit scoring works – or you just won't get it.

At this point I need to say something which will disappoint – there's no magical way to improve your credit score, unless there is a mistake of fact in the credit reference agencies' files. However, even though there's no exact science, there are things that will help.

Electoral roll. Always ensure you are on the electoral roll – it is the bedrock of all credit scores. If you're not, you will struggle. For those not eligible, send the credit reference agencies proof of residency – they will then add a note saying they've seen and verified this. The note will slow down the process as the application will be dealt with manually, but it should still improve your chances.

Keep up payments and never be late. Always try to follow at least the minimum repayment plan for your financial products. Even if you're struggling, don't default or miss payments. Doing this once or twice will cause problems that can cost you for years. Think of it like this – every late payment is effectively costing you £100 on top of the debt, every missed payment £250. In truth I've plucked these numbers out of thin air, as there's no way to quantify a poor credit score, but it's the right way to think.

If you are in difficulties, the clichéd 'contact your lender' is still the best advice. Hopefully they will try and help a little, as changing your repayment schedule is preferable to you defaulting – and though it will hit your credit score, it's better than a County Court Judgement (CCJ) against you.

Don't apply too many times. Lenders don't just look at your current situation, they try and predict your future behaviour. Potential over-indebtedness can cause rejection – scoring looks not only at your repayment history but at the likelihood you will repay in future. Multiple credit applications can count as evidence of possible over-indebtedness. It is important to note that there is a distinction between a 'credit enquiry' and a 'full credit check'. The latter goes on your file, the first doesn't, so if you just want a quote, get one, but ensure you ask what type of checks they will make. Providing it's not a 'full credit check' it is fine.

Avoid too much potential credit. Access to too much credit, even if it isn't used, can be a problem. If you have a range of unused credit cards, cancel most of them; this lowers your available credit and should help. As an added bonus, once you cancel unused cards, in approximately (though there's no guarantee) 18 months you should count as a 'new customer' again and be able to reapply for 'special introductory offers'.

Moving house hurts. If you're moving house, this usually scores you lower. If a move's on the cards, apply beforehand.

Marriage doesn't hurt, joint finances does. Marrying or living with someone who has a bad credit score shouldn't impact your finances, as third-party data (i.e. someone else's info) doesn't usually affect a score (and after the end of 2004 the rules will be changed). However, if you are 'financially linked' then it can have an effect on your score. Therefore even having a joint bank account for bills can mean you are co-scored. If your partner has a poor score, keep your finances rigidly separate and then at least one of you should have access to good credit.

Don't change your mobile, home telephone, utilities or car insurance before applying for credit. All of these may mean a credit search is performed which goes on your record. When a lender sees your credit reference file, it doesn't distinguish between whether this is a search from a mobile compnay or a loan company. As having many searches in a short space of time hurts your credit score, doing all these together can negatively impact on your ability to obtain new credit.

Evidence of stability is good. Those who own their home rather than rent, or who are employed rather than self-employed, tend to score more highly. Putting a fixed (land) line rather than a mobile number on application forms can help with security checks and improve your chances.

No history can be a problem. A limited credit history is a problem as it means lenders cannot predict your behaviour.

Money Diet Quick Fact Snack: Credit Repair Companies

Steer clear of any company that advertises that it fixes your credit score. They do it one of two ways. The legal method is to negotiate with a company after a CCJ has been served. If you offer them a settlement (not necessarily the full amount) a condition can be that the CCJ is wiped. Many companies do this for you, though they make you pay. However, there's nothing they can do you can't do for yourself, and if you need help, Citizens Advice Bureaus, Independent Advice Centres and the Consumer Credit Counselling Services should help for free anyway.

The other method is illegal. Some credit repair agencies advise you to perjure yourself and swear you didn't receive a CCJ even when you did. Once it's illegally wiped they try to quickly negotiate a settlement with the lender, before it is re-served. Don't just steer clear, turn the car right round and drive away at speed!

Credit Score Myths: The following do NOT impact your credit score

Others' info: Information about other people who live with you who aren't financially linked.

If you've been declined by someone else: Other lenders' declined applications – only the fact a credit search has been done is recorded.

Your sex, race, religion or politics

Who you current providers are: Your new lender won't know who you have cards with.

Checking your credit reference files: Lenders are not informed as to whether you check the files – it doesn't hurt.

This is a 'chicken and egg' situation – you can't get credit without a history, you can't get a history without credit.

If you can't get access to credit

A few lenders, like Capital One, the Associates and even Barclaycard, have special 'rate for the risk' credit cards. These have extremely high rates of interest, and should be avoided unless for the specific purpose of building or rebuilding your credit history.

To do this use the card for a little spending each month, but always pay it off in full, so there is no interest charged. Do this and after a year or two you should have a sufficient credit history to enable you to move towards more normal products. And a final thought – although it may be tempting, lying on your application form won't help. Firstly it's an offence, but also, if lenders can't corroborate your information, it's normally not used for credit scoring anyway.

two

THE BIG MEAL

THE COMPLETE, NO-HOLDS-BARRED, COMPREHENSIVE GUIDE TO SAVING MONEY ON MORTGAGES AND REMORTGAGES

Mortgage debts stay with us longer than badly cooked kippers. The wrong mortgage can add tens of thousands to your costs over the years. This chapter takes you through getting the very best-value mortgage possible, and how to improve your current home loan.

WHY BOTHER?

If someone walked up to you and offered you a legal twenty grand in cash with no strings attached, it's likely you'd grab it – in your teeth if you had to. Shave 1 percentage point off a £100,000 mortgage with 20 years left and you'd save £60 a month. Save this, and by the time the mortgage is paid off, you could have twenty grand.

It's just a stat, but it shows the scale of gain available. Paying off your home loan is the biggest financial burden you're likely to have, and by tackling it, you're likely to make the biggest single saving going.

The last few years have been an amazing time to get a mortgage or remortgage. Interest rates have touched their lowest for over 50 years. House prices have rocketed, which means those remortgaging are often borrowing a smaller proportion of their house's value – which should enable them to get, relatively, an even better rate than when they first took the house on.

Getting a Mortgage

Funnily enough, deciding whether to get a mortgage or not is easy. If you want to buy a house, unless you're very lucky, someone will need to loan you the money, and that means a mortgage, as all a mortgage is is a home loan.

The bigger the deposit you can put down, the easier it is to get a mortgage. Lenders will usually lend people on their own up to three-and-a-half times their income. These days some lenders will give more – in fact on rare occasions it is possible to borrow up to six times your earnings. For two people getting a mortgage together, it's normally possible to borrow either three times the income of the highest earner plus one times the income of the other, or two-and-a-half times their joint income. There are also a few lenders who don't use 'earnings multiples', but instead simply ask the question, 'What can you afford to repay?'

Money Diet Quick Fact Snack: Special Recipes to Create a Deposit

Raising a deposit to get on the housing ladder can be tough. Not having a deposit leaves a 100% mortgage as the only option and these are usually very expensive – meaning the interest rates are higher. While standard options involve help from your family – either they act as guarantors, so that if you can't pay they have to, or you get a loan from them – many people simply don't have this option. There are, however, a couple of more creative solutions that are possible.

Use a cheap credit card or personal loan. This should only be used by those who can keep a tight hold on their credit management. The idea is simple. Rather than an expensive 100% loan, borrow some or all of the deposit on a credit card (depending on your credit limit and the amount you need), preferably at 0%. A 95% mortgage is substantially cheaper than a 100% one, so overall you will be much better off. Even if the credit card rate is more than the mortgage rate, because the mortgage borrowing is so much larger, as long as you are borrowing the deposit just for the short term, and can prioritise paying it back, it's generally worthwhile.

Use a cashback mortgage. Some mortgages offer cash back to help with a new home's expenses when you get a mortgage. This can be up to 6% of the mortgage value. Providing the mortgage is MIG-free (i.e. free of a mortgage indemnity guarantee, see page 260), and extended-redemption penalty-free (see page 266), this can be used creatively to act as an effective deposit. If the cashback mortgage, as they sometimes are, is much cheaper than a 100% mortgage, then when contracts are exchanged (towards the end of the home-buying process) if the seller agrees, it is not necessary to hand over the full deposit. If it is agreed with the seller that the deposit will be handed over at completion, then the cashback may be used as the deposit and the overall mortgage will be at a cheaper rate.

Remortgaging

You don't have to move home to remortgage; all you're doing is swapping your current loan for a new one. Ask the question 'Is there a new mortgage available that's better and/or cheaper than my current one, where the benefits of switching outweigh the costs?' If the answer is yes, then buckle up and prepare for the ride, as it's time to switch.

However, there are more reasons to think about changing your current home loan than just the savings available. So let me try and anticipate a few of these reasons and see if any fit you.

The slap-on-the-wrist

'I've had my mortgage for years, why should I change it?'
Inaction is expensive. If you haven't touched your mortgage in years, it is likely you are paying your lender's Standard Variable Rate (SVR). These rates tend to move with the UK base rate (see page 262), which is set by the Bank of England. However, they don't necessarily move in exact proportion, as lenders can choose to move the rate willy-nilly, making themselves either more competitive or more profitable. Each lender's rate varies, but as a very rough rule of thumb it's 1.5 percentage points above the UK's bank base rate. Frankly, if you are paying the SVR and have been for years, then with only a few exceptions you are paying way over the odds.

Money Diet Quick Fact Snack: Remortgaging – a Definition

Remortgaging simply means changing your mortgage deal, whether with your existing lender or a new one. The main reasons it is done are to get a cheaper rate, because you are moving house, or to be able to borrow more on top of your existing mortgage.

The softlee-softlee-catchee-monkee
'I want to increase my borrowing and consolidate my loans.'
Rocket-paced house-price rises mean your home may be worth substantially more than the size of your mortgage. Remortgaging allows you to increase the size of your mortgage and borrow more at the low mortgage rate. Yet, remember, you are choosing a very long-term form of borrowing which will leave you actually paying quite a substantial amount in interest. It's also worth remembering that interest rates can rise sharply, so always ask yourself if you could afford to make the repayments if interest rates rose by 3 percentage points, or perhaps even more.

The ouch
'My endowment probably won't pay off my mortgage.'
Not fun, this one. If you are one of the millions of UK home-owners who have received letters from your endowment company warning your investment may not repay the mortgage in full when it matures, then remortgaging can provide a couple of useful solutions – see 'Interest-only mortgages', page 258.

The what-choice-do-I-have?
'I'm moving house.'
It isn't always necessary to remortgage when you move; many modern mortgages are 'portable', which means they can move with you. However, increasing the loan to do it will need agreement from your current lender. A house move is a good time to look at remortgaging as you may save substantial cash when you check out what is available.

It's worth noting your existing lender cannot force you to

> **Money Diet Quick-Fact Snack: Loan-To-Value ('LTV')**
>
> The actual interest rate paid on a mortgage depends on your LTV. As it sounds, this is the size of the loan compared to the value of the house. There are different LTV bands, and the lower the band you are in the cheaper the mortgage – bands are such things as a sub-75% LTV, or between 80% and 90% LTV, or over 95% LTV.
>
> For first-time mortgage holders, working out the LTV is easy. Simply take the value of your deposit away from 100%. For example, a 10% deposit is a 90% LTV. It is slightly trickier for those who are remortgaging. To find the LTV, divide the amount you have left to pay on your mortgage by the current value of your home. This means if your house's value has risen, your LTV will have decreased, which should mean you are able to get a better deal.

stick with it, though it could force you to pay any contracted redemption penalties (more on that in a moment). On occasion they may not give you their best bureaucratic efforts to help you move, but if things don't go smoothly the Mortgage Code lays down a complaints procedure for such an eventuality.

CHOOSING A MORTGAGE

Each individual lender's competitiveness varies depending on its current business priorities, but there's always one lender desperate for new business and willing to undercut its competitors. This means there's no such thing as the top mortgage provider.

A lender topping the mortgage table six months ago is likely to have made those special offers to increase its share of the market, and once it has hit its target, the probability is it will push its rates up, leaving it no longer the best.

Mortgage Type: Repayment or Interest Only

Mortgages come in two flavours – which to choose is the most important decision to make. When you remortgage, there is the opportunity to change the type, though.

Repayment mortgages

Here you repay the lender each month, and this pays both the original money borrowed (the capital) and the interest the lender is charging on the loan. At the end of the mortgage term you will automatically have paid off the mortgage in full.

Interest-only mortgages

Here, you pay the lender only the interest cost of the loan, while you agree to pay off the capital at a later date. Some people don't look at paying off the capital, and hope that moves in property prices or other investments will cover it, but the usual method is to set up an investment vehicle – the traditional one has been an endowment policy, which is a life assurance investment plan; however, ISAs, pensions and Peps have been used to do the same thing.

People *incorrectly* name such mortgages 'endowment mortgages', 'pension mortgages' or 'ISA mortgages'. This isn't just me being picky, but an important concept. The two products are not linked. You have an interest-only mortgage and separately an investment to pay it off. You needn't use that investment to pay off the mortgage; you could choose to use cash from another source. Sometimes endowments are 'assigned' to pay off a mortgage, but this should be changeable.

The big sales plank for interest-only mortgages is that if the investment performs well, the lump sum may be more than the amount needed, giving you a windfall at the end of the term. This is why many endowments were sold – yet the suggested repayment level of the combined interest and investment was usually set lower than a repayment mortgage. Unfortunately this often meant not enough money was invested, which is why for many people the endowment isn't coming close to repaying the mortgage.

If you have an endowment shortfall. There are a number of options, which can be either used separately or combined.

- Remortgage, and use the benefit of a cheaper interest rate to make up the shortfall.
- Switch either completely or partially to a repayment mortgage. This may be more expensive, but it means that at the end of the term your mortgage is guaranteed to be paid off.
- Pay more into the endowment. Well, I have to mention it as a possibility, though for most people it's likely to be a bad idea. However it may be worth seeing an Independent Financial Adviser to assess how well the endowment is likely to do.
- Set up a savings plan to make up the shortfall. Here you simply start paying money into another account to make sure you'll be covered. One way is to use a mini cash ISA (see 'Crash Diet', page 160) to get tax-free savings. This is quite a simple plan. And if the shortfall isn't as bad as expected, you'll have extra funds.

One final quick point. Many people when annoyed at a poorly performing endowment decide to surrender it. This is often a bad idea. Most of the benefit from an endowment is due to the bonus paid at the end of the term – surrender and you lose that. Endowments are one of the few subjects Independent

Financial Advisers shine at. (See 'Financial Fitness', page 101.) However, as a rule of thumb, if you are looking to surrender, you will be better off 'selling' the endowment. There is a market for second-hand endowment policies; buyers commonly advertise, and if you sell, you can get up to 30% more than surrendering. So always, always, always check this option out if you are considering getting rid of the endowment.

Money Diet Quick Fact Snack: Mortgage Indemnity Guarantees (MIGs)

MIGs are outrageous fees some lenders charge with mortgages where the loan-to-value (LTV) ratio is more than 90%. It is an insurance policy, yet – although you pay for it – it's not you it protects, but the lender, in case you default.

Some lenders use the term 'mortgage indemnity premium' or MIP, but it amounts to the same thing. Avoid them.

Not all lenders charge MIGs and that makes a huge difference. Someone with a 95% LTV would pay an MIG of around 1.5% of their house's value, or £1,500 on a £100,000 home. If you're mathematically minded then you can work out the MIG using the following equation. If not, just know that MIGs are complicated, expensive and should be avoided.

The Maths. You usually only pay an MIG if you're borrowing more than 90% of a house's value. The amount you pay is commonly defined as 7% of the amount borrowed above 75% of the house's value. To find out the cost of a MIG, key the following into your calculator:

$$(0.XX - 0.75) \times 0.07 \times \text{house value}$$

where XX is the percentage of your house's value that you're borrowing. (i.e. borrow 98% and you do 0.98 - 0.75, then multiply the result by 0.07 and then by the house's value).

> **Money Diet Wealth Warning: From Small Changes Do Big Savings Grow**
>
> While differences in mortgage percentage rates sound small – they have ENORMOUS impact. Cut the rate by 1 percentage point on a £100,000 mortgage and you save £60 a month.

Does this mean never get a new interest-only mortgage?

No. It's been a very bad decision in the past, but that doesn't mean automatically exclude it. The keyword is 'risk'. Take an interest-only loan and you must be aware of the 'risk' it may not be paid off in full. However, once you're aware of the risk, have considered it, understand it and planned for the worst, then an interest-only mortgage is still acceptable. Endowments have lost their sheen, and most new interest-only mortgages will be ISA-backed, taking advantage of ISAs' tax-free ability available to fund the mortgage. Yet this option suits very few – most people should stick with a repayment mortgage.

Types of Mortgage Special Offers

Mortgage 'special offers' is an unfamiliar term describing a common mortgage phenomenon. Companies try to tempt us in, hoping later they'll be able to bung the rate up and leave us clinging on, paying more for the rest of the term.

These special offers are the classic terms you'll have heard of: the 'fixed', 'discount' and 'trackers' or a combination of these. They usually last for two to five years, though they can be as short as six months or as long as 25 years.

Fixed rates

As the name suggests, the rate doesn't change, and interest rate moves are irrelevant. The best time to get a fixed rate is when UK interest rates are about to rise, as your rate remains static while others move higher.

Sweetener: the certainty of knowing exactly what you'll pay during the entire special-offer period. This means you can plan.

Money Diet Quick Fact Snack: Know the Difference

The Bank of England base rate. The basic cost of UK money is set by the Bank of England's 'Monetary Policy Committee'. Their job is to try and keep the country's inflation rate on a steady course. Their only weapon is the ability to change the rate at which the Bank of England lends money – the base rate.

When inflation (the rate at which prices rise) is too high, to slow the economy and stop people spending, they increase the cost of borrowing by raising the base rate. When inflation is too low, they need the economy to grow, so they decrease the cost of borrowing, reducing the incentive for people to save and encouraging them to borrow to spend.

When the Bank of England rate moves, other interest rates tend to move, too. This is because the base rate is roughly 'the standard price' for lending money. A good way to measure how competitive loans or savings rates are is to compare them to it.

Lenders' standard variable rates (SVR). Each bank or building society sets its own SVR; often it's referred to as the bank's standard mortgage rate. These move both when the Bank of England changes interest rates and if the lender wants to change its competitive stance. So if you're with a lender that's sold a lot of mortgages recently, it may increase its rate. Yet willy-nilly moves are uncommon; lenders are sneakier than this. They tend to move at the margins, taking advantage of changes in the Bank of England rate. If the Bank of England drops rates by 0.25%, a lender may subtly only cut its mortgage rate by 0.2%. Much more difficult to spot, but effectively still a rate rise. Watch out for these moves.

If you choose a fixed rate, simply be satisfied you can make the repayments, and even if rates drop don't worry. If the decision is made based on certainty, you still have it, so there's no point regretting what may have been. No one has an interest-rate crystal ball – so any choice you make is a gamble.

Rotten eggs: if rates drop, you're paying more than you need to. Fixed rates almost invariably stop you changing deal within the special-offer period, so get a fixed rate and you're stuck with it.

Final thought: many people wrongly assume the price fixed rates are initially offered at moves up and down with base rates. While there is some relationship, actually fixed-rate prices depend on the City's predictions of long-term rates. This means fixed-rate offer prices can be rising while UK base rates are falling. So be careful.

Discount rates

The important question is 'What is it discounted off?' The answer is usually it's a temporary discount off the standard variable rate (SVR). This is confusing as it depends on what level lenders set their SVR. For example, a 1 percentage point discount from a lender with an SVR of 6% is more expensive than an undiscounted mortgage from a lender with an SVR of 4.5%. Therefore with discounts it's not just size, but the usage that counts.

Sweetener: when the UK's interest rates are falling, your mortgage rate drops too, so if it looks like rates are due to drop, a discount is the one to go for. As it moves with base rates you won't feel you are paying much more than the market rate.

Rotten eggs: if interest rates rise, so does the cost of your mortgage. This means there's no security with a discount mortgage. Always ask 'Are repayments still affordable if rates rise by 2 or 3 percentage points?' If not, maybe the security of a fixed rate would be better for you.

Final note: some discount mortgages have a 'collar', a set minimum rate, and if the SVR drops below that, you won't benefit. If you're getting a discount mortgage because rates are going to drop, avoid collars like the plague.

Discount tracker rates/tracker rates

This is a recent – and welcome – innovation. Rather than the discount being off a bank's SVR, these discounts are off the Bank of England base rate itself. So a 0.5 percentage point tracker discount when the base rate is 4.5% means you pay 4% (though paradoxically even a tracker at + 0.5 percentage point, in this case a rate of 5%, could still count as a discount mortgage if it's lower than most SVRs). There are also now long-term tracker rates where, after the special offer, rather than reverting to the SVR it reverts to a tracker rate – e.g. base rate plus 1 percentage point.

Sweetener: the advantage over standard discounts is the lender can't interfere with the rate to suck in some extra profits. All the gain or pain of base rate moves is passed on directly.

Rotten eggs: the same problems as normal discount mortgages – no surety and if rates rise you will pay more.

Capped rates

The rate is variable – either based on the SVR, a tracker, or a discounted version of either of those – yet the maximum rate you can pay is fixed. In reality capped rates usually work like fixed rates, as the only time you don't pay the top rate is if the rate the loan's based on drops below the cap.

Sweetener: you effectively have a fixed rate if rates are rising, but a discount if there's a substantial drop.

Rotten eggs: Capped rates are usually higher than fixed rates, so you are consistently paying more. And if the rate never drops, you'd be better off with a fixed rate. However, if (as it'll rarely be) it's a straight choice between fixed and capped with exactly the same rate, go for capped.

Low SVR mortgages

Not, strictly speaking, a special offer, it's a relatively new beast in the mortgage market. Rather than a cheap rate for a couple of years, the low rate lasts the entire mortgage term. The internet banks Egg and Intelligent Finance, coupled with HSBC, lead the way on these.

Sweetener: there's no need to switch lenders every few years. So for those who really don't want hassle, this is the way to go.

Rotten eggs: the SVR may be low, but it isn't anywhere near as low as the best special offers. Those willing to ride the waves of the best mortgage rates are much better off sticking to the short-term special offers. Plus, these tend to be SVRs not trackers, so at some stage the bank may choose to make it less competitive. Even if you pick this nice easy mortgage life, you'll still need to keep an occasional eye on the market to make sure you are not overpaying.

Always Make Sure the End is in Sight

Whether you've a discount, fixed or tracker special offer, the most important thing is to keep a note of when it ends. It's very likely your mortgage repayments will shoot up, as you will be moved to the SVR rate. When this date is a minimum of three months away (after all, mortgage moves are easy to delay, but difficult to speed up) look at the mortgage market and consider remortgaging (again).

Money Diet Quick Fact Snack: Redemption Penalties

Many mortgage lenders tie you to their mortgage by contractually obliging you to pay a fine if you remortgage or repay the mortgage before the end of a set period. Redemption penalties are also known as 'tie-ins'. These penalties may be substantial, up to 5% of your mortgage's value (in certain circumstances even more), and can seriously impede any remortgaging benefits.

There are two types:

Not so bad: Standard Redemption Penalty. Here the penalty only lasts during the initial special offer period. This used to be the norm; now some new mortgages don't have any penalties at all. However, pick a good mortgage and you won't be looking to move until after the special offer period anyway. Though if you intend to overpay, in order to pay it off more quickly, in some circumstances redemption penalties may prevent that. The main time that standard redemption penalties are a real problem is with a five-year or longer fixed-rate offer, as there's a greater likelihood your situation will change over that time.

Always avoid: Overhanging or Extended Redemption Penalties. Here you pay a penalty for switching even after the special offer has ended. This often means that even though you're paying a high SVR you are still tied in with penalties. This can completely stymie remortgaging, even for those paying massively over the odds.

Other penalty triggers. Unfortunately it is not just remortgaging that may trigger redemption penalties. It is possible that overpaying, relocating or splitting with your partner (or anyone else on the mortgage with you) will do too; check these when you take a mortgage out.

Flexible Mortgages

Mortgage flexibility is chic, and rightly so – this innovation will save many people money. However, it's not necessarily for everyone. Flexible mortgages are usually at a higher rate than inflexible ones, and as each flexible feature tends to add to the cost, pick only those you'll actually use.

Flexible mortgages have four essential characteristics:

Overpayments. You can pay more than is needed, so the mortgage is repaid more quickly, and less interest accrues.

- £100,000 repayment mortgage over 25 years at 6.5% interest
- NO OVERPAYMENT – repay a total of £202,000
- OVERPAY £1 a day (£30 a month) – repay a total of £191,000 (pays off the mortgage two years earlier)
- OVERPAY £100 a month – repay a total of £172,000 (pays off mortgage six years earlier)

Underpayments, or taking a payment holiday. Decrease your payments, or even stop them completely if you have

---

Money Diet Quick Fact Snack: Using a Flexible Mortgage to Get a High Rate on Your Savings

It's possible to morph your flexible mortgage to earn more on your savings. This involves combining the use of overpayment and borrow-back facilities. To do it, pay all your excess savings into your mortgage, providing they can be withdrawn whenever you choose.

As the savings temporarily pay off some of the mortgage, you pay less interest. The overall impact is the same as earning interest on the savings, at the mortgage rate, plus there's no tax to pay on this. Therefore, your savings should easily outperform even the highest-paying savings account on the market.

---

other more pressing financial commitments or a lifestyle change, such as a new baby. Remember, though, the more slowly a mortgage is repaid, the more interest you pay in the long run.

Borrow-back. Allows you to reborrow money already repaid at the mortgage rate. This effectively allows you a personal loan – admittedly secured on your property, but at a much lower rate than would be available elsewhere.

Money Diet Money Magic: How to Flex the Inflexible

Like a chiropractor's manipulation, it is possible to encourage brittle old mortgages to bend in ways they weren't designed to. It isn't always easy, foolproof or perfect. Yet it is worth thinking about.

Overpayments. Nearly half of all flexible mortgage holders are only really concerned about the ability to overpay. By happy coincidence, this is by far the easiest to replicate, without any tricks at all, as most modern 'inflexible' mortgages permit overpayments, though lenders don't shout about it. The rules usually stipulate overpayments must be lump sums of a minimum of £250, and that they should be put towards paying off the capital, as only this decreases the interest charge. The only sticking point is if the mortgage is within its redemption penalty period. Technically overpayments may count as redeeming before the agreed time, however it's becoming increasingly common for mortgage companies to make exceptions.

To get round this: There's one other trick to play. Request a decrease in the term length of your mortgage. This means the necessary monthly payments will increase, effectively working like an overpayment. It's worth noting permission to alter the term is at the lender's discretion: they'll consider whether the new repayments are affordable or if you're overstretching your finances. Usually, though, it isn't a problem. There is also sometimes a one-off admin. fee of roughly £50. However, term changes tend to be permanent – they may let you switch back, but there's no guarantee, so all this needs careful consideration.

Underpayments. It's the opposite of overpaying: just lengthen the mortgage's term. It's worth remembering a longer term means permanent underpayments, and therefore the total interest charged on the mortgage will increase, but if it stops you defaulting, it may be worthwhile.

£100,000 Repayment Mortgage at 6% interest

Term (years)	Monthly repayment	Total repayment	Total interest	Compare to 25-year term
30	£605	£218,000	£118,000	£22,500 MORE
25	£652	£195,500	£95,500	N/A
20	£726	£174,000	£74,000	SAVE £21,500
15	£858	£154,500	£54,500	SAVE £41,000
10	£1,132	£136,000	£36,000	SAVE £59,500

Payment holidays. Thank heavens we're over half-way through the diet before I admit failure. I've squirmed, shaken and wriggled, but I'm scuppered, there really isn't a way to replicate a payment holiday. It is possible to use interest-free credit card special offers to pay the mortgage in the short term, but this leaves you with a debt repayment glut in the future. If you're in dire need, speak to your lender. They may allow some repayments to be missed, but it is likely this will harm any future applications for credit.

Borrow-back. To borrow back with a bog-standard mortgage, simply apply to the lender to increase the loan's size. Most allow this up to 75% of your house's current value, and with the rise in house prices, for most people this isn't a big problem. For more than that, the lender may well question the loan's purpose – however, if it's for home improvements they should be more generous.

If the amount required is less than £25,000, it can put lenders off slightly as they then need to comply with the bureaucracy of the Consumer Credit Act, though again household improvement loans are exempt from this.

Barring overpayments, these solutions don't come with the ease and fluidity of a pre-packaged flexible loan, and anyone who's likely to make regular use of the features should stick with those. However, many don't have this choice.

Daily calculated interest. The interest on a flexible mortgage should be calculated daily, or at least monthly. This way, as soon as you contribute, the amount owed decreases and so does the interest. Calculating interest daily as opposed to annually can be the equivalent of a 0.15% decrease in interest rate.

Current Account Mortgages – 'Hmmmmm'

Current account mortgages, originally popularised by Virgin One, are 'super-flexible'. A current account, mortgage and debts are wrapped together.

As your salary is paid directly, it automatically decreases the mortgage debt, so the interest decreases too.

You may note my 'hmmmmm' in the title: this is because while the concept is clever, the marketing of these accounts makes the benefits look a lot bigger than they really are. The most common trick is to sell them based on benefits available with all flexible mortgages, not just the additional current account features.

For example, £100,000 repayment mortgage over 25 years for someone with a £30,000 salary.

Standard mortgage: at 5.5% you'd pay £614 a month.

The hype: with a current account mortgage at the same rate, pay your salary into your account and spend all of it barring £100 each month and you'd save £26,000, paying the mortgage off three years and five months earlier. This is equivalent to a standard mortgage at just 4.05%.

The reality: most of this gain is due to the fact the £100 left in the account each month is an overpayment – in other words, it's equivalent to upping your monthly contributions. This feature is available with any flexible (and some not so flexible) mortgage. Strip this out and you are left with the pure benefit from putting your salary in, which is just £8.70 a month, £2,600 over the term.

This means the 'current account' bit is only equivalent to a gain of 0.1% in the interest rate, so if a current account mortgage is much more than 0.1% more expensive than a standard flexible mortgage, which they almost always are, the gain is wiped out. Only those earning big lump sums will find the 'current account' bit gains more substantial.

HOW MUCH WILL IT COST ME?
The Costs and Fees

1. Stamp duty

When you move house, the government usually gets a cut in the form of stamp duty. This is calculated on the value of the house, not the size of the mortgage. And it's the purchaser who pays the stamp duty.

There is one sneaky way to save on this –

Regeneration Areas. You'd be surprised at what counts as a regeneration area. For example, in London some 'up and coming' areas are demarked as such. Buy a property worth between £60,000 and £150,000 in one of these areas and there is no need to pay stamp duty – a saving of up to £1,500.

2. Penalties on your current mortgage (remortgages only)

It's important to check there are no redemption penalties to pay your current lender. If there are, ask exactly what they will be and factor this against the gain made due to the cheaper rate. If you are close to the end of the penalty period it may be worth waiting a couple of months.

Have-a-Go Hero!

Sample Letter for Those Trapped by Redemption Penalties

Mortgage Lender	My name
Profit Making House	My address
Extortionate Interest Lane	My street
Poundchester	My town
DOU 12P	My postcode

Today's date

Dear Sir/Madam,

I am writing to request further information on my mortgage policy. I currently have a **[NAME AND DETAILS OF MORTGAGE HERE, WITH REFERENCE NUMBER]**. I took this policy out on **[DATE MORTGAGE STARTED]**.

I am considering switching to another lender, as the rate it will charge me is much less than what I pay you. Please will you tell me:

a. What the redemption penalty cost will be if I switch my mortgage to another lender.

b. If there are any other costs you will add if I move mortgage.

c. If I do choose to stay with you, what better mortgages will you able to offer me than my current uncompetitive package? Please send me full details on each of these, together with examples of the new monthly costs, and details of redemption penalties or switching costs involved.

I would be very grateful for your help. I would appreciate a reply within the next 30 days.

Many thanks,

Me

Unfortunately, if the penalties are too large it won't be worth remortgaging. But don't give up hope – a few lenders allow their 'trapped' customers to switch to a limited selection of their other mortgages – not perfect, but definitely an improvement.

If not, 'holler' (see page 117): threaten you'll pay the fine and move regardless, in the hope they'll make you a special offer. Opposite is a short letter I've drafted for you. No promises it'll work, but it definitely shouldn't hurt.

3. Other remortgaging fees

It ain't just redemption penalties. There is a range of further costs to remortgaging:

Money Diet Quick Fact Snack: Rough Guide to Remortgaging Fees	Approximate Cost
Administration fee: this is your old lender's last snack on your cash. It charges you for the bureaucracy and paperwork involved in letting you go. (It's often also called a sealing or deeds transfer fee.)	£0–£150
Arrangement fee: paid to your new lender for setting up the mortgage.	£200–£400
Legal fee: you will need legal conveyancing when you remortgage.	£250–£400
Valuation fee: to assess whether your property is adequate security for the mortgage, the new lender will want a valuation. The bigger the house value, the bigger the fee.	£150–£500
Others: there may also be small fees for telegraphic transfer and checking insurance policies.	
TOTAL	£600–£1,450

Money Diet Quick Fact Snack: Get-Out-of-Jail-Free Card – 'Super-Portability'

There is a possible loophole for people trapped in by redemption penalties. Some loans are 'super-portable', which means move house and you are eligible to continue with the current deal or switch to any of that lender's other offers without penalty. If you have a mortgage with penalties, simply use super-portability to move to a non-penalty mortgage, and then remortgage with another lender. One person I mentioned this to saved £4,000 on redemption penalties and cut their rate. It's a small, but valuable, loophole.

Fees-free deals

Fees have a significant impact on working out the best deal. Many lenders offer special deals where their own fees are waived and cash is provided to pay the other fees. Fees-free mortgages tend to be, though aren't always, at a slightly higher interest rate.

Rule of thumb: the bigger the mortgage and the longer the special offer, the better off you are focusing on interest rates rather than fees-free option. As a very rough rule of thumb, with mortgages under £100,000 fees-free is better.

The Proof of the Fees-free Pudding

Fees-free winner: the borrowers

Omar and Irma Borrower have a £50,000 repayment mortgage lasting for 20 more years.

Current mortgage: Barstools Bank at standard 5.95% rate; no redemption penalties for moving.

Monthly repayments: £362.

Remortgage Option 1: Hardleyfixed Bank Fees-Free – 4.25% fixed for two years
Fees: no arrangement fee; legal and valuation fees are paid for you. Leaving just a deed transfer fee of £50.
Fee cost: £50.
Monthly repayments: £313.
Saving over two years: £49 x 24 months = £1,180 minus £50 fee = £1,130.

Remortgage Option 2: Notionwide Building Society – 3.89% fixed for two years.
Fees: arrangement fee £300 + combined £600 legal, valuation and deed transfer fee.
Fee cost: Estimate £900.
Monthly repayments: £302 a month.
Saving over two years: £60 x 24 months= £1,440 minus £900 fees = £540.

And the winner is ... the Borrowers would be £590 better off over two years taking the fees-free mortgage, compared to the cheapest-rate mortgage.

Pay-the-fees winner: the switchers
Wanda and Walter Switcher have a £200,000 repayment mortgage lasting for 20 more years.
Current mortgage: Barstools Bank at standard 5.95% rate, no redemption penalties for moving.
Monthly repayments: £1,447.

Remortgage Option 1: Hardleyfixed Bank Fees-Free at 4.25% fixed for two years.

Fees: no arrangement fee; legal and valuation fee are paid for you. This leaves just a deed transfer fee of £50.

Fee cost: £50.

Monthly repayments: £1,254.

Saving over two years: £193 x 24 months = £4,630 minus £50 fee = £4,580.

Remortgage Option 2: Notionwide Building Society at 3.85% fixed for two years.

Fees: arrangement fee £300 + combined £650 legal, valuation and deed transfer fee.

Fee cost: estimate £950.

Monthly repayments: £1,207 a month.

Saving over two years: £240 x 24 months =£5,760 minus £950 fees = £4,810.

And the winner is ... the Switchers would be £230 better off going for the cheapest rate Notionwide mortgage compared to the fees-free mortgage.

HOW MUCH WILL I SAVE?
First-time Mortgage

Ask the lender for the cost of monthly payments including any Mortgage Indemnity Guarantees, and compare. Ensure you are comparing like with like, though. For example, if you are planning to pay a higher deposit with one than the other, it's unfair to compare the monthly payments.

Remortgage Savings: Calorie Counter

There are some simple steps to follow to find out a rough answer. To aid in the calculation there's a Money Diet Mortgage Calorie Counter. Though before committing get accurate figures done.

Step 1. Use the Ready Reckoner on the following page to find the size of your mortgage and the decrease in interest rates the new mortgage offers over the old one.

E.g. £65,000 repayment mortgage decreased by 2 percentage points is a saving of £76 a month.

Step 2. Multiply the monthly saving by the length of the special offer.

E.g. The special offer lasts two and a half years (30 months), so the saving is £2,280.

Step 3. Take off the cost of any redemption penalties.

E.g. There are redemption penalties of 1% of the mortgage size, which equals £650. Therefore the saving is reduced to £1,630.

Step 4. Take off the cost of any remortgaging and broker fees for the specific mortgage.

E.g. This mortgage is mostly fees-free, so the total fees add up to only £200. Therefore the saving is reduced to £1,430 over the two and a half years. This is equivalent to an actual saving of £48 a month or £570 a year. Well worth it.

Money Diet Mortgage Calorie Counter

These tables are based on an original mortgage rate of 6%. They are not completely accurate for other interest rates, but should give you an idea.

Repayment, monthly interest

	£20,000		£30,000		£50,000		£65,000	
	Monthly Saving	Annual Saving	Monthly Saving	Annual Saving	Monthly Saving	Annual Saving	Monthly Saving	Annual Saving
0.25%	£4	£46	£5	£55	£8	£91	£10	£119
0.50%	£8	£91	£9	£109	£15	£181	£20	£236
1.00%	£15	£179	£18	£215	£30	£358	£39	£466
1.50%	£22	£265	£27	£318	£44	£531	£58	£690
2.00%	£29	£349	£35	£419	£58	£699	£76	£908
3.00%	£43	£510	£51	£612	£85	£1,021	£111	£1,327
4.00%	£55	£661	£66	£794	£110	£1,323	£143	£1,719

	£100,000		£150,000		£200,000		£500,000	
	Monthly Saving	Annual Saving	Monthly Saving	Annual Saving	Monthly Saving	Annual Saving	Monthly Saving	Annual Saving
0.25%	£15	£182	£23	£274	£30	£365	£76	£912
0.50%	£30	£363	£45	£544	£60	£725	£151	£1,813
1.00%	£60	£717	£90	£1,075	£119	£1,433	£299	£3,583
1.50%	£88	£1,062	£133	£1,592	£177	£2,123	£442	£5,308
2.00%	£116	£1,398	£175	£2,096	£233	£2,795	£582	£6,988
3.00%	£170	£2,041	£255	£3,062	£340	£4,082	£850	£10,205
4.00%	£220	£2,645	£331	£3,968	£441	£5,291	£1,102	£13,227

Interest only

	£20,000		£30,000		£50,000		£65,000	
	Monthly Saving	Annual Saving	Monthly Saving	Annual Saving	Monthly Saving	Annual Saving	Monthly Saving	Annual Saving
0.25%	£5	£63	£6	£75	£10	£125	£14	£163
0.50%	£10	£125	£13	£150	£21	£250	£27	£325
1.00%	£21	£250	£25	£300	£42	£500	£54	£650
1.50%	£31	£375	£38	£450	£63	£750	£81	£975
2.00%	£42	£500	£50	£600	£83	£1,000	£108	£1,300
3.00%	£63	£750	£75	£900	£125	£1,500	£163	£1,950
4.00%	£83	£1,000	£100	£1,200	£167	£2,000	£217	£2,600

	£100,000		£150,000		£200,000		£500,000	
	Monthly Saving	Annual Saving	Monthly Saving	Annual Saving	Monthly Saving	Annual Saving	Monthly Saving	Annual Saving
0.25%	£21	£250	£31	£375	£42	£500	£104	£1,250
0.50%	£42	£500	£63	£750	£83	£1,000	£208	£2,500
1.00%	£83	£1,000	£125	£1,500	£167	£2,000	£417	£5,000
1.50%	£125	£1,500	£188	£2,250	£250	£3,000	£625	£7,500
2.00%	£167	£2,000	£250	£3,000	£333	£4,000	£833	£10,000
3.00%	£250	£3,000	£375	£4,500	£500	£6,000	£1,250	£15,000
4.00%	£333	£4,000	£500	£6,000	£667	£8,000	£1,667	£1,667

Source: London & Country Mortgages

ADVERSE CREDIT MORTGAGES: HOW TO GET A MORTGAGE IF YOU HAVE A POOR CREDIT HISTORY

Normally mortgage companies lust after your business, but if you've a poor credit history they often won't play. It's not personal, just the result of computer predictions of your behaviour (see page 242 for more details).

What is Adverse Credit?

Adverse credit means anything that doesn't follow the usual pattern. The absolute worst case is a history of repossession, though a CCJ (County Court Judgement) or debt arrears can count too. Annoyingly, just being self-employed could mean you need to get a specialist mortgage, too. Adverse credit doesn't always mean you are forced to pay hugely over the odds. These days even some high-street lenders will still give you a mortgage, though their criteria are strict. In all cases if you've a big deposit, it'll help.

What to do?

Using a mortgage broker (see next bit) is a big advantage, though you need to be careful. In general avoid those that 'specialise' in adverse credit; often they're just there to take advantage. Some dodgy mortgage brokers are fronts for expensive sub-prime lenders. These offer mortgages to higher-risk borrowers rejected by the high-street lot, and stay profitable because they charge higher interest rates (which, they argue, reflect that risk).

Of course the worse your credit history, the more they charge. If you do have an adverse credit history it is often worth waiting a year before trying for a mortgage and making treble-sure you meet all your repayments in the meantime. This can make a big difference to the mortgage cost.

Getting an adverse-credit mortgage isn't a goal in itself

I tend not to think of sub-prime mortgages as a goal in themselves, but a sometimes-necessary way of rehabilitating credit. If it is necessary to get one of these higher-rate mortgages, ensure all the payments are met. Then, after a few years, you should be able to remortgage to a normal lender.

However, it's time for a BIG warning: there are some real sharks in this game, aiming to screw people in vulnerable situations and squeeze hideous amounts of cash out, so be incredibly careful.

Things to watch for if you're getting a 'sub-prime' mortgage

Interest rate. At its extreme this shouldn't be more than 4 percentage points above UK bank base rates (see page 262). If possible try for a lender whose standard mortgage rate is set in relationship to either UK base rates or the interbank lending rate (known as LIBOR) rather than an SVR.

Redemption penalties (see page 266). They're unavoidable in the sub-prime market, but ensure they don't last for more than three years. Longer penalties would prevent you from remortgaging after rehabilitating your credit.

Avoiding missed repayment penalties. Another big warning: don't *ever* get a mortgage with increased-interest penalty clauses for missed repayments. These can spiral you into disaster, heaping on bigger debts at the worst time. Some nasty operators structure their loans to maximise the chance of repossessing your property.

Do You Really Need a Mortgage?

I don't like being a party pooper, but if the mortgage is expensive it is very important to question whether it is worth buying a home at all. Stop and clinically consider if you can truly afford the repayments and, more importantly, whether you could afford them if interest rates rose by, say, 3%. If not, you're trapping yourself into further debilitating debt and running the risk of losing any home you buy.

WHERE TO GET FURTHER ADVICE — INDEPENDENT MORTGAGE BROKERS

Mortgage brokers are specialist advisers; it's well worth getting their help. For more details, see 'Get Mortgage Advice for Free' (page 207).

three £

SNACKS

THE PRECISION PLASTIC GUIDE TO THE PERFECT CREDIT CARDS

They say don't show favouritism to any of your children, but, alas, I can't help it. This is my baby. There are three types of credit-card user. I'll show you how to work out which type you are and then how to play the system in each case.

WHAT'S THE BEST CREDIT CARD?

On the bus, at a party, on a TV programme, eating a family meal, talking to a taxi driver or buying something at my local shop – there is one question that comes up without fail. 'What is the best credit card?' I've learned to stifle the exasperated scream trying to erupt from my stomach.

Don't think I mind being asked questions, I love what I do and am happy to help. People recognising me on the street and saying hello is a compliment (much better than surreptitious glances which leave me wondering whether it's because they've seen me on the telly or because my flies are undone). No, the reason I hate this particular question is I don't know the answer!

Before you cry, 'Fraud! I've heard him introduced as the Dumbledore of Debt, and he knows nothing,' the reason I can't answer is …

There is no one-size-fits-all credit card.

Credit cards involve not just interest rates, but a range of benefits, gimmicks and fringe uses too. All these factors can be used to sell us a card, but most cards are worthwhile for only one or two purposes. To beat the system you need a number of different ones – personally I keep six or seven active cards, but three is fine.

Yet don't just jump straight in and turn to the 'what to do' bits. The most important thing is to know what type of credit card person you are. Read the 'potential player', 'credit survivor', 'debt crisis' test on page 288.

BACK TO BASICS: WHAT IS A CREDIT CARD?

The plastic in your pocket is one of two very different animals: debit or credit cards. A debit card is a bit like an electronic cheque, so when you pay, the money is taken straight from your bank account. With a credit card (or store card, which is a limited-use credit card) you run up a bill for the month's spending. Then you either pay it off in full, so there's no interest charged, or you pay off a proportion of the bill, and interest is charged on the entire month's borrowing.

Used correctly, credit cards have many advantages over debit cards: extra consumer protection, the ability to delay payment, earn rewards and more (all are covered here).

Money Diet Quick Fact Snack: Hurdle Over a Cash Hump With a Credit Card

Almost all credit cards are interest-free for short-term borrowing – regardless of the published interest rate. Use it to buy something and the cash stays in your bank account until you pay it off. This is a useful way to delay or spread payments over a short time at no cost. It is possible to have nearly 60 days from the time you spend until the time the money must leave your account (about two weeks after you receive your statement). However, ensure you can pay off the entire bill in full, as leave even just £1 unpaid and you will be charged interest on the whole outstanding amount – negating any benefit.

However, use cards badly and all these are massively outweighed by one big disadvantage: expensive debt.

As a footnote, there is a third type of plastic – charge cards, the most famous of which is the green American Express card. These are a hybrid between debit and credit cards. You spend, build up a bill, and every month must pay it off in full. However, in truth, except for business people, this type of card has limited merit.

Visa and Mastercard (and Amex)

'What credit card do you have?' If you just answered 'Visa' or 'Mastercard' we've work to do – almost undoubtedly you've the wrong plastic. You should've answered who the provider is. Is it a Barclaycard? HSBC? First Direct? Associates? They set the interest rates and terms, so this is where the difference lies. If you don't know, then you chose it for the wrong reason.

Visa and Mastercard are card-transaction companies; they do the processing when you buy or pay for things, and send back the details to the card-provider. The actual differences between Visa and Mastercard are virtually nil; just a few technical issues. There may be slightly more significant issues of acceptability when you travel abroad, but I wouldn't let it impact the choice of card.

American Express (Amex) is slightly different. It only offers its own and affiliated cards, so you can't get a Barclaycard Amex, for example. Also, American Express is accepted less often in the UK than Visa or Mastercard, so sometimes paying for a meal on it is tough. Most of this revolves around the way the three companies charge retailers, but I shall restrain myself from information overload on that right now.

HOW CARD PROVIDERS MAKE THEIR MONEY

The big bucks come from interest earned on money lent. And when I say big, I mean BIG! Some cards have more interest than Melinda Messenger would generate at a stag night.

Fines, Grand Designs and Transaction Fees

Interest isn't the only credit-card-provider income stream:

Fines. Late-payment fines, cash-withdrawal fees and other penalties all add to their coffers. The easiest way to avoid a late-payment fine is to use a direct debit. For those who automatically pay off the bill in full, this is easy. If you can't afford to do that, at the very least set up a direct debit to make the minimum repayments. You can (and should where possible) always add to the payment by sending a cheque each month, but at least this way you'll never be fined.

If you are fined, most lenders will usually wipe the fee (the first time at least) if you call them and honestly say you forgot; just ask – surely £25 is worth the phone call.

Money Diet Quick Fact Snack: WOW! How Much They Charge in Interest

This really is worth a moment's consideration. The average high-street bank charges around 17% on credit-card debts, yet pays just 0.1% on interest on the money kept in its current account. Now think about this: when you keep money in a current or savings account, you are effectively lending the bank money. It can take this cash and lend it out to someone else, or, worse still, back to you, as credit-card debt. Admittedly banks have expenses, but in simple terms, over a year:

Lend it £1,000 in your current account and it pays you £1 (80p after tax).

It lends you £1,000 as credit-card debt and you pay it £170.

Almost makes you want to become a banker, doesn't it?

One final thing to check: some providers want 'cleared funds' in their account by the deadline day. This means your cheque needs to reach them at least three days before the deadline date, to prevent a fine.

Grand designs. To squeeze every last pound from us, plastic-providers try to flog us two additional extras.

Repayment protection insurance, in the event of accident, sickness or unemployment. Often this is automatically included, so you actively need to tell them if you don't want it. This is expensive protection; it's usually proportionally much cheaper to use a general 'income-replacement policy' which pays a proportion of your salary if such problems arise.

Card protection is the other oft-sold plan. Here if you lose your card(s) and make one call, all will be cancelled. You can always call all of your card providers yourself, but some like the peace of mind. Remember that, as they usually deal with *all* your cards, don't sign up for a policy with more than one card provider. Plus 'advanced' and 'premier' packages are often pants, offering little more for a lot more cost. Be careful – sometimes you'll find your cover is automatically 'upgraded'; do always check whether there's a cheaper option available and ask to downgrade.

Transaction fees. Almost every time a transaction is made, retailers pay up to 2.5% of the spending to the card company, generating revenue even from those people who never pay interest. Ultimately we pay for this in the form of higher retail prices. However, the transaction fee is often used to off-set the cost of credit card reward schemes. Use one of these correctly and you'll gain. (See page 300.)

There's a final, less tangible, benefit for providers – credit cards allow banks to 'cross-sell'. This means they use the data gleaned from your credit-card custom to build a profile on you and try and flog you other goods.

ARE YOU A POTENTIAL PLAYER, A CREDIT SURVIVOR OR IN DEBT CRISIS?

To decide the way to play the system, first work out exactly what type of credit-card user you are. This, unfortunately, isn't your choice; it's determined by your financial situation.

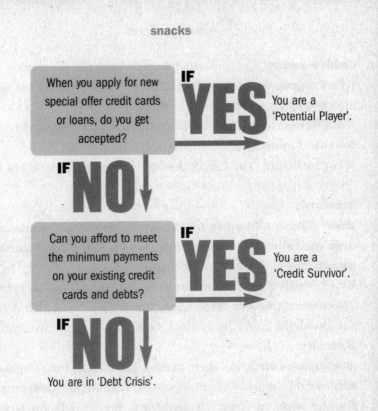

When you apply for new special offer credit cards or loans, do you get accepted?

IF YES You are a 'Potential Player'.

IF NO

Can you afford to meet the minimum payments on your existing credit cards and debts?

IF YES You are a 'Credit Survivor'.

IF NO

You are in 'Debt Crisis'.

To explain:

Potential players

Who? Anyone who can apply for new credit cards, and scores well enough to get introductory offers.

Why? You're a 'player' because do it right and you can beat the system.

What to avoid? Choosing the wrong cards – it's tragic. I can hear the toilet flushing your money away.

What to read? 'The Potential Player's Precision Plastic Guide' (page 290). 'Free Cash' (page 311). However, even potential players can gain by reading 'The Credit Card Shuffle' (page 315) too, as it offers good hints for general credit-card housekeeping and saves you over-applying for credit.

Credit survivors

Who? Anyone meeting their current debt repayments, but unable to get new special-offer cards.

Why? You're surviving – but could thrive, by rejigging existing debts and minimising your interest.

What to Read? 'The Credit Survival Technique' (page 314).

Debt crisis

Who? Those who can't meet current debt repayments and can't get any new mainstream credit (ignoring specialist consolidation or 'rate for risk' loans).

Why? Missing repayments causes debt problems to spiral. The amount owed could increase due to fines, and unless you act, the debts could get critical. Deal with it immediately, it's a priority.

Is it unsolvable? No. There are no quick fixes, but people do successfully improve their situation, rehabilitate their credit and get back on track. Realising you are in debt crisis is a massive first step back. .

What to Read? 'Food Poisoning' (page 335).

THE POTENTIAL PLAYER'S PRECISION PLASTIC GUIDE
Be at the Cutting Edge

There's no such thing as a bad credit card, just a bad credit-card user. Use the right card for the right purpose and you'll win. Get it wrong and they'll skin you for every penny. Shifting when it suits *you*, not them, makes you a 'credit-card tart'. If you're a potential player (see page 289), then pick a card, any card.

How to Be a Tart: Picking Your Premier Plastic
(card types detailed in following pages)

Do you already have debts on your current cards?

IF YES

Balance Transfer Card
Shift your debt to a new card with a special rate. Use a separate card for spending on – follow the 'NO' path to decide which one.

IF NO

Do you regularly spend on a credit card?

IF NO

Reward Card
Even if you've never used a credit card before, providing you have a little discipline, you should start. Credit cards paid off in full each month are a more rewarding weapon than cash or debit cards and you gain additional consumer protection.

IF YES

Do you pay off the bill in full each month?

IF YES

Reward Card (see above).

IF NO

Are you happy to change cards every six months or so?

IF YES

Purchases Card: Best Intro Rate
Be a tart. Use the card which offers the best introductory rate for purchases – hopefully at 0%.

IF NO

Purchases Card: Lowest Standard Rate
If you prefer a 'stable relationship', stick to the credit card with the lowest possible standard rate.

Who's My Baby? Picking Cards for Specific Uses
(card types detailed in following pages)

Your main card isn't right for every use. I'm not suggesting you have every type of card, but think through which of these events are common in your life, and pick secondary cards accordingly.

Is this an everyday UK purchase? **IF YES**

Purchases Card
Use the main card selected for purchasing.

IF NO

Are you buying from a UK retailer or provider? **IF NO**

Overseas Spending Card
Anyone who either buys from abroad or goes on business or holidays overseas can gain substantially using one of these special cards.

IF YES

Is it for a large electrical or white-good purchase? **IF YES**

Special-Use Card
Some cards offer free warranties and short-term protection against loss, theft or accidental damage. At certain times this is well worth having.

IF NO

Are you buying something for a Christmas present? **IF YES**

Price Promise Card
Find it anywhere else cheaper and these will refund the difference. This way buy it in time before Christmas and you can claim back any reductions made in the January sales.

IF NO

Are you purchasing a holiday or trip abroad? **IF YES**

Travel Insurance Card
Use a card offering free travel insurance policies.

IF NO

Main Card
Stick with your main card for all other transactions.

DIY Credit Card Rough Calorie Counter – How Much Will You Save?			
Decrease in interest	£1,000 debt over 1 year	£5,000 debt over 3 years	£10,000 debt over 5 years
1%	SAVE £10	SAVE £151	SAVE £510
3%	SAVE £30	SAVE £463	SAVE £1,592
5%	SAVE £50	SAVE £788	SAVE £2,763
10%	SAVE £100	SAVE £1,655	SAVE £6,105
18%	SAVE £180	SAVE £3,215	SAVE £12,877
32%	SAVE £320	SAVE £6,500	SAVE £30,075

The Card Types: Detailed Recipes

The very best card of each type changes with pulse-raising speed. Like the Crash Diet, each category has 'suggested ingredients', yet things change, so always follow the logic when you pick. My site, www.moneysavingexpert.com, which is free, is designed to complement the Money Diet. I compile the best buys there manually, not by computer selection. This is important. Cards are too complicated to categorise by numbers.

Purchases cards

Credit cards are perfect for borrowing, as they're extremely flexible, allowing you to borrow what you need and pay back when you can. Credit cards charge interest on the entire amount borrowed if you don't clear the debt in full. Therefore borrow £1,000 and repay £950 and you will pay interest on the entire £1,000 for that month. If you had been able to find the extra £50 you wouldn't have paid anything at all. For anyone who borrows without clearing the debt in full, every month, even for just two or three months a year, then by far the most important consideration is the interest cost.

> **Money Diet Quick Fact Snack: Cards That Charge Even if You Pay Them Off in Full**
>
> A very small number of cards charge interest even if you pay the bill in full. These should be avoided. The way to tell is if they don't have the usual 40–60 days' interest-free repayment period that is standard on most cards (separate to interest-free introductory offers). Lloyds TSB and MBNA are common culprits of this type of card offer.

Purchases: be a tart. This is the cutting-edge method, and it's way cheaper than any other. If you want to be a tart (and who wouldn't?), the rules are simple. Be wantonly disloyal and brazenly switch to the best new offers. There are usually more than 20 cards offering 0% introductory interest rates.

Top tarts can keep the interest they're charged at 0% as at the end of the special offer, they simply apply for a new offer and shift the existing debt. This doesn't mean they don't pay the card back – there is always a necessary minimum monthly repayment (usually 3% of the outstanding balance or £5,

Calorie Counter: Purchase Card

Spend £500/month over a year, repaying only the minimum each month (1)

	Interest rate	Interest cost
High-street card	18.9%	£540
Stable relationship card	7% (2)	£200
0% intro rate for 6 months followed by 15%	0%, 15%	£300
Tart: Two 0% intro rates for 6 months	0% (3)	£0

(1) making 3% or £5 monthly minimum repayments (2) lowest possible rate (3) debts shifted to a new 0% intro offer started after first intro rate ends

---

Money Diet Wealth Warning: Store Cards – The Devil's Debts

With store cards like Burtons, BHS or Kwik-Fit you can spend only in a specific store or group. Interest rates can be upwards of 30%. There is never an excuse for borrowing on a store card; even the very few that don't charge horrendous rates are no better than average high-street credit cards. For stores these cards are gold dust. They sell you the goods, get their cut of the interest, and can build up valuable information on your spending. Avoid them or, better still, get your own back (see 'Financial Fitness', page 134).

---

whichever is greater). It's also necessary to be careful of the impact on your credit score (see page 244). Choosing the right tart card is easy – just ask 'Who gives new cardholders 0% interest for the longest amount of time?' A standard offer is six months, nine is usually possible and the odd specially targeted internet and direct-mailing offers have lasted up to a year.

Tarting takes effort and organisation, but it pays. Always remember to take precautions, though: note down when the 0% rate ends in your diary; put it on a post-it stuck on the wall or write it on a loved one's forehead; and make sure the debt is paid off or moved. Fail to do this and all your tarting gains will be washed away as the interest rate shoots up and you have to pay. (See 'Know Thyself', page 56, for the impact of bad tarting.)

Suggested ingredients. Egg; Mint; Marbles; Halifax; Morgan Stanley; MBNA; Tesco Visa; Nationwide; Lloyds TSB, Accucard.

Purchases: stable relationships. Tarting isn't easy in any walk of life; it takes time and effort and can impact your reputation, in this case to gain credit. The alternative is a stable relationship; simply find as low a 'non-promotional' rate as possible – under 10% is a winner. Do remember most standard rates are variable, so they can change over time, though competitive standard-rate providers tend to stay that way – but still always monitor what you're paying. Two recent innovations should help this: the Co-Op Bank offers cards with a low rate that is fixed for five years, and Northern Rock offers a 'base rate' tracker.

Suggested ingredients. Co-Op; Northern Rock; Cahoot; Intelligent Finance; Halifax Web Card; Smile.

Balance transfer cards

Anyone paying interest for existing debts on a credit card or, worse still, on a store card should immediately consider a balance transfer – a shrinking potion for interest bills. Transferring a balance means the new provider pays off the debts on your current cards for you, so you now owe it the money instead, at a hopefully lower interest rate. When you apply for a new card with a balance-transfer special offer, tell the new provider what cards and debts you have and it should pay them off for you up to its credit limit. Very occasionally there are fees of 1.5% for balance transfers – it's always worth checking.

Tarts' transfers. There's a hoard of cards offering 0% transfers for six to nine months for new cardholders; after that the interest reverts to the card's standard rate. Work out if you can pay the debt off within the 0% time period. If the answer is yes, then whether you want to tart or not this is the right method, as since you're not being charged interest it's easier to pay off more quickly.

If you can't repay within the 0% period, these cards can still

> **Money Diet Quick Fact Snack: 'Super Balance Transfers'**
>
> A number of cards offer what I call 'super balance transfers'. This means that rather than just allowing balance transfers to pay off another card's debts, they also provide a facility officially demarked to pay off an overdraft, which actually allows you to pay the money into your current account. This is a very effective mechanism for getting cheap and flexible debt as once the money is in your current account you can use it to pay off whatever you want. Or you could just earn interest on money lent to you for 0% (see 'Free Cash', page 311).
>
> *Suggested ingredients.* Egg; MBNA; Abbey; Alliance & Leicester; Virgin, Mint.

be useful. Shift your debt every time the special offer ends to another 0% balance transfer card. Those with good credit scores can continue to use this method for a substantial number of years.

You should always transfer in the month before the special offer ends, to avoid all interest charges. Therefore apply for a new card around four to six weeks before the introductory offer ends. One common mistake is to think that as the interest is 0% you needn't repay anything – but if you do that you'll be fined; always meet the card's minimum repayments.

Two quick tips. Before your special offer period ends, try calling the card company and asking for an extension. It doesn't always work, but you may just find you get 0% for longer with no extra effort (see 'The Credit Card Shuffle', page 315 for more details on existing-customer balance transfers).

Be mindful when transferring balances to different cards which are managed by the same company; for example Alliance & Leicester and Abbey cards are both effectively run by MBNA (look in the terms and conditions to find out). This

Calorie Counter: Balance Transfer Cards			
£5,000 debt over 6 months (just making the minimum 3% repayments)			
Card	Interest rate	Interest cost	Saving
High-street card	17.4%	£390	–
Transfer to a 0% rate for 6 months	0%	£0	£390
£7,500 debt paying £225/month until balance is cleared			
Card	Time taken to repay	Interest cost	Saving
High-street card (18.9%)	46 months	£2,840	–
Life-of-balance transfer at 4.9%	37 months	£560	£2,280
Continual tarting at 0% (if possible)	34 months	£0	£2,840

can impact on the offer you are given, as the company will look at its total exposure to your risk.

Suggested ingredients (tend to be the same as purchase cards). Egg Visa; Mint; Marbles; Halifax; Morgan Stanley; MBNA; Tesco Visa; Nationwide; Lloyds TSB; Capital One.

Lazy transfers. For anyone with longer-lasting debts for whom tarting by rotating 0% offers isn't going to happen, use 'life-of-balance' transfer cards, where the special-offer rate lasts until the entire balance transferred has been paid off. The rates can be as low as 2.9% during special promotions, but the usual best offer is around 4.9%. These represent an easy and very effective way to cut the cost of debts. Again, you must make the minimum payments, but it is an easy way to be assured of low interest if you are prepared to transfer.

Interestingly, the best life-of-balance transfer rates are lower than the lowest standard rate for purchases. This means if you're not a tart but need to make a big credit-card purchase,

---

Money Diet Wealth Warning: Misbalanced Transfers

There are two major potential problems with balance transfers. Both occur when the special offer is only for balance transfers, not normal spending – something especially common with 'Lazy Transfers'.

Problem 1: The Obvious. Things bought on the card are NOT at the cheap balance transfer rate (e.g. 4.9%), but at the higher spending rate (e.g. 18%).

Problem 2: The Devious. When you repay the card, the card company can choose what happens to your repayments. Usually it chooses to pay off the cheap (4.9%) debt first. This means you're not repaying the expensive (18%) spending debts at all. They sit there with the interest growing and growing, and there's nothing you can do apart from pay all the balance transfer debts first.

This has such an impact that in most circumstances even using your balance transfer card only for balance transfers, and another card at a higher interest rate (e.g. 20%) for spending is actually cheaper – as you can choose to prioritise paying off the more expensive debts first.

So, how do I put this subtly ...?

Never, ever, ever, ever spend on a card with a special offer only for balance transfers. Just transfer the balance, then lock it away, cut it up, or eat it. *(Safety note for any precocious children reading – 'eat it' is just for emphasis, not genuine advice!)*

Similarly, though it's less common, if a card just has a special rate for purchases, similarly never do a balance transfer on it. If the special offer rate is for both, you're fine, providing it lasts the same length of time.

NB See 'The Great Barclaycard 0% for life loophole' page 138.

spend on your normal card, then move it to a life-of-balance transfer card immediately for a perpetually lower rate.

Suggested ingredients. Blue American Express; British Airways American Express; Capital One (certain cards); HSBC; LloydsTSB (certain cards); Barclaycard; Mint.

Reward scheme cards – something for nothing

This is where it gets fun. Anyone who doesn't need to borrow on a credit card can make money in a simple way, so if you don't have plastic, it's time to get it. (For a less easy, but more profitable way, see 'Free Cash', page 311). Credit-card reward schemes provide flights, days out, vouchers or cash to reward you for spending on the card. The more spent, the more you collect.

Pay in full or be a fool. There's a golden rule – only ever pick a card based on loyalty schemes if you pay the balance off in full *every month* without fail. Then you avoid any interest charges. Crucial, as the gains from even the best reward schemes are massively outweighed by any interest. To avoid accidental interest charges, set up a direct debit to automatically pay off the card in full. This isn't always easy – providers' forms may just have boxes for 'minimum monthly payments' and 'pay a fixed amount'. However, cross these out and write 'pay off in full each month' and most card companies will honour it – but do always check it has been set up. The other possible hurdle, an annual fee, is, these days, mainly a thing of the past. If there is an annual fee, it will suck back any reward gain, so keep away.

> **Money Diet Quick Fact Snack: It's Always Good to Have Protection**
>
> Another advantage of credit cards over cash or debit cards is an additional legal protection due to Section 75 of the Consumer Credit Act, cunningly known as 'Section 75 protection'. While the name isn't sexy, the result is. Buy anything costing over £100, and the card company is jointly liable with the retailer for the sale. Thus, if the retailer goes bust or the goods aren't delivered, the credit card company may have to step in to compensate you.

You're paid to spend. For those who do pay in full, reward schemes are something for nothing as you gain each time you spend on the credit card. Therefore forget cash, forget debit cards, always use your reward credit card! And be paid every time you spend. (It is very rare for rewards to be paid on balance transfers or cash withdrawals.)

When points don't make the prize choice. There are two types of credit-card reward scheme – cashback and points. Cashback is simple: a proportion of your spending is returned to you in cash. Usually it's totalled up and paid annually, either on the anniversary of the account opening or a fixed date. With points schemes, points or miles are awarded for spending and may be used to redeem gifts, flights, trips, days out or holidays. The reason most reward cards pay points is because this completely mystifies the actual value of the reward itself. There's a feel-good factor for getting points, but it's often false.

On the other hand cashback has two huge advantages: you know exactly how much it is worth, and it's flexible. Even the widest-ranging scheme, AirMiles, is massively restrictive compared to the spending range of cold hard cash.

Money Diet Quick Snack Fact: Credit Card Reward Schemes

'Nectar Is Pants' – Martin Lewis, BBC Radio 5, 2002

You may gather from the above quote that I've never been a big fan of the Nectar points scheme. To be fair, when used purely for Sainsbury's shopping, it's not too bad at all, but as Barclaycard's credit-card reward scheme it ain't hot. The title's a quote from Nectar's launch, rather than a current comment, so by the time you read this, they may have improved the scheme and people will happily be earning Nectar points galore, leaving me sued for misleading info. Then again, I could also walk into McDonald's and see Prince Charles scoffing a Big Mac with Paul McCartney.

Cutting through the hype, at launch the value I calculated of the Nectar points awarded for £100-worth of Barclaycard spending was a paltry 29p; as I write over a year later, it's not changed. Admittedly, it's better than the cards that give no rewards, but only just. It may be Nectar, but it ain't no honey.

Multi-earn points are a red herring. One tool used to flog reward schemes is the 'multi-earn factor', where, as well as earning points on a credit card, they may be earned elsewhere too. With Nectar it's shopping at Sainsbury's, BP and others, as well as spending on a Barclaycard. However, the biggest multi-earn scheme by far is AirMiles, which can be earned in many ways, but is the prime reward of the NatWest and RBS credit-card range.

Multi-earn provides a foolish feel-good factor. Sticking with Nectar at launch as the example, all spending in Sainsbury's using the Nectar card earns 2 points. On £100 spending this gets you £1.14 worth of points; the marketing then extols using a Barclaycard to pay, earning more points – 1 per £2 spend – which means a further 29p worth. Overall this is a total of £1.43 in Nectar points. Yet pay instead with a 1% cashback card and you'd get the same initial £1.14 of Sainsbury's spend points plus £1 in cash on top – much more rewarding.

Actually comparing rewards schemes is excruciatingly difficult. Trust me, I once spent a depressing Christmas fortnight analysing the real value of the 50+ different schemes on the market. (It felt like even if I picked my nose, points would drop out.) The results further bolstered the standing of cashback. The average point scheme returned 69p per £100 spent, and many of these had annual fees, whereas cashback cards averaged 86p per £100 and none had an annual fee. The reason is simple: it's easy to see if you're getting a bad cashback deal, so they don't try it on as much.

Suggested ingredients: the best-paying reward schemes. Reward-card schemes tend not to change too often, but when they do the changes can be substantial. Traditionally the best-paying reward schemes come from companies where the rewards are their own products, as therefore they are actually

Calorie Counter: Reward Credit Cards			
The return on £15,000 a year on various standard credit cards as at 1/12/03			
Card	Scheme	Return per £100	Return on £15,000 spending a year
GM card	Discount of Vauxhall	£3	£450
Circle Rebate/ Blue Amex	Cashback	£1	£150
NatWest	AirMiles (flights, days out, shopping)	£0.47	£70
Barclays	Nectar (flights, days out, shopping)	£0.29	£44
HSBC	No rewards	None	None

only forking out the cost price, not the retail value, plus they get ancillary marketing gains.

For a number of years the GM Visa card has been top of the tree, paying £3 per £100 spent – twice as much as the next best; however, this cash only counts as a discount off a new Vauxhall car bought from a dealership. Well worth it for Vauxhall buyers – pointless (forgive the pun) for anyone else.

The two other consistent players are the Thomas Cook Card, which usually gives around £1.50 per £100 spending off its own holidays, and the BAA Worldcard, where you can get discounts off its parking worth up to £2 per £100 spent on the

---

Money-Diet Quick-Fact Snack: Cut Up Your Charity Affinity Credit Card

No, I'm not Scrooge; by all means give to charity – but for the same effort you can give more by scrapping these cards. Sign up for a charity card and the charity usually receives between £2.50 and £18. After that, most charity cards donate around 0.25 per cent of the purchase value – that's 25p per £100 spent. This is a very small amount, and as technically it's a royalty from the bank, not a donation from an individual, the charity can't reclaim tax through the gift-aid scheme (for full details see 'Crash Diet', page 000).

Instead, use a cashback reward card, paying 1 per cent, and donate this cash to charity and as well as getting more, it gets the tax break. While this takes more discipline, the difference is huge. For £16,000 spending a year (not unreasonable if it replaces debit-card and cash transactions) on a charity card it would receive around £40 including the sign-up fee. Use a 1-per cent cash back card you'll receive £160 cash back; donate this and the charity can reclaim £45 on top, or £105 more if a higher-rate taxpayer donated all their gains. In total, that's £265 rather than £40. Of course, the 'pay in full or be a fool' reward-card rule still applies, so only do this if you pay off your card in full.

card and a free upgrade to first class on the Heathrow and Gatwick Expresses, without even using up your points.

If none of these tickle your fancy, then it has to be cashback, the very best of which pay a 1% return on your spending, or £1 per £100 spent, in cash. AirMiles lovers may gnash teeth at this, but AirMiles cards actually tend to be worth less than 50p per £100 spent – not a bargain. The only thing to watch for with cashback is if you are a very high spender – many cards have maximum cashback limits; it may mean you need two cashback cards to cover a year's spending.

Suggested ingredients: cashback reward cards. Blue American Express; Circle Rebate Card (Capital One); Nationwide Cashback; Halifax Cashback Card; Morgan Stanley Cashback Card; Alliance & Leicester; Abbey Cashback; Accucard; More>Than; Easy Money.

Overseas spending cards

Going abroad doesn't mean taking a holiday from being ripped off. There are tons of hidden charges on credit cards used abroad, in addition to the normal interest charges. Yet, with the right card, plastic is the cheapest method of overseas spending. There are, however, some hidden and unbidden charges:

A hefty 'load' on the exchange rate: card exchange rates are based on the highly competitive Visa or Mastercard wholesale rates. Yet almost all debit and credit cards secretly add a 'load', which makes the exchange rate around 2.75% worse. This 'load' isn't billed as a separate item on your statement, it's smuggled into the exchange rate and just adds to what you pay.

> **Money Diet Quick Fact Snack: Spend on the Card, not With Cash**
>
> The fact that there's this additional cash-withdrawal charge and, potentially, interest means using the card to pay for things abroad is always cheaper than withdrawing cash and spending it. Spend as much as you can on the card, using it to pay for even very small purchases.

They snack when you withdraw cash: withdraw cash when abroad and as well as the 'loading' there is a fee on top. This is usually either 2% or £2, whichever is the higher. On credit cards this fee applies in the UK too, yet most of us never experience this as we use debit cards at home, so we avoid it. However, some debit cards don't work overseas, and those that do usually add the cash-withdrawal fee too. This fee is separate from anything the overseas bank may charge you on top for using their machines, something especially common in the USA.

An 'interesting' addition: there's another danger to credit-card cash withdrawals – those who are usually protected from any interest charges, because they pay off their balance in full each month, may lose this protection when withdrawing cash. Some cards charge interest on cash withdrawals even if you pay off the balance in full – it's another sneaky terms-and-conditions note.

Therefore there are three things to ask credit- and debit-card providers before going overseas:

- What is the foreign-exchange loading? Is it different in Europe compared to the rest of the world?
- What is the cash-withdrawal fee?
- If I withdraw cash on my credit card, and pay off the balance at the end of the month, will you still charge me interest?

The only problem is many card companies' customer service staff mightn't know the answers to these questions, especially to the last one – I've been misanswered a number of times. So get them to check rather than just answer off the top of their heads, and if necessary ask for proof in writing.

Money Diet Quick Fact Snack:
The Cheapest Way To Get Overseas Cash Before You Go

While the right credit card is the best way to spend abroad, it's often useful to have at least enough foreign currency to get you from the airport to your final destination when you travel. This means buying it here. For either Travellers Cheques or foreign currency, beware the over-hyped 'commission-free'. This is pretty much irrelevant; it's the exchange rate that really impacts on the cost. Let me show you by example:

Sneakyboy Travel: Commission-free
Exchange rate: £1 buys 17 Money Diet dollars
Pay £100 and get MD$1,700

Honest Martin's Bureau de Change: Commission charge £1.50
Exchange rate: £1 buys 18 Money Diet dollars
Pay £100 and get £98.50 worth of currency, which at this exchange rate buys MD$1,770

So Honest Martin's pays more even though it charges commission. As exchange rates change daily, there is no hard-and-fast rule of who's cheapest. Ignore all sales pitches and simply ask what you will get for your cash, including all commissions or fees – e.g. 'How many US dollars for £100, after all charges?' **Suggested ingredients.** Post Office; Marks & Spencer; Thomas Cook.

Abroad saving: Some cards reduce their overseas charges and sell themselves based on this. Often there is no loading at all on these cards, making the exchange rate ultra-competitive, and the cash withdrawals are cheaper too. This is very sassy marketing – the aim's to put the card in your pocket when you go abroad, and hope you'll use it all year round in the UK. Money Dieters will realise that isn't the right thing to do – instead just get these cards for use only when you are abroad.

Not only do these cards beat other credit cards, they also usually beat every other holiday cash method. On a day when the exchange rate was €1.42 to the pound, an American Express Bureau de Change charged £735, including commission for €1,000 in Travellers Cheques, while spending the same amount on an overseas specialist credit card cost just £705.

Suggested ingredients. Four cards consistently trumpet their

Calorie Counter: Overseas Spending Card

Spend £1,000 and withdraw £750 worth of overseas currency

Card	Load	Cash withdrawal fee (higher of)	Load on £1,000 worth of Euro spending	Cash withdrawal of £750 worth of Euros (A)			Total cost
				Load	Cash withdrawal fee (A)(B)	A month's interest (if paid off in full)	
Standard card	2.75%	£2.50 or 1.75%	£27.50	£20.60	£19.50	£13 (C)	£80
Specialist overseas card	0%	£1.50 or 1.5%	£0	£0	£13.50	£0	£13

(A) 2 x £200, 2 x £100, 3 x £50 worth of Euros; (B) ignores any overseas bank charge; (C) 17% interest

overseas charges: Liverpool Victoria; Nationwide; Saga, and Lombard Direct. Also current account holders with Nationwide may find its debit card best of all. Yet always check nothing's changed by asking the questions listed on page 306.

Special-use cards

There are further gimmicks and gizmos aplenty, especially from high-street banks, in order to draw attention from their interest rates. Yet there's nothing stopping you buying the goods on the card for the additional bonuses, then paying the debt off in full or transferring it to another, cheaper card.

Purchase protection. Buy goods on the card and if they're lost, stolen or accidentally damaged within a set number of days, you get a refund. It's very useful for higher-value goods that aren't covered on household policies.
Suggested ingredients. Nationwide; Barclaycard; Halifax; Saga; Virgin; Tesco (about 30% of cards offer this).

Extended warranties. Salespeople often push expensive extended warranties for white goods or electronic goods. Yet while warranty prices are high, the chances of breakdown are low, and the repair costs not too expensive. All in all, buying warranties is rarely worth it. However, some cards offer a free second year's warranty providing breakdown cover if you pay for goods on the card – worth taking advantage of.
Suggested ingredients. Barclaycard; NatWest; HSBC.

Travel insurance cards

Buy travel tickets on some cards and there's free insurance. This cover is rarely adequate, apart from on some Platinum

> **Money Diet Quick Fact Snack: Black is the New Gold**
>
> The only card colour that makes a difference is black. Many people like the prestige of a Gold or Platinum, so they're now used as a sales technique, but it means nothing. Capital One's minimum-earning threshold for a Platinum card is just £10,000 a year – not much above full-time earnings at minimum wage. Black, however, still has cachet. Yet cachet doesn't pay the bills – focus on the cost not the colour; after all, with annual fees of £250 plus, and interest rates that aren't noticeably better, it'd need to provide some serious add-on benefits, and you'd need to take full advantage of them, to be worth shelling out that amount.

cards. Don't confuse travel insurance with travel accident insurance, which is free on most cards but only pays out in the event of an accident while actually on a plane, train, bus or car trip. Also note, most free travel insurance from credit cards requires the entire package to be bought on the card: pay for just the deposit, or just the remainder, and you won't be covered.

Suggested ingredients. Travel accident insurance: over 50% of available cards (not really worth focusing on it). Travel insurance: Tesco; American Express; MBNA; NatWest; Lloyds TSB.

Price promise cards

Buy goods on the card and find them cheaper anywhere else within a set amount of time, and a price promise card will refund the difference. The service should be free, but occasionally it will cost a fee. Usually the goods must be specifically branded and proof of price reduction is always required – a retailer's flyer, internet page, or note signed on the retailer's paper should do. These cards can be used to play a special trick to get Christmas presents at January sales prices (see 'Unlucky for Them, Lucky for Us ...', page 143).

Suggested ingredients. Barclaycard; Royal Bank of Scotland cards.

POTENTIAL PLAYERS:
FREE CASH – BE THE ULTIMATE TART

I started explaining this technique in the year 2000, when the first 0% balance transfers started. Since then, coupled with other ad-hoc credit-card cash tricks, I estimate I've made over £1,600 in pure profit from my plastic. Others have gained too. My favourite e-mail came a year after I wrote about this technique in my *Sunday Express* column. It went something like this: 'When we first read about Free Cash, we didn't think it would really work, but gave it a go anyway. We've spent our lives being skint, but we've made about £400 each since and are taking our five- and seven-year-olds on holiday for the first time in their lives. Thank you.'

Though it's not difficult, Free Cash isn't for the forgetful – it requires care and attention. If you've any doubts, don't do it, as play it badly and you'll pay. Also if you've any other credit-card debts, forget it; concentrate on minimising their interest costs. As this isn't for beginners I'm assuming you've read the rest of the credit-card section before reading this. For those ready to take credit-card companies for every penny, this is how.

The Basic Premise

Credit-card 0% offers mean they lend you money for free. Save that money at the highest interest rate possible to earn on it, plus get cashback too if possible.

Step 1: Game

To start you need to max out your new special offer 0% card and get that money in your current account. There are two routes.

- ■ *Balance-transfer bonanza.* A number of credit cards, such as Egg and Abbey, allow 'super balance transfers' (see page 297), allowing you to move money directly into your bank account. Providing this is at 0%, game on. Get it to pay the maximum amount into your current account (fees can be charged for balance transfers, so first check this doesn't apply). You can also do this using the special cheques many other credit cards offer – but then there's sometimes a 1.5% fee, which squashes much of the gain.

- ■ *Alternative: The purchasing prizes method.* Use a 0%-for-purchases card for all spending, instead of debit cards, other credit cards and cash transactions, but only make the monthly minimum repayments. This leaves your wages unspent, allowing the equivalent amount to build up in your current account. (Warning: this requires self-discipline. Seeing the money build up is very tempting, but it isn't the same as real money, it's just that the debt is elsewhere – don't spend it.)

  Cashback bonus. A few cards offer cashback on spending (see page 305) and 0% interest. If you're using this method, you'll be paid cashback too.

Step 2: Set

Overall now the extra cash in your current account should match the 0% debts on the card. Move the cash into the highest-interest *safe* easy-access savings you can find – either a mini cash ISA (see page 160) or a savings account (see page 156).

> **Money Diet Quick Fact Snack: Make Even More With an Offset Mortgage**
>
> Those with mortgages or loans allowing the use of savings to offset their costs should instead put the money in there (providing you can access these savings instantly) for even more gain – as the 0% money will be temporarily paying off your mortgage (see page 267).

Then you'll earn interest on it while the credit card charges you nothing. However, remember you still need to meet the minimum repayments on the credit card, so the debt will lessen gradually (use a direct debit to ensure it's always paid).

- ■ *Purchases prizes method note:* As the money will be dripping gradually into your current account, rather than wait for the whole lot to build, move it into your savings account as and when.

Step 3: Match

You can bag the free cash after your card's 0% period ends. However, to keep earning, shift the debt on to a new card using an interest-free balance transfer offer and leave the cash in the highest-interest savings account. It's also possible to build more 0% debt at the same time by starting again, using more cards. Some high-credit scorers claim to have had up to £40,000 worth of 0% debts at any one time – but always ensure ready access to the same amount of cash to pay it off.

> **Martin's Money Memories: All Your Baskets in One Egg**
>
> At one time internet bank Egg paid the highest credit-card cashback at 0% interest, whilst also offering the highest-paying savings account. This meant it lent me money for free, and then paid me 6% on it. Poetry.

Calorie counter: free cash

Ready Reckoner: Roughly How Much Free Cash You Can Make per Year			
The amount of interest-free debt			
Savings rate (after tax)	£1,000	£5,000	£12,000	£30,000
3%	£30	£150	£360	£900
5%	£50	£250	£600	£1,500
7%	£70	£350	£840	£2,100

Suggested ingredients. Egg; Morgan Stanley; Tesco; Mint; Nationwide; MBNA; Abbey; Alliance & Leicester.

THE CREDIT SURVIVAL TECHNIQUE: WHAT TO DO IF YOU CAN'T GET ANY NEW CARDS

All the 'precision plastic' tricks and potential profits are stymied for those with a low income, or less than perfect credit history. Funny how lenders like to give money to those who already have it …

Yet, as long as you can cover the minimum repayments, I've got a system that will cut your interest charges and repay your debts more quickly.

It's worth pausing for a second before that, though. Good financial health is precious: take a moment to consider that you're surviving, but what would happen if you didn't? Do the Financial Blitz (page 7), work through the Money Diet Monthly Calorie Counter (page 33) and read 'Food Poisoning' (page 335) too, as there's advice there that's relevant. And even once we've reduced the amount of interest you pay, don't let it become an excuse for borrowing more.

The credit card shuffle: slip, slide, shuffle and groove
This is my four-step interest-reduction dance. Don't confuse 'shuffling' with 'switching' – the key to the shuffle is moving money around between existing, not new, debts. The shuffle is a Money Diet workout – cue flared trousers and gyrating hips.

First, a Simple Question

Do you have more than one credit card?
- ◼ If YES: use Steps 1, 2, 3 and 4.
- ◼ If NO, but you have an overdraft facility: use Steps 1, 3 and 4.
- ◼ If NO, and no overdraft facility: use Steps 1 and 4.

Note: Don't give up at any point – Step 4 can work even if 1, 2 and 3 aren't possible.

Step 1: the Slip

Slime up to your provider and ask it to cut the rate
Call your current credit- and store-card providers and ask if they will *slip* your interest rate down. Some providers have automatic 'interest-rate-matching policies', so if you've other cards at cheaper rates, they will match it. Even without any of that, it's truly silly but simply asking can work, and intimating

---

Money Diet Safety Disclaimer: The Credit Card Shuffle

The Shuffle is designed to save you money, not make you look cool at a nightclub. The author and publishers take no responsibility whatsoever for embarrassment or injuries caused by trying to actually shimmy to the Shuffle.

---

you're thinking of shifting to another card works even better. Be confident, be polite, be charming and try to think of a reason your rate should be cheaper. It's amazing what deals customer service reps have the power to authorise.

Step 2: the Slide

Can the debt be moved?

It used to be that all special balance-transfer offers (for an explanation of the term, see page 296) were for new cardholders, whereas existing cardholders were just offered the card's standard rate. Yet momentum is changing, and existing-customer deals are springing up, as providers are scared of

Official Balance Transfer Rates for Existing Customers (Sept 2003)	
Card	Existing customer balance transfer rate
Abbey	Offer rate decided on individual circumstance
Alliance & Leicester	Offer rate decided on individual circumstance
American Express Blue	9.9% life of balance
Barclaycard	6.9% life of balance
Cahoot	Standard 8% rate
Egg	5.9% for five months for some customers
HSBC	3.9% over short term
Lloyds TSB	5.9% life of balance (on main card/targeted offers on others)
MBNA	Offer rate decided on individual circumstance
NatWest	No fixed policy, but targeted offers available
Mint	No fixed policy, but targeted offers available
RBS Advanta	No fixed policy, but targeted offers available
RBS	No fixed policy, but targeted offers available
Tesco Standard	14.9% only

continually losing customers. Barclaycard started this – unsurprising, it's the biggest card so it has most customers to lose – and others are catching on. Existing customer deals aren't as good as new customer offers, but are much better than most cards' standard interest rates. So call your provider and ask it the following questions to see if you can *slide* any debts over.

- If I transfer a balance from another card, what rate will you charge me?
- What is the maximum debt I can have on this card? (In other words, the credit limit.)
- Will you increase my credit limit? (Provides more flexibility for the shuffle.)

The table opposite indicates the types of offer available; they will change, but shouldn't move too substantially.

Step 3: the Shuffle

Move the debts

Now you've minimised all current interest rates and discovered at what rates transfers are available, *shuffle* the debts, using balance transfers. The aim is to fill up the credit limits on the cards charging the least interest. Even if no special rates were offered, you should still be able to shift the money to the cheapest standard-rate card.

Those with just one credit card, and an overdraft facility, should compare their rates. If the overdraft rate is more expensive, spend on the credit card instead of from your bank account, releasing the pressure on the overdraft, and allowing your earnings to pay it back. Effectively this moves the debt to the cheaper rate on the credit card. If the overdraft is cheaper, then simply pay as much as you can off the credit card.

Credit Card Shuffle: A Possible Complication and a Possible Solution

A problem arises if a card offers a cheaper rate for balance transfers to it than the existing debts on it. This adds an expense due to the way the card companies allocate repayments (see page 299 for an explanation). It's still better to do it than not – but there is a way round it. It may sound silly, but first shift the debt onto another card, and then move it back, effectively converting the 'purchase debts' to 'balance-transfer debts'. If the credit limits don't allow it, shift as much of the debt as is possible. An example should help:

Justin Case has two credit cards:

Card 1: Obey Notional Misercard
Standard rate: 17.9%; balance: £700; credit limit: £3,000.
Balance-transfer rate: 9.9% until all the debt transferred is paid off.

Card 2: Critical Two Weasel card
Standard rate: 16.9%; balance: £1,200; credit limit: £2,000.
Balance-transfer rate: the standard 16.9%.

The Obvious Method

Simply transfer the Critical Two balance to the Misercard.
Total debt: £700 at 17.9% and £1,200 at 9.9%.

The bank will automatically allocate the repayments to the cheap debt, meaning the 17.9% debt isn't paid off until the £1,200 is cleared. It's a saving, but more is possible.

Money Diet Method

First transfer the Misercard debt onto the Critical Two card.
Situation: £1,900 debt now at 16.9%.

Then, once the debt is definitely on that account (call and check), transfer all the debt back to the Misercard.

Situation: £1,900 debt, all at the 9.9% rate

One note of caution here: usually there shouldn't be any problem doing this but, very occasionally, providers may spot what you're doing and kibosh the transfer back.

Step 4: Get Into the Groove

Focus your repayments

At this point you have the lowest interest rates possible. The final step is to focus repayments to pay off the most expensive debts first. To do this, pay the minimum repayments on all debts, except the most expensive. Throw all the cash you can at paying that off. As soon as it is paid off, shift focus to the next highest-rate debts and continue until all debts are repaid. This will reduce the interest cost, even if the other steps above aren't available. If you have an overdraft, check its rate, too – if it's the highest rate, make sure it is paid off first.

One final trick: even with minimum payments you will gradually pay some debts off the cheapest cards. Every six months or so, do balance transfers again to move debts from the most expensive card to fill up the credit limit on the cheapest.

Calorie Counter: Doing the Shuffle – a Real-life Example

A friend with some debt worries came to talk to me last August. She had a range of cards and had been turned down for new credit. After having done a budget with her (and, trust me, that makes her seriously brave – I'm tough) we managed to squeeze £300 a month out to pay off the debts. As she was worried about dancing alone, I decided to partner up and Shuffle with her. At the start her debts looked like this:

Initial Situation				
	Debt	Rate	Credit limit	The potential interest cost if cards repaid in full with £300/month payments
Barclaycard	£2,500	17.9%	£3,500	£545
Tesco Card	£1,750	14.9%	£4,500	£220
Debenhams Store Card	£1,750	29.9%	£2,000	£485
TOTAL	£6,000	18.7%	N/A	£1,250

The average interest rate was 18.7% and with the £300/month it'd cost her £1,250 in interest to pay them all off.

What we did. Barclaycard was willing to slip down her interest rate to match Tesco's, but this turned out to be irrelevant, as it also offered a 6.9% balance transfer for existing customers with the rate lasting until the entire debt was paid off.

The first thing we did was move all the debt off Barclaycard to the other cards, so it was empty. This enabled us to move all the debts back onto the card at the transfer rate, rather than the spending rate. After Barclaycard was filled up, the rest went to Tesco, at its standard rate. This left the hideously expensive store card paid off. To finish, my friend started focusing on repaying the costlier Tesco debt, with only the minimum going to the cheaper Barclaycard.

Post Shuffle Situation				
	Debt	Rate	Interest (prioritising expensive debts)	Saving
Barclaycard	£3,500	6.9%	£325	£220
Tesco Card	£2,500	14.9%	£200	£20
Debenhams Store Card	£0	29.9%	£0	£485
TOTAL	£6,000	9.0%	£525	£725

The result. Overall, the interest to be paid until the time the cards are paid off was reduced from £1,250 to £525, more than a 60% saving. And remember, there were no new cards here; just using the ones she had, but more efficiently.

four

MORE SNACKS

PUKKA PERSONAL LOANS

For a simple product, there are more fences to leap than the Grand National. However, get it right and loans are an effective way to borrow. This chapter also includes a sneaky way to beat even the cheapest loan on the market, by 'perverting your plastic'. Newspapers may shriek 'UK in debt crisis', but for most households it isn't debt itself but its punitively high interest that's the crisis. Yet, get a loan the right way and it is possible to cut the cost by over 70%.

BACK TO BASICS

Traditionally personal loans are the way to borrow between £1,000 and £25,000. They give you cash, you spend it on whatever you want, and repay a fixed amount off each month for a set term. The rate of interest agreed at the loan's start is fixed, which is useful when certainty counts. So for a lump sum for a car, kitchen or even holiday, loans are a reasonably convenient way to do it.

Like credit cards, most personal loans are 'unsecured',

which is good. Unfortunately while loans should be simple, there are a range of hurdles to leap over. However, don't be too worried – read on and you can outjump Colin Jackson. Before getting into the nitty-gritty, I want to ask you three questions:

1. Do you really need to borrow money? Loans are a long-term commitment – you should consider whether you can afford it, and if you are sure you'll always be able to repay.

2. Do you have access to other borrowing that may be cheaper? If you have credit cards, overdraft facilities and a mortgage, then it's likely you already have access to substantial amounts of borrowing. Don't simply plump for a loan because you need a lump sum. Follow the explanations in the rest of this section to see what's cheaper, plus see my half-price plastic personal loan technique (page 330).

3. Will they loan you the money? As with credit cards, your credit history impacts on your ability to borrow. It's necessary to work out whether you're a Potential Player, Credit Survivor or in Debt Crisis (see page 288). Potential Players should just read on. Credit Survivors shouldn't really be borrowing more, but a loan at a decent rate may be slightly easier to get than a credit card, so it can be a good way to reduce your existing debt's interest rate. Focusing on mainstream rather than cutting-edge lenders makes this more likely. Also, if you can't get loans the standard way, check out if you have a local Credit Union, a small community-run organisation that may be able to help. Those in debt crisis shouldn't be considering further debts, and should turn straight to page 335.

PERSONAL LOAN E NUMBERS – WHAT TO AVOID

Lenders have an arsenal of weapons to shoot up the price of personal loans and, rather obviously, the best way to get a cheap one is to avoid them. To push the Diet theme probably slightly further than I should, they're a bit like E numbers. They may look good, may even help the taste, but can seriously damage your wealth over the long run.

E101: Insurance Costs

This is the big one – it can cost thousands. Loans are advertised based on the APR – the standard measure of interest. The lower the APR, the cheaper the loan. But (and this is a but so big even Jennifer Lopez would be impressed) this is only for loans WITHOUT Payment Protection Insurance (PPI).

PPI covers repayments if you have an accident, get sick or are made redundant, and can cost thousands. Yet it is *never* included in the APR. This shouldn't happen. The law says insurance costs should only be included in the APR if the loan cost is compulsory. Lenders therefore almost never make PPI compulsory, they just push it heavily. In fact, many lenders treat it as a default setting; in other words, unless you specify you *don't* want it, you'll get it. All this is so they can advertise cheaper loans, and make most of their profits on expensive insurance policies. PPI is also damn difficult to cancel.

This doesn't mean PPI is bad – just be careful, and read my sneaky way to slash its cost in 'The Crash Diet', page 215.

Martin's Money Memories:
I Almost Paid £550 a Minute to Hear a Sexy Voice

Sorry to disappoint; I'm not about to confess to a skeleton in my closet. This is still about PPI. I once called Northern Rock Bank's call centre to test how it sells insurance. A lovely woman answered. She was polite and charming with a voice so husky it'd make Benson & Hedges proud.

Martin: 'I'd like a loan, please. I want to borrow £10,000 over five years.'

Sexy Northern Rock Woman: 'Certainly, Mr Lewis. No problem. It's £248 a month.'

Forearmed with Northern Rock's prices, I knew this was the 'with insurance cost', though neither I nor the nice woman had mentioned PPI. As a good honest chappy I thought it best to clarify.

Martin: 'Does that include insurance?'

SNRW: 'Yes, you're fully covered with this loan.'

Martin: 'Do I need the insurance?'

SNRW: 'We wouldn't advocate you not to get it; it's advisable you do. But obviously the choice is yours.'

In the midst of this five minutes of huskiness is a teeny-weeny financial fact. She had automatically quoted a with-insurance loan. I was prepared, but how many people can work out in their head in under five seconds the cost per month of 8% interest applied to a decreasing £10,000 loan balance over five years? Frankly, even with a spreadsheet it isn't easy.

Plus, she never asked whether I was self-employed, or other issues which potentially devalue the insurance. It was just automatically added. It would've been easy to sign for the loan, which had the cheapest advertised APR, thinking it a good deal, without realising about the extra for insurance. And don't think that this is small change; the insurance cost £2,700 over the term – substantially more than the interest cost.

E102: Penalties for Paying Off the Loan Early

Loans have redemption penalties. Did you know? Pay a loan off early and most lenders usually add a couple of months' worth of interest, but you tend only to find out when you try it. If there's any chance you may want to repay before the term ends, always check, and go for the few that don't.

E103: the Rule of 78

This is truly devious. Let's just admire lenders for their chutzpah. They claim the 'Rule of 78' makes loans fairer. Actually,

---

Martin's Money Memories: Virgin on the Ridiculous

I'm not a fan of many of Virgin's money products. Almost all are launched in a blaze of publicity, and claims of originality, but often underneath its consumer-friendly claims are ordinary products often at rates that don't unduly worry the best-buy tables.

When Virgin joined the loans market its press release headlined it'd take on 'hidden-charge sharks'. It argued most loans had hidden costs to paying off early and its loans didn't have redemption penalties.

Normally I'd ignore a new loan launch with far from competitive interest rates. Yet this whiter-than-white spin made many newspaper articles, so I took a peek. This loan used the Rule of 78.

I know it's sad, but it genuinely made me angry. The Ro78 is the most secretive of loan charges, yet Virgin claimed its loan could be repaid without any early repayment penalties.

Just look at the impact.

Borrow £10,000 at its then 9.7% rate and repay after 1 year.

Using Rule of 78 calculations: total interest paid £975.

Without Rule of 78 calculations: total interest paid £880.

A £95 hidden charge that supposedly didn't exist. Virgin on the ridiculous.

Money Diet Quick Fact Snack: Doing the Maths on the Rule of 78

WARNING: This isn't 'need to know'. For nerds only.

Calculate the interest. Work out the total amount of interest payable over the life of the loan by taking the amount borrowed away from the total cost (for non-insured loans).

Assign each month its reverse number. Take the number of months and assign this in reverse order to each month you're due to pay off (e.g. over two years, the first month is month 24, the second month 23, the third month 22, etc.).

Calculate interest in proportion. The amount of interest assigned per month is worked out by dividing that number (e.g. for the fourth month over two years it's 21) by the total of all these numbers (i.e. 24+23+22+21 ...+3+2+1 = 300). So, in this example 21/300th of the total amount of interest. Told you it was complicated.

P.S. It's called the Rule of 78 because the total of all the months (1+2+3 ... up to 12) in one year adds up to 78.

---

it's a further redemption penalty by another name. The government has announced it is looking to ban it, possibly as early as autumn 2004.

The Ro78 is a hideously complicated hidden formula, which means early repayments are artificially allocated towards repaying the interest, not the capital. Basically, pay the loan off early and any prior repayments won't have made much of a dent, leaving more to repay than you'd think. This can make paying a loan off in the first year or two much more expensive, so if that's likely, find a non-Ro78 loan; in fact a flexible loan's probably best (see below).

E104: Bizarre Tiers

As a general rule with personal loans, the more you borrow, the lower the interest rate. Most banks set their tiers at standard rates. For example:

- £1,000 to £4,999 – 11.9%
- £5,000 to £9,999 – 8.9%
- Above £10,000 – 7.9%

However, a couple of lenders deliberately set theirs in bizarre places. For example:

- £1,000 to £5,050 – 12.9%
- £5,051 to £10,050 – 8.9%
- Above £10,051 – 7.9%

Most people borrow rounded amounts for loans. Yet in the above example it would be substantially cheaper in total to borrow £5,060 than it would to borrow £5,000. Keep an eye out.

E105: It's Not Just the Size, But How Long it is

Remember, the loan term plays a part in the cost. The longer you borrow for, the higher the total cost you pay, as the interest stacks up for longer.

Questions When Buying A Loan

Now you know the tricks, and have decided whether to get PPI or not, ask prospective lenders:

- How much will I have to repay in total over the life of the loan?
- Does it have redemption penalties?
- Does it use the Rule of 78?

Simple as that!

Money Diet Quick Fact Snack: Flexible Personal Loans

Based on the flexible mortgage system, the idea is you have a borrowing facility where you define the amount repaid. There are three tenets.

Overpay: pay the loan more quickly without any penalties at all.

Underpay: pay less than the recommended amount, within set limits.

Borrow-back: borrow back some of the money repaid, within set amounts, if you need more.

Interest and PPI are only paid on the outstanding amount. Flexible loans can be a great deal for people with uncertain finances. The rates tend to be good, but a little higher than the cheapest standard loans. The only real negative is that the interest rate usually isn't fixed, so the lender reserves the right to increase it, something you're protected from with a normal loan.

Flexibility can also be achieved using 'offset' loans. Here you have a loan linked to a savings account, so they balance each other out, and you only pay interest on the total amount you're in debt.

Suggested ingredients. *Full flexibility:* Cahoot. *Partial flexibility:* Intelligent Finance; Egg.

Suggested ingredients: no-insurance loans. Northern Rock; Liverpool Victoria; Sainsbury; Tesco; Lombard Direct; Cahoot; Nationwide; Halifax.

Suggested ingredients: with-insurance loans. Intelligent Finance; Nationwide; Cahoot (and try the cheapest 'no-insurance loans' as well).

Suggested ingredients: loans you may redeem early. Egg; Intelligent Finance; Cahoot.

Calorie Counter

Borrow £7,500 without insurance over five years with a typical high-street branch loan at 15.2% and the total repayment is £10,530 – that's interest of £3,030. Use instead a provider with a cheap rate, usually around 6%, and the total is £8,735, of which £1,235 is interest – substantially less than a third of the cost.

Yet it all changes with PPI loans. Here the cheap APR advertiser charges £10,790 in total, but loans that offer cheap insurance can undercut this even with a higher APR. In the example below (real costs at the time of writing) it's another £730 cheaper due to its much less expensive insurance. (Also see 'Loan Insurance', page 215.)

£7,500 over five years	Rate	No Insurance		With Insurance		
		Monthly payments	Total cost	Monthly payment	Total cost	Unnecessary cost
Branch loan	15.2%	£175.45	£10,530	£218.80	£13,130	£3,070
Cheap insurance loan	8.3%	£152.37	£9,140	**£167.60**	**£10,060**	**None**
Cheap APR advertiser	6.3%	**£145.58**	**£8,735**	£179.79	£10,790	£730

HALF-PRICE PLASTIC PERSONAL LOAN OR OVERDRAFT

This is where loans get sexy – well, for me, anyway. It is possible to massively undercut even the cheapest loans on the market by perverting your credit cards. This isn't a technique for beginners. It needs an understanding of the way credit cards work. Read the Credit Card chapter (page 283) first, focusing especially on balance transfers, to provide the building blocks.

The Premise

The cheapest credit-card balance-transfer offers undercut the cheapest loans. Therefore use them to replicate a loan.

There are two types of balance-transfer offer to choose from:

The ultimate: Moving debt around from 0% card to 0% card via repeated balance transfers is always cheapest. Yet, especially for longer-term borrowing – three years plus – there's a risk you'll forget or credit-scoring issues will deny continued access to such terms.

Cheap and safe: Life-of-balance transfers are actually very similar to loans, as the rate is fixed at the outset. The cheapest are usually 4.9% (or 2.9% if you're lucky) – much better than loan rates. For all but ultra-toned Money Dieters I'd plump for this method. And my explanation below assumes you have.

How to Pervert Your Plastic

To create your own bespoke personal loan, apply for as high a credit limit as possible on the new 'life of balance card' then, if it's approved, you're ready to start. I'm assuming you already have an existing credit card; if not, then you'll need to apply for a standard card as well.

To consolidate existing credit card debts. Simply transfer the balances directly to the new card.

To make a big one-off purchase. Pay for it with your existing card and immediately transfer the debt to the new card.

331

To make a range of cash purchases or to cut the cost of existing personal loans or overdrafts. The cheapest option is via an existing 'Super Balance Transfer' card (see page 297) so you can pay the cash straight into your current account. If that isn't possible, some credit cards offer cheques, usually at a charge of 1.5% (even with this it should still work). Write one of these to pay into your bank account. Then simply transfer this card's debt to the life-of-balance card. (Those paying off existing loans should read the next section, page 333.)

As soon as this debt appears (speed is important, as some cards charge interest on balance transfers for every day they're in your account; don't wait for the statement), transfer it straight across to the life-of-balance transfer card. The only exception is where the debt is on an intro 0% offer. However, most life-of-balance cards put a time limit on when you can make the transfer – e.g. not beyond six months after getting the card – so ensure you don't miss out.

Watch Out

Even at 4.9% life of balance, be careful. Never use it for spending – do that and the lender biases your repayments towards paying off the cheap debts first (see page 299). So, simply transfer the balance, then stick this card in a drawer.

To Truly Replicate a Loan

Repay a fixed amount each month; this pays the debt off much more quickly than sticking to the minimum. Credit cards are more flexible than loans, so you can also pay off more if you choose. Yet always keep repaying the loan; if you just choose to make the minimum repayments you'll end up paying a stack more interest due to the extra time it takes.

CALORIE COUNTER

£5,000 loan repaying £150/month	Interest rate	Months to repay	Total interest	Saving
Standard branch loan*	15.9%	44	£1,630	N/A
Cheapest standard loan*	6.8%	37	£560	£1,070
Life-of-balance transfer loan system	4.9%	36	£380	£1,250
0% rotating transfer loan system	0% then 0%	34	£0	£1,630

*No PPI

WHAT IF I ALREADY HAVE AN EXPENSIVE LOAN?

Prior to the Money Diet you may have signed up for an expensive personal or car loan. Now we need to cut the cost. Unfortunately, it isn't as simple as just moving to a cheaper loan. Two things may make it more expensive than you think.

Redemption penalties: pay loans off early and you can be fined (see page 326). This is worse if you have payment protection insurance (PPI) as you may need to repay the whole policy.

The Rule of 78: again, repay early and this calculation method adds to your cost (see page 326).

Can You Save by Switching?

Most people will be able to save by switching, but sums need doing. First find out the following information – just call your existing lender and ask.

1. How much, including penalties, will it cost me to repay the loan in full? Answer equals REPAY amount (e.g. £3,200).

2. If I stick with this loan, how many repayments do I have left and how much are they? Multiply the number of payments by the repayment amount and you get the KEEP PAYING total, (e.g. 32 months at £125 per month = £4,000).

If you're switching to another personal loan

Ask the new lender how much is the total cost to borrow the REPAY amount over the same number of months as the existing loan. (Or even pay it off sooner if you can afford to.) The answer is the NEW LOAN amount (e.g. 'How much will it cost me to borrow £3,200 over 32 months? Answer: £3,600).

Now, quite simply, if the NEW LOAN amount is less than the KEEP PAYING amount, it is worth switching (e.g., in this example you'd be £400 better off).

If you're switching to a half-price plastic personal loan

The calculation is the same, except it's more difficult to work out the NEW LOAN amount, as credit-card providers don't give this type of quote. If you're not a spreadsheet junkie, but have access to the internet, then use a loan-calculator (or Nationwide has a credit card calculator), plug in the interest rate and the amount you think you can repay; this should give you the NEW LOAN cost.

If not, the only other route is to call up the cheapest personal loan you can and ask for a quote. As the credit-card interest rate will be lower than this (or you wouldn't be doing it), if it's worth switching in the case of a personal loan, it'll be even more worth doing with the cheaper credit-card rate.

five

FOOD POISONING
DEBT CRISIS – WHAT TO DO

THERE'S ALWAYS A SOLUTION
NO MATTER HOW BAD THE DEBT

Debt Crisis isn't a title to inspire confidence. However, no debt
problem is insolvable. There's always a way back. Debt crisis
has many causes – radical financial change such as losing a job,
illness, divorce or death; an inability to plan; a tendency to
overspend, and many more. Frankly, at this point I don't care
how you did it, let's just work out how we get you out of there.

First, remember debt isn't isolated from your other
finances. So use the rest of the Money Diet to minimise your
costs. If you've crippling debt, don't just follow my 'cut bills
without cutting back' advice, though, it's time to cut back!
(See Financial Fitness, page 27.)

ARE YOU REALLY IN DEBT CRISIS?

Let me repeat my definition of debt crisis. If you have debts
and you cannot meet the minimum repayments, this is a

crisis, even if it's only in the short term. Yet, anyone who spends more than they can afford is moving towards crisis and should consider taking stock and starting to act.

A common mistake is to think that missing a few months' payments isn't a big deal. It is – and the reason's simple: it can start a debt spiral.

A debt spiral. Miss payments and your credit score descends more quickly than Homer Simpson on a doughnut. Late-payment fines may be added, more interest piles up, on both the original debt and on the fines, and you owe substantially more. Then, even if the 'short-term bad time' ends, the debts are now much bigger, and you can't reduce the cost using new cheaper debts due to your now reduced credit score.

This isn't a scare story, but a call to action. If you can't meet your payments, sort things out. Right now. Today. The sooner it's done, the less serious it will be – and the quicker it'll be over. Some people wait years before dealing with their debts – by then the action needed is drastic and their ability to play the system is severely restricted.

WHAT TO DO
If it's Only Just Happening

If you think you're going to be unable to meet your minimum payments soon, then you may not yet have damaged your credit score. In that case, you may still be a 'Potential Player' and able to minimise the interest costs by shifting the debt, and by reducing expenditure using the Money Diet, forestalling the debt crisis before it happens. See pages 54 and 69.

If You're in the Quagmire

It's a two-step process.

Step 1: Do the money diet 'financial blitz'

Reduce all your expenditure to the minimum as soon as possible. Cut back on all non-essential spending and see how far this takes you towards being able to meet your requirements.

Step 2: Go and see a debt counsellor

This really is very important. I'm not talking about any of those companies that advertise on the TV, promising to consolidate your loans and fix your credit, no matter how glamorous the celeb promoting them. They can be hideously expensive, damage your credit score and leave you locked into unnecessary debt for years (see 'Debt Consolidation Companies', page 339). Instead, a number of free debt-counselling charities or non-profit agencies will give you detailed personal one-on-one advice on what to do.

The four I'd plump for are:
- The Consumer Credit Counselling Service.
- Citizens Advice Bureaus.
- The Federation of Independent Advice Centres.
- National Debtline.

All are completely free. They all operate in slightly different ways, so there is nothing wrong with trying more than one of them to see which you prefer. There are also a good range of local agencies who may be able to help – just ensure they're genuine advice centres and provide free, unbiased advice.

Now you may be asking, 'Hold on, isn't he going to tell me

Money Diet Quick Fact Snack: Debt-Consolidation Companies

These are the most palatable of the companies looking to profit out of debt crisis. They advertise for homeowners to loan to, and offer to pay off all your other loans, so you owe them one easy, simple, low monthly payment. Let's examine just what this means:

Homeowners: These companies are actually giving you a 'secured' loan, so if you can't pay up they can make a claim on your home. In effect this is what a mortgage is, yet these companies may charge two or three times the mortgage rate. Why not first see if you can remortgage (see page 255) at their cheaper rate.

Consolidation: 'One nice, easy monthly payment.' This is a nice sell; it makes the whole thing seem harmless. Yet there is no benefit purely from having all your money in one place. You only benefit if the interest rate is reduced – yet often they don't mention their interest rates because they can be more expensive than other forms of lending. Five loans with cheap interest is better than one loan with high interest. Don't buy this spiel.

Low monthly payment: Though attractive, because you can meet the repayments, be aware of the consequence. The loan is usually spread over a much, much longer time than your current debts. It may mean paying it off for 10 or 20 or 30 years and therefore thousands of pounds in extra interest. Again, compare this to the cost of putting the money on a mortgage.

More available for a holiday: This makes me want to growl. It's unfair temptation. They're trying to get you to borrow even more. Of course, if you're in debt crisis the idea of a holiday to get away and forget it all seems wonderful – but doing it with their money will cost you for years.

Re-encouragement to spend: These companies tend not to do a budget. That's dangerous: you're often in crisis because you've overspent. Budgets are crucial. And please remember, even if they clear your credit cards, don't use them again. It'll get worse.

Lock-in penalties: No, you didn't hear this in the advert, because it tends not to be mentioned. Some of these companies will lock you into the loan, with big penalties for repaying early, so you're stuck with them, and stuck paying interest year after year after year. Plus these penalties are on a secured loan and may mean even if you just want to move house, you have to pay a large Rule of 78 penalty (see page 326).

---

what to do here? Isn't that what the Money Diet's about?' In this case, no, I'm not. And there's a simple reason. These folks are good, free, one-on-one advisers who will help you. They are not in it to make money out of you, they're just there to help you out of a problem. And if I'm really honest, they're better than me at it. I'm a Money Saving Expert, a system player, yet those in debt crisis move outside the system, it's different. Debt crisis is tricky and can be complicated. There's nothing wrong with getting help. I'm a huge fan. Don't wait until you are in debt crisis; see them in conjunction with doing the Money Diet if it looks like you are going to have problems.

They aim not to be judgemental. They will help prioritise your expenditure. Often people assume that banks, doorstep loan collectors or credit cards are the first people you should pay. Actually you should focus on keeping the heat and electricity on, a roof over your head and food on the table.

On occasion debt-counselling services will negotiate with lenders for you. This may involve freezing your interest, making agreements to pay the debt sooner or just buying you a bit of time and space. The dreaded terms 'Individual Voluntary Arrangements' and 'bankruptcy' may be mentioned. Actually they're not so bad in reality. Going bankrupt stops anyone else demanding money and closes off any routes creditors have. The worst debt e-mail I've ever received was a man who had £260,000 on credit cards and a salary of under £30,000. I don't understand how he was lent so much, but I directed him to the free debt counsellors. He was advised to go bankrupt. He did. A while later he got back in touch – his life wasn't brilliant, but the pressure was off his shoulders and he was sleeping for the first time in years. It ain't no bed of roses, but I'd still call it a solution.

What Not to Do

Don't go to debt-consolidation agencies, debt-management companies, credit-repair companies, door-to-door lenders, loan sharks, cheque-cashing companies or any of the other businesses who prey on people in crisis. They may promise no-nonsense easy cash solutions, but in the long run you'll pay, and in the worst case you will have people knocking on your door, not taking no for an answer.

If you're already involved with such companies, still see the free debt-counselling agencies and get some advice. They may be able to extricate you, or at least help balance the payments.

Martin's Money Memories: Unedited: Their Words, Not Mine

Debt can be more than a financial crisis – it can be very dark. Let me be honest, I've never been in debt crisis. I don't know what it feels like. Yet I'm often asked for help by people who are. The following 'memory' is something I thought long and hard about before putting in. I hope I've done the right thing. I hope if you're in debt trouble it'll encourage you to talk to someone about it.

One day, a woman posted in the chat section of my website, www.moneysavingexpert.com. She had run up debts without telling her husband, and he had just lost his job. She said she couldn't see any other option than killing herself. I was scared for her and didn't really know what to do – the money side, yes, but I'm not a counsellor. So I took advice from someone who was, and wrote a careful reply to try and say the right thing.

The first person to reply after me was Andrea, one of the site's regulars. She simply extended a hand of friendship, said things were never as bad as they seemed, and 'Why not send me a personal message? I'll bring the virtual coffee, if you bring the biscuits.' I'd be lying if I tried to pretend my eyes were dry after I read it.

More people replied. The following are a couple of posts I've selected. Their words, not mine ...

Light at the end of the tunnel: 'Just to let you know there is light at the end of that very dark tunnel. I, too, got into £8,000 worth of debt as a student. When I started working I added to this a further £7,000 bank loan thinking I could pay it all off with my newly acquired wage. I WAS WRONG – BIG TIME!!!! Solicitors' letters ensued, and so I contacted the Consumer Credit Counselling Service. With a debt management plan created by them I have slowly paid off £10,000 in three years. By the end of this year all my store cards and credit cards will have been paid off, and by 2005 everything else will be too. It was hard initially not to be able to buy 'things' and I didn't have a holiday for two years but instead saved up and went to Australia this March – yes, just by saving and not spending. I learned money-respect the hard way and I'm not going down that road again. Try the CCCS – it worked for me.'

The best decision I ever made: 'Over two years ago, I started getting into money troubles. I was earning in excess of £75k p.a!! I lost my contract and couldn't pay off loans. I was feeling the strain. The mortgage was falling behind. Just when I thought things couldn't get any worse, my wife announced she couldn't carry on like this and we separated. I moved back in with my parents and thought that maybe this would see an end to it all – nope. My half of the loans still left me with more than £20k of debt. I had a new job paying me £16k p.a – just enough to cover my outgoings and maintenance payments, leaving me little spare to go and see my son twice a month. I was advised the only solution was personal bankruptcy ... the words alone filled me with dread. The day arrived for court, I was ushered in to see a judge. Five minutes later, I was officially bankrupt.

Now I am debt-free, but have tight constraints for another 2.5 years until the bankruptcy period is over. But it isn't all that bad. I know exactly what my salary will be and have no more worries about being chased by creditors. I come to the end of the month and know I have a little money left to go towards my son's birthday and take him away for a week. It has to be in the UK – not glamorous, but what the hell? My advice for anyone who is in a similar situation ... Please do not make the same mistakes as me and leave everything, thinking it will all go away – it doesn't. The feeling I get now, knowing that there will be an end to all of this soon, is indescribable. Hopefully, someone reading this may make a similar decision – it is the best one I have ever made.'

I wish I could tell you I knew what happened to the suicidal woman. She never did post again. I pray she read the messages and advice and sorted the problems out. If you're in debt crisis, please deal with it – there are people who will help you for free. Use them.

A FINAL £THOUGHT

... I Hope the Money Diet No Longer Works

If the entire nation followed the Money Diet properly, this book would become worthless. There'd be no more 0% credit cards, there'd be no more top-paying savings accounts, direct marketing would stop, branding consultants would have to change careers and start driving school buses. Providers would learn marketing gimmicks would fail, so they'd give up, and there'd be nothing for us to take advantage of any more.

Maybe that's a bit too much to ask for. So I'll finish with an easier hope – the same one I started with ... I hope you save some money.

Martin

INDEX

index

Would you like a personal Money Saving Makeover with the UK's only Money Saving Expert, Martin Lewis?

Enter our *Money Diet* free prize draw to win a face-to-face consultation with Martin Lewis during tea at The Ritz – enjoy a bit of free glamour while completely re-evaluating the way you spend and save your money.

Send the answer to the following question, along with your name, address, telephone number and email address (optional), on a postcard by 30th June 2004 to:

The Money Diet Prize Draw

Ebury Press Marketing Department, PO Box 4313

20 Vauxhall Bridge Road, London, SW1V 2SA

Martin Lewis's fantastic website containing top money saving tips is at which web address?

  a) **www.moneysavingexpert.com**

  b) **www.flashthecash.com**

  c) **www.skinflint.com**

Terms and Conditions:

The first correct entry to be drawn will be declared the winner.

The draw will take place on 16th July 2004.

The winner will be notified by 30th July 2004.

No employees from The Random House Group Ltd or participating retailers may enter.

Entries only accepted from within the UK.

Entrants must be over 18.

No purchase necessary.

The judge's decision is final and no correspondence will be entered into.

It is a condition of entry that the winners agree to the use of their name, address and photograph in publicity material. However, we will not archive or utilise any entrant's name or address for anything unrelated to this competition.

No cash alternative.

Prize does not include transport or any additional expenses.

The promoter is The Random House Group Ltd, 20 Vauxhall Bridge Road, London, SW1V 2SA.